GET OUT OF
DEBT NOW

GET OUT OF DEBT NOW

HOW TO GAIN CONTROL OF YOUR FINANCIAL AFFAIRS ONCE AND FOR ALL

Fred Graver

Little, Brown and Company • Boston • Toronto

For Ann O'Grady —

who married me for richer or poorer,
and got a little bit of both

FIRST EDITION

The author is grateful to the publishers for permission to quote
material as noted below.

M. Evans and Company, Inc. for excerpts from *Levin's Laws:
Tactics for Winning without Intimidation* by Edward Levin.
Copyright © 1980 by Edward Levin and Patricia Linden.
Reprinted by permission of the publisher, M. Evans and Company,
Inc., New York, N.Y. 10017

Rawson, Wade Publishers, Inc. for excerpts from *Super Threats*
by John M. Striker and Andrew O. Shapiro copyright © 1977 by
John M. Striker and Andrew O. Shapiro. Reprinted by permission
of Rawson, Wade Publishers, Inc.

LIBRARY OF CONGRESS CATALOGING IN PUBLICATION DATA
Graver, Fred.
  Get out of debt now.
  Includes index.
  1. Finance, Personal. 2. Debt. I. Title.
HG179.G72   332.024'02   81–18634
ISBN 0–316–32415–9   AACR2

BP
Designed by Susan Windheim
Published simultaneously in Canada
by Little, Brown & Company (Canada) Limited
PRINTED IN THE UNITED STATES OF AMERICA

CONTENTS

FACING IT   32

How Much Do I Owe? How Much Do I Have? •
Getting a Fix on Your Position • The High Cost of
Living in Debt • In Case of Emergency . . .

EMERGENCY SITUATIONS   44

Buying Time • The Six Most Common Emergencies

MAKING A PLAN YOU CAN STICK TO   54

Getting the Family Involved • Inflation-Proofing Your
Budget • Cash Only, Please • Setting Priorities
• Contacting Your Creditors • Time for a Pat on the
Back • Negotiating—Putting Your Mouth Where Your
Money Is (Or Should Be) • Getting Help from a Credit
Counselor • Consolidating and Refinancing

YOUR CREDIT REPORT   86

Credit Bureaus • What's on My Credit Report? •
Other Uses of Your Credit Report • The Investigative
Report • Reviewing Your Credit Report • Issues
Surrounding Credit Report

ACKNOWLEDGMENTS

I owe a large debt of gratitude to Mary Tondorf-Dick, who kept me to what the reader needed, while allowing for what I wanted to say.

To Carol Mann, for her faith in me and in this book.

To the many people I interviewed — for their time, expertise and, above all, their honesty. I spoke with creditors, collectors, counselors, debtors, lawyers, and clerks in my attempt to break down the "wall of fear." I would particularly like to thank Ellen Broadman of Consumers Union, Paul Olsen, Robert Cialdini, David Samuels of the New York City Office of Consumer Affairs, Bernard Sennet, Jerry Taylor, Alan D. Reffkin, and Linden Wheeler of Sears. And sincere thanks also to those who asked that I not identify them.

For their inspiration, and careful review of sections of this book, I'd like to thank Nancy Teeters of the Board of Governors of the Federal Reserve System; Luther Gatling, Director of Budget Credit Counseling Service in New York; James Fishman, Deputy Attorney General of New York State; Kenneth Rosen; and Dorothy Eisenberg.

Finally, I owe a debt I can never really express, let alone repay, to my wife Ann O'Grady and my children, Joshua and Ann Claire, whose support, encouragement, and love enabled me to write this book.

The best parts of this book belong to the above. Errors of fact or judgment are my own.

GET OUT OF DEBT NOW

IT'S NO SIN
TO BE BROKE

IT HAD BEEN A LONG DAY for Francis Benson. A junior account executive in a large advertising agency, Francis had all the trappings of success: nice clothes, a co-op apartment with a river view, a classy imported sports car, two expensive vacations every year, charge accounts at all the major stores. At any of the restaurants Francis and his wife frequented, the maître d' and the waiters knew him by name, and had him marked as a successful member of the affluent society. (Not to mention a good tipper.)

What really was going on in Francis's life showed him to be a product of the affluent society, but not in a way you would expect. Francis's long day had begun just five minutes after coming to the office, when a representative from MasterCard contacted him about his long-overdue bill. The mail contained an anonymous-looking yellow envelope, in which he found a threatening letter (the second) from his summer landlord — Francis had bounced the last month's rent check on his (long ago depleted) overdraft-protected account. The landlord, whom Francis figured to be the excitable type anyway, was threatening to sue.

When Francis called home, his wife Diane told him the grocer had pleaded with her when she was shopping this morning, asking when their account would be settled. She was frustrated and a little desperate. There were very few of the local merchants to whom she had not made a late payment or passed a bad check at least once. She felt deeply that each of them mistrusted her every time she made a purchase — even when she was paying cash.

The phone calls and the mail disturbed Francis for the whole day, his uneasiness staying with him through two important meetings (in which he had not been at his best) and lunch with a friend (where he found his ears perking up at the mention of the word "bankruptcy" at the next table).

Francis and his wife had been playing a kind of financial brinksmanship for several years now, and with their combined earnings — close to forty thousand dollars a year — the brink had seemed a pretty comfortable place to be. They held three Master-Card accounts from three different banks; two of these banks had also given them Visa cards. While they had to pay their charge cards — American Express and Diners Club — every month in full, Visa and MasterCard allowed them a low minimum payment, offering them more and more of their weekly income for what the economists called "discretionary" purposes. Even after the credit crunch of 1980, when their cards each had hefty fees slapped on them for "annual membership," the credit-card life was ultimately very attractive to them. Everything they had, they spent. There was always more — more credit, more cash to be advanced, more of a balance covered by their monthly minimum payment — where that came from.

In the last couple of months, though, it had been harder and harder to make all the payments on their bills. The minimum payments had begun to look like maximum payments, and the seemingly bottomless well of their overdraft checking account had dried up. Francis and Diane realized a very basic fact very quickly — they had been borrowing *money* for the past few years, and *money* would have to be paid back.

They began to decrease the use of their credit cards and started putting off one creditor to pay another. Their savings were completely depleted. The ultimate frustration, Diane thought, was that so much of each paycheck was earmarked for bills that were one or two months overdue, that paying current bills (which, alone, would have been within their means) had to be put off—they began to feel they were living in a time warp. They could never, she felt, catch up.

Both Francis and Diane knew that they had squandered a considerable amount of money. Their current debts totaled close to $15,000. Even the possessions they had to show for their years of spending—their clothes, home appliances, their stereo and videocasette recorder—took on the look of souvenirs after the holiday had long been forgotten. Worse yet were bills for meals and entertainment barely remembered.

The collectors hounding them placed the couple squarely in the category of "deadbeat," and accused them of spending money they never intended to repay. Although Francis and Diane knew they never intended to defraud their creditors, they both knew they had been less than honest with themselves. Their first reaction was to blame the creditors for lending them so much money so easily. Now, they realized they had been willing customers, and the day of reckoning had finally come.

With their combined incomes working in a sound debt-management program, and by following principles similar to those outlined in this book, Francis and Diane cleared themselves of their debt problems within a year. In the course of repaying their debts, they learned that the real power of their income was best realized in their own hands, not in the hands of their creditors. They removed themselves from the credit card syndrome, and learned some important lessons. They've vowed never to get overburdened with debt again.

Thanks to the fact that they had two healthy incomes to put to work on their problems, and that they were able to commit themselves to a year-long plan, Francis and Diane got off the brutal hook of debt pretty easily. For Neil Johnson, it wasn't so easy. Married while still in college, Neil had graduated with three thousand dollars in student loans to be paid, a wife who still had to finish her undergraduate study, one child, and no job. He was lucky to find work for a new magazine opening in his city, and spent long, hard hours on this ambitious project. Sometimes the magazine wasn't able to give Neil his full paycheck, which frustrated him—but not to the point of quitting, since jobs offering as much experience were hard to come by; once the magazine had established itself, the problem of pay shortages would end. But the magazine folded just as his first student loan payments came up, and Neil found himself strapped.

Luckily, the commercial bank in his neighborhood had no idea of what shaky financial grounds the magazine was on, and Neil had used his job as a reference to get one of their bankcards. He began to borrow cash advances from the card to pay off his student loans, and he and his wife promised each other that this was the only debt that they would acquire with the card. But Neil had trouble finding another job, and their cash flow worsened. The only money coming in was from his wife's part-time job in the college admissions office. Swallowing hard, Neil and his wife found themselves charging more of the day-to-day expenses on their credit card.

When Neil finally found work — in a job that just about paid him a living wage — his wife had finished school and was starting her own career. Unfortunately, her own student loans, which would come due in several months, would increase their debt to $6,000.

Neil's wife finally began work as a teacher, but they had to buy a new car for her daily commute. And they now had to pay for day care for their child. Their two incomes amounted to little more than what they needed to keep up on past debts and to meet day-to-day expenses. It left nothing for out-of-the-ordinary items such as clothing, vacations, gifts and the like, which were financed by using credit cards.

The scenario played itself out. In three years from Neil's graduation, he and his young family amassed a total debt of $12,000. The daily realities now included dunning letters, harassing phone calls from bill collectors, and the unavailability of credit of any kind. The future looked bleak to Neil — neither he nor his wife were due for a windfall, and there was no place $12,000 could come from in any reasonable amount of time.

What Neil shared with millions of other people in this country is a sense of frustration, embarrassment, and confusion over the mountain of debts that can accumulate — for any of us — in a short period of time. With 25, 30, even 50 percent of your take-home pay going to your credit bills, where can you turn for assistance? How can you ever hope to get out of debt?

The Chinese have a saying: "A journey of a thousand miles must begin with a single step." Beneath the pile of bills that faces you every month lies a simple, straightforward way of getting out of debt. You *can* manage your debts. You *can* repair a terrible credit record. You *can* pay off all your bills without getting even further in debt. Read on.

GET OUT OF DEBT *NOW*

In 1978, the OPEC ministers asked Robert Simons of Chicago to redo his household budget. They asked him to do it again in 1979, and twice in 1980. In fact, every time the OPEC sheikhs started to rattle oil drills instead of sabers, Robert did his budget over. Every increase in the price of a barrel of OPEC oil led to an increase in the price of Robert's heating oil and his gasoline bill. Being a traveling salesman covering three states and the winters in Chicago being as harsh as they were didn't help much.

So, with great regularity, Robert Simons would pull out the canceled checks, the bills, and the calculator. He would add up his income, add up his expenses, and wince when he saw how close the two were coming.

Robert didn't think of himself as being in debt. He was always able to pay back any loan he had taken. His credit cards were usually up to date. (Oh, sure he let them slide when he hit hard times — but that's what cards are for, right?) But recently he had begun to worry about the chunk of his regular income that went to pay back his credit cards. His tax return for 1980 showed close to $2,000 in interest charges alone. It was a nice deduction, he thought, but he could have put that money to good use during the year.

Robert could see that the expense of living with credit cards was going to be more than he could afford in the coming years — especially if the economists who were calling the eighties "the decade of austerity" were right. But getting off credit seemed like an impossibility — how could he stop using credit, pay back his bills, and still maintain his life-style? It was a puzzling, complex problem.

Although he was far from facing the emergencies described by some of the cases in this book, Robert Simons is typical of the *average borrower* who needs to begin a debt-management program to meet the tough economic realities of the eighties. Credit is going to cost more and more, and the necessities of life are going to leave less and less of your income available to pay for credit. If the eighties are going to be a decade of learning to live with cutbacks in our resources, of learning to use what we have more wisely, then you, as a consumer, are going to have to think of credit as one of those resources. This book will show you how, by employing resources that are not so costly, and are readily available.

An article in the July 1979 *Good Housekeeping* magazine portrayed a family that was helped considerably by credit counseling. Tom and Joan Vander Putten of Ridge, N.Y., owed $10,369 to creditors. "We had every charge card you could get your hands on," Tom said. "We had cards from the department stores, the oil companies, the banks, you name it. I hate carrying cash. I like going into a store and buying whatever I want. I'd begun to feel affluent and that made me feel good."

Tom and Joan's financial trouble began when Tom entered into his own business, an air-conditioning repair service. The nation had slid into a recession, and the market for Tom's services was reduced considerably. They borrowed to get through the slack periods, and ended 1974 owing $6,000. They obtained a consolidation loan, but that improved their situation only slightly. Tom dropped his business venture and went to work for an established firm, but his salary wasn't enough to cover their already-acquired debts.

They began "skimming," paying each creditor a little each month — often less than the stated minimum payment. "At one point," Tom reported, "my paycheck had to be divided into 23 different pieces, with each creditor getting no more than $5."

Calls began to come at all hours from collectors, and their check-cashing card was rejected at the grocery store. At this point, bankruptcy seemed like the best option. Instead, they entered credit counseling, and in three years had paid off their $10,369 debt. It was a long, hard climb, but they learned to budget, pulled together as a family, and are out of the burden of debt.

Overdraft checking. Minimum payments. Overdue notices. Skimming. Credit counselors. Consolidation loans. Bankruptcy.

Do you recognize yourself in these stories? Do these innocent words cause you to wince a little because of your own financial condition? I've recounted these incidents of debt for two reasons — to help you see how debt pervades and influences many lives, and to show that you are not alone in having credit problems.

I have found, in my research for this book, that consumer credit is one of the most powerful and yet most unexamined aspects of every person's finances. Credit is the second largest factor in most family's finances — the first being the paycheck. Yet, we pay more attention to the bite taken out of our income by a rise in the price of a gallon of milk than we do to the transaction fees placed on our credit cards. The milk may only cost us another dollar every month, while our credit costs may increase by five to ten dollars without our so much as blinking. Why?

We have been sold credit as a way of life. If the interest charges go up on our cards — well, the convenience of having the card is worth it. If the bank charges us a fee because we pay our bill off every month — well, that's life. If the combination of interest, transaction fees, yearly fee, and late charges amount to 30 percent interest on what we've borrowed, and cause us to have less and less money left over every month — hey! That hurts!

This book begins with a simple message for the average person wondering how she or he will survive the coming decade of austerity: *get out of debt*. Avoid it like the plague. When push comes to shove, either with credit restraints like those of the spring of 1980, reduced income potential, or declining profits at the banks, personal debt is where it's going to hurt first and hardest.

Many people already understand that message. Bankruptcies are at their highest levels ever. Bankruptcy is one sure, easy way to get out of debt. It's also one very dangerous way to get out of debt. For reasons I'll go into later in this chapter, bankruptcy is not only the last alternative — it's also the worst, although it is still, for many, the only. The best way to get rid of debts, rebuild your credit standing, learn from your mistakes, and get on a sound financial footing is to set up a debt management program; work with your creditors, a counselor, or a lawyer; and begin to pay off your bills.

If you are one of the millions of people in this country who are under the severe burden of debt, the suggestion that you can get out of debt now might seem far from reality. Such doubts, misperceptions, and frustrations keep you returning again and again to the revolving credit merry-go-round, and keep you farther and farther behind. The first step toward getting out of debt now is the step you take off the credit merry-go-round. After that, there is a great deal of hard work to do, and a lot of personal commitment needed. But you will be free of the emotional and financial enslavement that consumer debt can produce. And, from that first independent step, you will *feel* out of debt now.

This book will arm you with the means of getting out of debt. It provides real tools for anyone who has serious consumer debt problems and offers you a way of determining exactly how much money you owe, how you can most easily and quickly pay those bills, and how you can get back on your feet. You'll find out what all your alternatives are as a debtor, what your legal rights are, and how you can put them to use.

In the chapters that follow, you'll also find out what you are up against at the bank, the finance companies, the collection agencies, and with their lawyers. Since most people who are in debt don't understand how the credit industry operates, their ignorance provides the creditor with an enormous advantage. And creditors, for the most part, would like to keep it that way. They do so by using the wall of fear. This book will guide you, the overextended, indebted consumer, over that wall of fear and through the credit industry.

THE WALL OF FEAR

The first thing I'm going to do is break down the wall of fear that exists between creditors and debtors. That wall of fear leads to misunderstanding, anxiety, and frustration for the person who owes money. Bill collectors know that the person who owes them money is in a weak position — they've got file cabinets full of statistics to prove it. And they play that weakness for all it's worth.

The credit industry has become an empire in this country because it has learned how to sell debt, and it has learned how to pounce on the victims of the system.

This book is going to show you what *they* are made of, who they are, what they can and can't do, what they want from their customers, and what they will finally accept. I'm going to tell their secrets, because that's the only way you will be on an equal footing with them. And once you get on an equal footing, you'll be able to come to terms — literally — with them.

We're going to go behind the scenes whenever possible. I'll show you what a collection agent has on his desk when he's on the phone to you, what a loan officer looks for on your credit rating, and we'll even try to make sense of the binary logic of the computer at your local bank.

The wall of fear is what keeps every contact by a collector or creditor focused on you. They come across the wall of fear to get money out of you, but you can't (or at least aren't supposed to) cross the wall to find out just what is expected of you. It's a very effective technique. If you were a collector, you might use it yourself. But — it is just a technique. It's not the reality of the situation.

The collector, no matter how threatening or difficult he may be on the phone, is doing a job — nothing more, nothing less. Certainly it isn't a very pleasant job: he or she often feels lied to and abused. And it *is* sometimes true that debtors lie — out of fear and ignorance of the consequences of their not being able to pay their debts.

Of course, the most difficult, abusive, and objectionable collectors do their job best and get the most money. If it isn't the direct threat of that collector that gets you to pay up, it's the "good-guy/bad-guy" approach, which relies on the threat of the abusive collector lurking in the background, that works best. And the creditors who are lax or "understanding" are forgotten, paid only on the rare occasion when you have a little extra to give them.

But, in fact, that isn't usually the way you want to pay your bills. And it usually isn't the way it would be best for you to pay your bills, both for you and your creditors. Your ability to control weekly and monthly finances is severely hampered by the wall of fear. While you might think it best to pay the bills that have been outstanding the longest, you often don't, because another creditor has been hounding you harder.

Creditors use the wall of fear because it works. The less you know about them, the better they can operate. Secrets have a way of becoming more powerful when they are covered up. Although banks will charge off more than $750 million this year in bad debts, you don't generally know this. So if you've got a late payment with Citibank, they can make you feel that their entire organization is going to collapse around your head if you don't kick up the $85 you owe them.

HOW DEEPLY IN DEBT ARE WE?

We are in the midst of a national debt crisis. Americans, those happy-go-lucky spenders, owe over $318 billion to credit cards, auto loans, checking overdrafts, and other forms of installment credit. Over $58 billion of that is in credit cards alone. (These figures are as of June of 1981.)

This tremendous surge in borrowing has put many Americans in a position where they are embarrassed by the debt load they carry. In many cases, people in debt find themselves wondering just how they got as far into debt as they have. When the collectors begin to call, they can even find themselves confronting the thought that they have become deadbeats because of their inability to pay their bills.

In fact, statistics show that only one percent of the people who are taken to court for default are "classic" deadbeats — those who use credit with no intention to repay. In the Spring 1981 issue of *Credit World* magazine, Dean Ashby, a credit collections expert, asserted that "about 20 percent [of people with credit] tend to overestimate their ability to pay for what they desire. They offer collection problems but basically are worthwhile risks."

Never before have people relied so much on borrowed money to keep up their standard of living. A quick breakdown of the national debt averages offers little consolation to everyone who owes money. Every man, woman, and child in this country owes, as of June 1981, $5,900. (Not literally, that's the average debt.) In

January through February of 1981, repayments of loans ran at 21.1 percent of after-tax income. (The largest chunk of repayment dollars out of income came at the end of 1979, when consumers were paying back an average of 22.7 percent to installment loans.) The high level of debt affects our economy in other ways, as well. As household debt climbs, people have less to put into buying additional goods, or to save. At the end of 1980 and beginning of 1981, for example, consumer credit hit a drastic slump. It was only in February 1981 that a major increase in credit use was seen, and many experts said that consumer confidence in the economy would take even longer to recover.

Debt has become so much a part of our daily life that we rarely remember that most things we "own" do not, really, belong to us.

Debt can do incredible damage to people who owe money, and who owe it in a big way. The "safe" debt in this country is estimated to be 20 percent of take-home pay (not including mortgage payments), and as we have seen, the national average is running around 22 percent. But there are millions of people who owe 30 to 40 percent of their take-home pay.

How do these statistics translate into actual costs?

The typical American family, with an income of $17,000 to $20,000, pays a monthly rate (according to the Federal Reserve) of $500 for mortgage and taxes, a $175–200 car payment, and $200–300 on credit cards, checking-overdraft accounts, and retail credit. The figures total 50 to 60 percent of take-home pay going to debt service — half of which goes to consumer credit payments alone.

During the years 1975–1980, the amount of household debt (consumer and mortgage) has increased nearly 100 percent, from $652 billion to $1,250 billion. The effects that could be triggered by such a debt burden range from an enormous rise in bankruptcies (which we are seeing) to a lengthening of the recession due to the inflexibility of household budgets, many of which are tied to extended repayment plans. A five- or ten-year recession, according to some economists, is a real possibility. And much of the lengthening of that recession is due to the consumer's entrenchment in debt service. What happened, simply, is that many of us borrowed simply to keep from falling behind.

One aspect of consumer debt that is often overlooked is second-mortgage borrowing. Homes, of course, are the typical family's major asset, and inflation has given us an incredible rise in the worth of homes, creating large equities that can be borrowed upon. The new borrowing has taken the form of second mortgages, which is seeing a large national surge. The increase in mortgage debt in 1979–1981 is about 30 percent, largely because of entries into the area of selling second mortgages by commercial banks, finance companies, and specific second-mortgage firms. The Federal Reserve estimates that *half* of the new mortgage debt has been used for nonhousing purposes — consumers are not putting on aluminum siding, converting their basements, or adding on new wings to their homes. They have, it seems, been taking vacations, buying clothing, and handling the necessities of life.

Based on figures released by the Federal Reserve in August 1981, let's see how consumer indebtedness breaks into various categories:

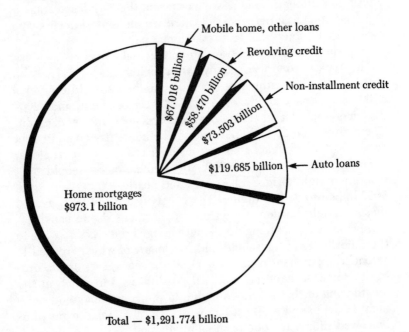

Mobile home, other loans

Revolving credit

Non-installment credit

$67.016 billion

$58.470 billion

$73.503 billion

$119.685 billion ← Auto loans

Home mortgages
$973.1 billion

Total — $1,291.774 billion

Allowed to go on its merry course, consumer credit can wreak economic havoc on your household. You can begin to lose the ability to make independent, responsible choices about your money. And the real potential of your income and earnings can be lost to a future of credit repayments.

UNLEASHING THE POWER OF THE HOUSEHOLD ECONOMY

The techniques in this book have a sound economic base. Each consumer, and each household, in America is an independent economic unit and should work to preserve his or her ability to control his or her own financial destiny. If this independence is threatened, as it is by the kind of bullying that collectors and creditors employ, then a large chunk of the consumer market is threatened. More and more families are servicing more and more debt today, and it is essential that they know how they can get out of debt wisely.

When a consumer finds himself overloaded with debt, one of these economic units is drastically affected. For whatever reason, that person has stopped functioning efficiently and effectively as a part of our economy. He has lost control over his financial destiny.

What this book attempts to do, to a large extent, is to put that control back in the hands of the consumer. People should be given the right, in debt or not, to say what their money is going to be spent on and how. Certainly, we all make promises in the form of credit and loan agreements, and these promises should be kept, at practically all costs. But owing a debt to a creditor does not mean that you have to hand over your personal and home finances to the quickest and fastest bully on the block.

There is no small coincidence between the loose, almost cavalier attitude taken by the sellers of credit and the rise of a cavalier attitude about credit among debtors. We are in the midst of a debt crisis because credit has become an end and not a means. Since the birth of the national bankcards, a little over a decade ago, our perception of why we borrow money has altered drastically. People who never would have gone to a bank to arrange a loan for the purchase of a television or furniture *were* willing to use credit cards for these things — thereby taking a bank loan, although they didn't think of it that way. For the banks the making of loans became the wholesale marketing of credit. With a bankcard, we were told, we had clout. We were accepted. Our identities were complete.

What is missing in this exchange is attention to the essential element of repayment. No ad tells us that it is chic or sophisticated to pay back what we have borrowed. As was discovered in the late seventies, many creditors were guilty of selling credit to people who couldn't afford it — the system was calculated to absorb those losses. There is a kind of seduction and intoxication involved in the easy-credit world. But implicit in this seduction is a threat of future problems. Sooner or later, the bills have to be paid.

What is being threatened by our attitude toward credit is an essential economic freedom — the right to choose. The creditor's right to choose whom to lend to is threatened because a lax attitude makes it almost impossible for him to tell who is credit-worthy or not. And the debtor's independence and right to choose is threatened when he has to, in effect, pay on demand to the largest screamer among his creditors.

The enormous rise in consumer debt has not been without its attendant difficulties for the banking profession. According to the *American Bankers Association Bulletin* on delinquency rates, the third quarter of 1980 saw a fifteen-year high of 2.94 percent of outstanding credit balances delinquent. At the end of the second quarter of 1980, the *Bulletin* had stated that "the expansion [of consumer credit] of the past five years has come to an end, partly as a result of high inflation, heavy debt loads, and energy dependence."

By understanding that a great deal of responsibility needs to be reintroduced into this exchange, that credit is a necessity in our economy, and that responsible borrowing and lending are absolutely essential for the continued smooth functioning of the economy, we've come a long way toward breaking down some of the common misconceptions in the relationship between lenders and borrowers. And perhaps we've contributed a little to the economic health of the country.

WHY *NOT* GO BANKRUPT?

Because of the weak economy, the Federal Bankruptcy Act of 1978, and the new ability of lawyers to advertise their services, bankruptcies rose to incredible levels over the years 1977–1980. In the first full year under the new law, nearly half a million people filed for bankruptcy.

Bankruptcy seems like an easy way to wipe out your debts and get a fresh start. In fact, it is easy — that was the intent of the federal act. But, because it's easy doesn't mean that there can't be severe complications and aftereffects to bankruptcy (described in detail in "Bankruptcy: Strong Medicine").

I wrote this book so that people could have alternatives to bankruptcy as a way of getting themselves out of debt. Certainly, there are many people for whom bankruptcy is the only solution — and for them, it is a good solution. But bankruptcy is being sold to people in the same way that debt is being sold, and buying a bill of goods without knowing what your alternatives are, or what is in store for you up ahead, won't be of any help to you at all.

There are three factors that complicate bankruptcy. I describe them in complete detail in "Bankruptcy," but it's important for you to be aware of them, and to know why the energy and commitment you devote to a debt-management program can protect you from the pitfalls of bankruptcy.

First, there is a moral and ethical problem which arises in many people when they go through bankruptcy. This problem has nothing to do with your preconceptions about whether or not you feel, at the outset, that bankruptcy is right or wrong. This emotional and psychological factor arises in many people, and causes them to feel a loss of self-esteem which can take a while to regain.

Second, there is a "creditor's backlash" that exists against those who have wiped out their debts through bankruptcy. I call this a backlash because it is occurring as an industry-wide reaction to the bankruptcy trends, not based on any specific rationale. It is too early to assess exactly which factor, or combination of factors, has caused the rise in bankruptcy. But at this point, creditors have, for the most part, established severe credit restrictions against bankruptees.

Finally, if you have any property at all to protect from seizure by the court in a bankruptcy proceeding, you will need a lawyer. As I'll show in various points in the book, getting a good lawyer is a very hard thing to do, particularly in the consumer credit and bankruptcy areas. One of the most common pitfalls in going through bankruptcy is having a lawyer who does not and *cannot* represent you properly.

The best reason for not going bankrupt is that you can, in average circumstances, manage those debts by developing a sound budget, working with your creditors, and building a plan of debt repayment that will wipe out your bills, reestablish your credit rating, and place you on a sound financial base for the future. All of these approaches and alternatives are spelled out in this book.

WHAT ARE THE EMOTIONAL EFFECTS OF SERIOUS DEBT?

The experience of carrying heavy debt cuts far deeper than merely into the savings accounts and wallets of the American family. It cuts right into their emotional life as well. At the root of the majority of marital and family problems in this country is the problem of money. And that problem is often made worse by the lack of knowledge people have about what they are dealing with when they deal with the credit industry.

Additionally, the guilt, frustration, and embarrassment that most people feel about their debt is often unnecessary — once you understand the many ways credit penetrates and influences our lives, you can see that the blame for being in debt should not be limited to the person receiving the bills.

"Almost invariably, the first effect of serious debt on a family is a cycle of guilt and blame," says New York psychotherapist Paul Olsen. Olsen has counseled quite a few families in stress situations, and spoke with me about the effects that debt has on them.

"There is a lot of feeling, which comes out in the debt collection process, that the consumer has been hyped, and now he is being persecuted and badgered for something that he may not have really wanted in the first place."

I asked Dr. Olsen about a comment made to me by a vice-president of a major bank, who stated that "the banking relationship is like a family, and the bank is like the parents, and sometimes the children get a little out of line with what we have allowed them to have, and then we have to bring them back into line." Olsen commented that such a pattern was common in the debtor/creditor relationship, but the banker had neglected to mention one factor: "The parent in this case does not acknowledge that he has seduced the child.

"The credit people," he went on to say, "will not take the responsibility for having said, in a tacit way, that if you don't buy, you're a loser. If you don't buy, you are hurting the economy, the family, the whole fabric of life."

When a person becomes overextended, and collectors begin to hound him for his payments, the effect within the family can be devastating. According to Dr. Olsen, "The first thing that happens, invariably, is that the head of the household is blamed. The discussions of money turn into some kind of personal attack. 'It must be Pop. It's his fault' — or whoever is earning the money. 'You got us to this place.' The rest of the family doesn't take any responsibility for the pressure or the situations they may have put the head of the household in, since that person is supposed to provide for them.

"Then, the person responds by saying, 'But I thought this was a cooperative venture.' But it's not like that at all. Then, the fear, the anxiety begin to creep in. People's fantasies begin to come up — that the house will be foreclosed, that they'll be on the street. These are primitive fantasies that come out.

"Very often, that's the first sign of the cracking of a marriage. The money problems really start to churn up any other things that are lying at the root of the marriage. I would say the vast majority of marriages with problems use money as their battling ground."

Very often, as well, a family finds itself in serious debt because of an external crisis — for example, someone may need expensive medical treatments, or the main wage earner may be out of work for a long period of time. The crises compound themselves.

"Families who have been poor," Dr. Olsen claims, "respond better to an external crisis. There's a greater pulling together, they'll probably be more adaptable, and there's less of a mystique about the loss involved. 'I've been there before,' they think, 'I've seen this before.' People who have been princes and princesses, who have been comfortable all of their lives, are devastated. They have a tremendous loss of self-esteem. They feel, 'You're no good. You lost your job.'"

Even when the causes are not external, when the bills have just slowly been piling up to an unpayable amount, there is still that feeling of "I didn't do it." Resentment enters the picture. The debtor tends to blame the spouse, the children. He thinks "If we didn't do this, or buy that, then . . ." Dr. Olsen relates this to an attempt to save face, to keep from looking at the problem realistically.

The irony, Paul Olsen claims, is that the self-denigration people feel, this sense that debt equals worthlessness, is also imagined. It's not real. As he says, "Who *really* cares? Who's keeping score? This society has intrinsically no means to do anything to you. There are no debtor's prisons. Although you might not believe it at the time, you can go through bankruptcy, and your neighbors won't stop talking to you. But there is always a strong sense of personal failure connected to being in debt."

Conversely, there is a sense of personal triumph in harnessing the energies within yourself and your family when you work to get out of debt. No matter which method described in this book you use to get out of debt, I guarantee that you will feel a sense of self-reliance and achievement that no amount of credit could buy.

WHO IS IN DEBT? AND WHY?

Practically everyone in this country owes money to someone for goods or services they have already received.

The files of the Consumer Credit Counseling Service in New York show a profile of the average debtor that looks something like this:

He is the head of a three-person household with a gross annual income of $15,000. He owes an average of $8,000 in consumer debts to nine different creditors, and he and his family are spending $400 a month more than they earn.

At first glance, the most startling fact in this profile is that the average debtor in CCCS owes half of his gross income to creditors. But there are other national statistics that show a large segment of the debtors in this country owing something to closer to two or three times as much money as they make each year. And these statistics show that debt crosses all class and social lines — it is no longer a lower-class problem, but a distinct issue of the middle-class squeeze.

In 1954, William Whyte, in his classic book *The Organization Man*, coined the term "inconspicuous consumption" to describe the process in which "luxuries" — a new dishwasher or a second car — can become "necessities" by way of peer pressure. Whyte coined another term, "budgetism," to describe how the young families of the fifties were able to keep up with the Joneses. Budgetism could just as well be used to describe how many of us survive — let alone keep up with the Joneses — in the eighties.

Budgetism is the ability to go from month to month, rhythmically, gracefully, on the wave of new monthly statements from credit cards and installment agreements. We discover the high balance that can be maintained by a combination of minimum payments, and we stick with it. It's a kind of financial brinksmanship practiced widely today.

The fastest growing segment of new debtors is young people, earning $13,000 to $30,000 per year, who want the good things of life right now, and feel that they have a strong future to mortgage. They are the primary members of a class that has its roots in the early sixties — the indigent debtor — those who possess what once was only the property of the wealthy, but who have no means of their own outside of their ability to obtain credit. Inconspicuous consumption, budgetism, and the indigent debtor are phenomena that have become fixtures on the American scene. By understanding them, we can begin to sense the vast numbers of people in debt, and understand why.

You can ride the wave of consumer debt pretty far, although there are few who can arrive on shore all in one piece. Since creditors, for the most part, won't act as guardians of your assets, judging whether or not you are carrying more debt than you can repay, it is fairly easy to build up sizable obligations before you begin to show signs of trouble. And when the trouble begins, the whole house of cards can come down.

HOW DO YOU KNOW IF YOU'RE IN TROUBLE?

You know the feeling. Looking at the bills, you ask yourself, "How did it ever get this bad?"

It's not just the person receiving dunning notices in the mail, getting frequent calls from collectors, or feeling that bankruptcy might be the only solution who is in, or heading for, debt trouble. We have become so sold on debt as a way of life that many of us are in credit trouble and don't realize it. Or we realize it once a month, and then forget about it.

Before you say to yourself, "Oh, this book isn't for me," take this simple quiz and see where you stand.

- Do you spend more than 20 percent of your take-home pay on monthly installment bills, not including mortgage payments?
- Are you juggling payments to your creditors?
- Have you recently had to borrow cash with your credit card to meet household expenses?
- Do you find it impossible to get money into a savings account?
- Have you needed a debt consolidation loan within the last twelve months?
- Are you currently being telephoned by a bill collector or collection agency?
- Do you secretly suspect that your credit card spending has gotten out of control?
- Are you worried every day about your debts?
- Is there frequent stress in your household because of overdue bills?

You don't need a scale of one-to-three correct answers to know if you're seriously in trouble. If you answered "yes" to enough of these questions to cause concern, you owe it to yourself to gain control of your financial affairs . . . once and for all.

And this book can help you.

THE AMERICAN WAY OF DEBT

You could lay all the economists in the world end to end, and they still wouldn't reach a conclusion.

— American folk saying, circa 1980

DEBT IS BOTH good and bad. It allows people to raise their standard of living and increase their "productive capacities" — those comforts which make it possible for them to work and live day to day. But it also carries a certain amount of risk, especially when people borrow beyond what they will be able to pay back with future income. Excessive debt among many people gives rise to economic conditions that are unstable. *But* if too many people stopped using debt to buy the things they wanted, our economy would grind into a recession.

Americans owe money in a number of different ways: home mortgages, installment contracts, charge accounts, personal loans, and credit cards. Some people use credit on a day-to-day basis, charging everything from washing machines to toothpaste. Others use it only for major items such as automobiles. Some debt, such as mortgage debt, is stretched out over a lifetime. Installment credit and credit cards are, or should be, short-term debts, which cost more and carry a higher risk for the lender.

People can do one of two things to put their money to work in America — lend it or use it to service debt. While Shakespeare warned us, "Neither a borrower, nor a lender be," *New York Times* economic columnist Leonard Silk cheerfully flies in the face of literary criticism when he claims, "That might be the dumbest thing that Shakespeare ever wrote."

Consumers, in fact, are the largest lending segment in our economy. We lend our money through savings, taxes, and direct investments. Checking accounts and N.O.W. accounts in commercial banks are loans that we make to the banks, which they have promised to return — either on demand or after a specified period. Likewise, at savings and loan associations, or at a life insurance company, when we make a payment on a policy or deposit funds, there is a promise to return the funds on request or upon fulfillment of some contractual obligation.

Just as you believe that money in a checking account is an asset for you, lenders consider the money you have borrowed from them as an asset. (Contributing to the confusion of this essentially simple matter is the inequity of interest rates. While you pay 18 percent or more on your credit-card loans, you receive 5¼ percent on your N.O.W. account. Most people, therefore, don't consider themselves lenders, and think themselves wise when they borrow heavily, and pay back with "inflated" dollars.)

As I said in the last chapter, each household in America is an important economic unit. When households in great numbers lose a degree of their economic independence due to overobligations to creditors, it has a serious effect on the smooth functioning of the economy. To begin to understand how this works, and how consumer debt functions as an important part in all of this, let's take a look at the place households have in the American economy.

You can do a quick balance sheet for your household that would follow this form:

By subtracting the current spending and taxes from the current income, you get what is called current savings. Now, a family's current savings can go in three directions: capital goods (durables — things which you expect to last, such as washing machines and refrigerators — and services), investments (treasury bonds, certificates of deposit, money markets, savings), or reducing liabilities (paying off debts).

If you have no savings — that is, no amount of money set aside and available to be spent when and how you want — you automatically increase your liabilities. You go into debt, thereby obtaining the funds needed to purchase capital goods, to invest, or (in the case of many people overburdened with debt) to pay off other debts.

To keep everything flowing smoothly, the households with savings get together with the households who are increasing their liabilities — at the bank.

A SHORT LESSON IN BANKING

So here we are, on Friday afternoon, at the place where the basic transactions of a consumer's money take place — the bank. While you and I wait in line to deposit our hard-earned wages — thereby channeling some of our current savings into investments (passbook deposits, N.O.W. accounts, etc.), or reducing our liabilities (paying off a loan) — we can look over to the "platform" where bank officers are assisting others who wish to increase their liabilities, by borrowing.

There are two major types of banking businesses in the United States: commercial banks and thrift institutions. "Thrifts," who promote themselves by saying they are "people banks," include savings and loans, mutual savings banks, and credit unions.

By lending existing funds to customers, thrifts essentially take money through one window and lend it through the other. Their responsibility lies with their depositors, since they must make money with funds that they lend so that the depositors can earn interest. (The picture at the thrifts, as I write this, is changing somewhat — they are in financial trouble, and as an industry have, in effect, become deregulated and are allowed to offer credit cards and pursue more aggressive lending policies. But their essential function remains the same.)

Commercial banks, however, lend in a very different way. They create money, by the power given to them by the Federal Reserve. When a loan is made by a commercial bank, the bank writes a check to the debtor, sometimes simply depositing the amount of that check in the debtor's account. By law, commercial banks are forced to keep a percentage of that loan, *not* the full amount, on reserve — in this way, they protect their deposits. The percentage which they must keep on reserve comes out of their deposits, as well as funds they may borrow for a short time from other banks, or from the Federal Reserve. The rest of the loan is "created."

Here's an example. One afternoon Citibank gets a deposit of $150 from a customer. This is enough money to make up a 15 percent reserve on a $1,000 loan. They loan Schmidlap, a carpenter, $1,000. He promises to repay the loan, with interest.

Schmidlap walks down the street to the lumberyard for goods. He spends the $1,000, which the lumberyard deposits in their bank, Manufacturer's Hanover.

Manufacturer's Hanover takes the $1,000 and turns it into over $6,000 in loans. The loans help create jobs, build business, help consumers buy the things that they need, etc. The economy is kept active.

But wait a minute, you say. What about the original $150? Where did that come from? What if *that* was just "created" money? Where does it all end? (Or begin, for that matter?)

If too much money is piped into the economy, we get inflation.

Remember that. As simple as it sounds, that one sentence is why we had a credit crunch in the spring of 1980. It is why, as I write this in the spring of 1981, the prime rate jumps over and under the 20 percent mark, and the Dow-Jones is riding a roller coaster shaped by wildly fluctuating bond prices. (Don't worry, Schmidlap, you don't have to return the money. It's not your fault.)

To a greater or lesser degree — no one has really determined — bankers contribute to inflation. In an interview with the *New York Times* in April of 1981, Gaylord Freeman, retired chairman of the First Chicago Corporation, was quoted as saying, "The underlying cause of inflation has been a lack of self-discipline in our society. Nobody likes inflation, but everybody likes the causes of inflation. Banks are no different. If we accept the concept that a money supply increasing faster than the increase in goods and services is a main cause of inflation, it's easy to see how the banks are involved. Banks create money by making loans. And when the loans are made for such things as trips to Hawaii, they're even more inflationary than lending to a manufacturer. Even though the Federal Reserve controls a bank's lending through its reserve requirements, a bank can always borrow uncommitted reserves from another bank and expand its lending."

Inflation means that every dollar you have is worth less. Than what? That's sometimes hard to say. If you are living in an inflationary economy, as we are, the dollar after one inflationary cycle is worth less than it had been worth before the cycle began. The before-cycle dollar, of course, was worth less than its predecessor. Many economists use the 1970 dollar as our last measure of a pre-inflationary cycle currency. The dollar in mid-1981 is worth about half as much as the 1970 dollar.

In order to maintain the stability and integrity of the dollar, the Federal Reserve Board controls the creation of new money. Their decisions and the actions they take to control inflation are largely the result of their monetary policy. Monetary policy influences the total amount of credit available, and its cost.

The Fed does its job in a number of ways, which we are going to look at in a few pages. One way is by controlling the amount of reserves banks need to keep when making loans. This was the basis of the spring 1980 credit crunch, and the sharp hike in interest rates in the spring of 1981.

INFLATION AND THE CREDIT CRUNCH

Long before I began to write this book — when I was applying for a car loan, actually — I asked a banker to explain to me how interest rates were set. "Banks sell money," he told me. "It costs us something, and we make a profit when you buy it from us. Interest rates are what we charge you." He then went into an explanation of the influences on the prime rate, the federal funds rate, the Federal Reserve, and the credit markets. None of it made any sense to me — I was still trying to figure out whether or not the money he was lending me would put an FM radio in my car.

But what he was telling me was important, and I should have listened more carefully. Anyone who borrows, even if he or she is in the middle of paying back loans, is affected by the fluctuations in these rates.

Over the last few years, the fluctuations in interest rates have been big news, largely because of the policies of the Federal Reserve Board. In 1979, the seven governors of the board announced that they would attempt to control inflation by restricting the money supply, and not by controlling interest rates as they had been doing. Interest rates, then, became the tool by which bankers and investors anticipated, battled with, and profited from changes in the money supply and the inflationary climate in general.

Up until recently, you and I were unaffected by these fluctuations, since consumer loans were covered by strict usury laws, which held the interest rates charged to as low as 12 percent. Those days are *gone*. State legislators, in desperate attempts to keep the credit-card operations of the major banks in their states, or attract those same operations to their states, are providing some very attractive packages to those banks. The packages include elimination of usury rate ceilings and significant tax breaks. In some cases, banks will have to pay only 3 percent on their bankcard profits. (More about this in "Can They Do This to Me?")

As the usury laws come off, the price of credit will rise and (don't bet on this) fall in more direct correspondence with the cost of money to the banks than we have witnessed before. Now, more than ever, it is important for you to have a working knowledge of how economic policy affects your life. Until you are out of debt, it is doubly important, since most of these new laws are being enacted with retroactive provisions, which could raise the rates on consumer loans made months ago.

The link between economic policy and consumer credit was most amply demonstrated in the spring of 1980. On March 27, 1980, the secretary of the treasury, G. William Miller, entered a national press conference and, in full public display, cut his family's credit cards in half. Just two weeks before, Miller, President Carter, and other members of the administration had imposed an unprecedented series of credit controls on the country. The economy was being hit by strong double-digit inflation, the country's major banks had raised their prime interest rates (the rates quoted for their best customers, although many loans to "best customers" are discounted from the prime), and for the fourth time in as many months Washington was faced with finding a solution in one of two areas: the government sector or the consumer sector.

As you can imagine, it wasn't much of a debate. As Miller was slicing his cards, millions of Americans were being taught a difficult economic lesson. Perhaps you experienced, firsthand, some of the direct effects of the credit crunch. Credit was suddenly harder to get. You may have received a letter from your bank, stating that it was raising its interest rates and reducing available lines of credit. Maintenance fees, membership fees, and transaction fees were being levied. If you were in the market for a home, you discovered that mortgage money had all but dried up; the major mortgage lenders were quickly devising new lending structures that would allow them to tie the rate of a loan to the current rate of interest.

The more you relied on credit in your life, the more drastic the effects of the crunch were. Applications for every type of personal loan were being rejected practically out of hand. Consumers were being asked to make larger monthly payments on loans which they had already obtained, particularly installment credit agreements from department stores and bankcards.

Did the President and the Fed ask for all of this? What had we done to deserve this?

In the first place, all that the Fed and the President actually imposed, according to Governor Nancy Teeters of the Federal Reserve Board, "was a margin requirement on the creditor."

Remember Schmidlap? When he borrowed the $1,000 from Citibank, the $150 they kept in reserve was the margin required by the Fed. What the Fed told creditors, according to Governor Teeters, was that "If they expanded their consumer credit beyond what it was on March 14, they'd be subject to a reserve require-ment. In the case of nonbank creditors, they would be subject to a reserve requirement just like a bank. The public perception of that was not that at all. The public thought that the President had told them to tear up their cards.

"There was a great deal of shock aspect about all of this. Consumers took a long look and said, 'They're right. We are too deeply in debt.' They began paying off, until September and October of 1980, when they began using credit again."

One of the ironic consequences of the credit controls is that they increased credit-card profits in a way that the Fed and Congress had not expected. According to a House panel report issued in January 1981, "For many years creditors had sought ways to increase interest rates on credit, speed up repayment plans and charge annual fees for credit cards. When credit controls were invoked in March it gave those creditors an excuse to raise costs to consumers while blaming the Federal Government for their actions." The panel also commented that "although it was unnec-essary, unethical, and perhaps a breach of contract, 86% of the creditors who could do so chose to apply drastic new credit terms to their customers' past purchases." The study showed that some creditors increased monthly minimum payments by 150 percent, and interest rates by one-third.

In January 1981, Jack Anderson reported in his column that many banks turned the crunch into high profits. "The Fed," he wrote, "left it to the banker's discretion to choose the way they would curtail credit to their customers. And for some bankers, greed proved to be the better part of discretion."

A final word. S. Lees Booth, the senior vice-president and national director of research at the National Consumer Finance Association, in an interview in *Credit* magazine, commented: "The major lasting effect of the credit controls was the new pricing of lender services."

Equally ironic was that, as the Fed controlled the supply of credit available, the small businesses, the homeowner, and the consumer lender took the brunt of the banks' holding back on credit. "We went out of our way to say, 'Make sure that you continue to make loans for homes and automobiles and small businesses,' and the banks just did what they wanted," claims Governor Teeters.

HIGH INTEREST RATES — A FACT OF LIFE?

The big question, of course, is whether or not all of this monetary policy is doing any good at all. Monetary policy, for one thing, seems to signal rises in interest rates all across the board. When the money supply seems to grow too large, the Fed reduces the reserves held by commercial banks by selling these banks "securities," taking the money for the sale from the bank reserves. Since the banks have less reserves on hand from which to make their loans, they raise the interest rates so that their overall profit will not be affected. The bankers, as we have seen, are no dummies. When the Fed announces as innocent a statistic as a simple rise in the money rates, the bankers don't even wait for the reserves to be reduced. They just raise the rates — out of habit, anticipation, anxiety, or whatever it is that bankers operate out of.

An example which, at one fell swoop, demonstrates just how simple this process is and how complexly it is woven into the psychology of bankers and investors occurred in late April 1981.

On Friday, April 24, the Fed drained money from its system in order to tighten the money supply. Estimates of just how much money was drained ran from $2.5 billion to $10 billion. Securities dealers, who follow closely the buying and selling of those items by which the Fed controls reserves, had a hard time figuring just what the Fed was up to. Was the Fed dissatisfied with money supply growth? Would this be a short-term strategy that the Fed was employing, or a long-term one?

The prime rate began to go up. The next week, Chase Manhattan Bank led the surge by raising their prime from 17½ to 18 percent. Other banks followed. The prime rates across the country lined up, Indian style, on Wednesday, April 29, and in the meantime, the federal funds rate began to fluctuate wildly.

Now — the federal funds rate is the rate banks charge each other for loans that they make "overnight." Although in many cases the loans are, literally, for overnight periods, others are two-, three-, or four-day loans. The banks are forced into the position of borrowing this money from each other when they are trying to protect their reserves. And especially so that they won't be caught short on Wednesday of any given week, when they have to settle accounts with the Fed. If their reserve positions are not settled by Wednesday, the banks are in trouble.

(At last, we all have something in common with these high-level financiers. We all know what it's like to come up short when it's time to settle our accounts.)

Back to April 1981. By Thursday, the federal funds rate had risen to 21 percent. Those who had been trading in the credit markets told of how, in the beginning of the week, the Fed had been trying to correct the mistake they had made in the previous week — draining too many funds — by buying securities. There was one small problem — there were no securities to be bought. The situation became so desperate that the Fed sought help from the Treasury, which placed between $6 billion and $7 billion into special accounts at commercial banks.

There is a punch line to this story. On Friday, May 1, the Federal Reserve announced that the nation's basic money supply had risen by $4.2 billion in the week ended April 22. One economist summed the situation up by saying, "I think the Fed knew about these big money supply numbers, and it has been tightening already. That explains why the short-term rates went up so much this week."

Oh. So they knew all along, did they? And in the meantime, another nail was driven in the high-interest-rate coffin. The steady pattern of money supply figures, banker psychology, and costly money had played itself out again.

The result of this kind of group action is the economic roller coaster we've been riding on for the past few years. I related that long example to you to demonstrate just how ingrained those knee-jerk responses to the money supply are. Whether or not these interest rates will cease their convulsions in the near future, and whether or not any of this will have done any good, is not the concern of this book. The fact that high interest rates and inflation are going to be a major influence on the life of every debtor in this country is.

Jim Boyle, director of governmental affairs at the Consumer Federation of America, has been one of the most outspoken critics of the Fed's policy of fighting inflation by raising interest rates. He cites the depression of the auto and housing industries, the large increases in the Consumer Price Index, the number of small businesses that have been driven out of business by the high-interest policy, and the decrease in productivity caused by interest rates that discourage borrowing by businesses for new plans — all of these — as evidence of high-interest destruction of the economy.

"In human terms," says Boyle, "the higher interest rates are particularly devastating. When less creditworthy individuals borrow to meet their basic needs, they particularly feel the sting of higher interest rates. And the less creditworthy an individual is, the larger the interest rate increases.

"The higher interest rates make it much more difficult for low- and middle-income Americans to attain financial security. The high rates help push more and more families, who must borrow to purchase necessities, into an economic pressure cooker, with destructive effects on family stability and cohesion."

Apparently, there are very few people looking out for the consumer. You can expect higher interest rates, greater restrictions on credit, and *very expensive* credit, with costs far beyond the simple interest rates, in the near future. Other companies that thrive on high interest rates will flourish as well. Collection agencies expect business to boom as high rates slow bill payments. The banks will fluctuate their interest rates with the prime, and the state legislators will allow them to make those hikes retroactive.

Consumer, look out for yourself. Get off the credit merry-go-round now.

FACING IT

I don't like to think about debt. I don't like being in debt, thinking about the ways we've handled it poorly, ways we've mishandled our money — going over it's depressing. I feel bad because it seems like we don't have any resources to deal with it. It's painful!

— A CALIFORNIAN

ALTHOUGH THE PREVIOUS CHAPTERS may have increased your understanding of why people go into debt, and might have given you a better perspective on your own debt situation, there comes a time when education must stop and action must begin. This is the chapter where we get down to business.

The chapter following this deals with emergency situations. If you are currently being threatened by a creditor or collector, you can combine the steps in this chapter with the advice you'll find there.

At this point it's important to get as complete a picture of your assets, liabilities, and contractual obligations as possible. The goal of the worksheets included in this chapter is to find out how much money you owe, whom you owe it to, and where the money will come from to pay them back. From here, you can begin to see clearly which alternatives will work for you, and how long it will take you to get out of debt.

We'll investigate the terms of your credit agreements as well, so that you can understand better the nature of your obligations to your creditors. The chapter after next will discuss how to get your own home and your family in shape for getting out of debt, where you can turn to for help, and how to build a solid, dependable repayment schedule.

For many people, getting out of debt is a two- or three-year process. There are long-term debts that need to be settled, and only a limited amount of financial resources to deal with them. If you think of that process as a long journey, then this chapter will provide the map for that journey. Most of the steps that you have to take in this chapter and the chapter after next occur outside any contact you may have with your creditors. If you are having debt troubles, these steps will occur before you contact your creditors to discuss your debt with them, or before you have to face them in legal and semilegal confrontations. If your debt problems are simpler, the steps here will help you manage them with greater efficiency. Some of the steps in these chapters will take a week or two to complete.

There's some hard work in these chapters. There is a great deal of hard work involved in getting out of debt. But the picture doesn't look so bleak when you've got it laid out in front of you. Emotionally, you'll probably feel as though you've gotten out from under debt after you take these first few steps.

HOW MUCH DO I OWE? HOW MUCH DO I HAVE?

The first things you have to pull together are the basic records of your personal finances:

1. Paycheck stubs.
2. Canceled checks for the last three months.
3. All bills — monthly bills for utilities, phones, etc. All credit-card bills, insurance bills. If you are unable to apply the monthly balances on these bills to a yearly estimate because the amounts fluctuate considerably over the year, call or write your creditors and request copies of last year's bills. Tell them that time is of the essence. They usually cooperate, especially if you owe them money.
4. Sales contracts and credit agreements. Again, if you don't have copies of these, obtain them from your creditor or the place where you bought these items.
5. Bank statements, loan books, other bank documents.

Other items will be specified in the worksheets.

The first thing to do is to make a complete list of everyone you owe money to. Every creditor, account number, address, and phone number. If you have been contacted by these people, list the names of the persons you have spoken with, and if possible the dates when you spoke with them. Later, this information will be important in setting priorities for whom you'll pay back first.

There are two worksheets in this chapter, and one in the chapter after the next. The first worksheet will give you a sense of your overall financial position. The second will show your net worth. In the chapter after next, a third worksheet will give you a day-to-day picture of your income and outgo.

GETTING A FIX ON YOUR POSITION

This can usually be done by using your checkbook and paycheck stubs. (If you're confused about the process of filling the chart out, an example follows.) In this worksheet, expenses that you must meet every month are separated from expenses that occur annually or semiannually, but not on a monthly basis. Among the items you should be careful of are medical and dental bills, and other items that may not be easy to predict, but have the potential to wreak havoc on any budget.

MONTHLY INCOME
Your take-home pay _____
Spouse's take-home pay _____
Other regular income _____
    1 TOTAL _____

MONTHLY EXPENSES
Rent or mortgage _____
Food _____
Utilities _____
   (If any utility takes up
   more than a third of
   your utility payments,
   or if it is subject to fluctuations over the year,

ANNUAL EXPENSES
Taxes (not deducted from
   pay or included in
   mortgage payment) _____
Insurance (not paid
   monthly) _____
Medical and dental
   bills _____
School costs _____
Major purchases and
   repairs _____
Vacation _____
Clothing _____

break it out from the
total here and list
immediately below.
List as utilities: oil, gas,
water, sewerage,
phone, and electricity.)

Savings and investments _____

Insurance _____

Charitable contributions _____

Transportation and auto _____

Entertainment _____

All other _____

2̲ TOTAL _____

Other (subscriptions,
club memberships,
gifts) _____

TOTAL _____

Divide the total of annual
expenses by 12 to find
the amount that should
be set aside every
month to cover these
expenses. 3̲ _____

PAYMENTS ON CURRENT DEBTS

Personal loans
(list lender and purpose)   *monthly payment*   *balance*

_____   _____   _____

_____   _____   _____

_____   _____   _____

_____   _____   _____

Charge accounts and other installment payments

_____   _____   _____

_____   _____   _____

_____   _____   _____

_____   _____   _____

4̲ TOTALS _____   _____

Add totals 2, 3 & 4   (2) Monthly expenses
+ (3) 1/12 Annual expenses
+ (4) Payments on current debts
_____

TOTAL

This is what you have "going out" every month. Subtract what you
have going out from total (1), your income.

(1) Monthly income
− (2 + 3 + 4)
_____

Your current saving or debt

If your payments exceed your current income, you are seriously in debt — as if you hadn't known already! Don't panic — this book will help you reduce the amount of your monthly payments so that they are more in line with your income and your needs.

If you have anything left over, and have included all payments due on old debts, the remaining amount is available either for saving or for servicing new debt — maintaining payments on what you borrow.

Let's look at an example of a typical worksheet. Tom takes home $1,200 a month. His wife Mary stays home with her infant daughter, but earns $250 a month after taxes doing part-time work at home. That gives them $1,450 a month. Their mortgage payment totals $565, which includes taxes on the property. Food equals $240 a month, and other monthly expenses add with the food and mortgage bills to equal an even $1,000.

Tom and Mary's annual expenses, which include $40 a month for car insurance, $100 a month for medical and dental bills, and a $50 saving every month for their yearly vacation, gives them a total of $320.

With $130 a month remaining in their budget, Tom and Mary face a total of $279 per month in payments for personal loans, charge accounts, and other installment payments. (Oddly enough, these payments place Tom and Mary in debt although they are slightly below the "20 percent of your take-home pay" guidelines. It is the basic necessities of life which are really putting them behind the eight ball.) Their installment debts appear on their chart as:

TYPE OF LOAN	MONTHLY PAYMENT	BALANCE
Auto loan	$109	$2616
Bank loan	$100	$1785
Washer and dryer on credit card	$25	$450
MasterCard	$23	$825
Visa	$22	$764

Obviously, Tom and Mary can't afford to take on more debt. Additionally, it will be two years before they can regard themselves as being comfortably out of debt.

What if Tom and Mary stopped using credit completely? If they used their $130 a month to pay off their debts, without any adjustments in their budget (and with the cooperation of their creditors), it would take them 49 months — over four years — to pay off all their debts, although some of the debts would be wiped out before then.

There are many steps Tom and Mary can take — credit counseling, bankruptcy, or their own debt-management program. Each step involves different demands on them and on their finances. Whichever way they go, you can see the kind of intricate, complex set of circumstances that can arise when you enter into a plan for getting out of debt.

Now that you have an accurate picture of your debt limit, and perhaps how badly you are above it, it is worthwhile to take a look at your net worth. You may be able to liquidate some of these items to get out of debt, keeping others as a security blanket. On the other hand, it might be nice just to know you've got *something* to show for all those credit bills.

As you can see, this worksheet can't be answered completely in one sitting. Here's a guide to help you look for the accurate answers to some of these items:

- Check with an institution that sells U.S. Savings Bonds to determine the current value of yours. Current value is rarely the face value — it's either more or less.
- The cash value of your life insurance can be determined by a table in your policy or by the agent of the insurance company. This only applies to whole life, not term. The same goes for the surrender value of any annuities you own.
- It might be impossible to determine the present-day value of your pension or profit-sharing plan, since you aren't supposed to receive these monies until you retire. But, your personnel office should be able to tell you what the cash value of your plan would be if you quit your job. If you have an Individual Retirement Account or a

Keogh plan, list its current balance, minus the penalty for premature withdrawal.

- It's important to get the exact market value of your home. Find out what similar houses have sold in your area (you can find this in a local land records office), or ask a real estate agent for an estimate of your home's current value. Do the same for any other real estate you own.
- The *Wall Street Journal* can tell you the current value of your investments. Your broker can help with this, too.
- There are a number of books with current used-car prices, but the Kelley Blue Book, available at most commercial banks, is perhaps the most reliable source. For help with other vehicles and boats, contact your dealer.
- Listing the value of household furnishings, etc., is *very* difficult, since there's no real market for these items. A safe estimate would be to calculate what 25 percent of the original price would be, then halve that. This is what a pawnshop would probably give you, without any haggling.

Of course, filling out the rest of the form won't be as difficult. Most people to whom you owe money do you the favor of reminding you monthly of your obligations.

When you've completed this worksheet, it's easy to compute your asset-to-debt ratio. It's an important step to seeing where you stand.

Sometimes, a person who owes a large amount of money can take heart in the fact that the borrowed funds have been put to good use — for anything from medical care or tuition, to their home, to necessary household items. Also, you might find items on this worksheet which can be used to help you get out of debt — property (such as a car, a boat, or some other "luxury" item) that can be leased, rented, or sold, cash in bank accounts that is earning less interest than your loans are charging, and so on.

THE HIGH COST OF LIVING IN DEBT

Credit costs vary. Unless you pay attention to the cost of credit, you can end up paying more than you have to. We'll look at two purchases — one of them expensive, one relatively inexpensive —

Your Net Worth

ASSETS

Cash on hand and in checking accounts   _____
Cash in savings accounts   _____
Certificates of deposit   _____
U.S. Savings Bonds (current value)   _____
Cash value of life insurance   _____
Surrender value of annuities   _____
Cash value of pension plan   _____
Cash value of profit-sharing plan   _____
Market value of home   _____
Market value of other real estate   _____
Market value of business interests   _____
Market value of securities   _____
Market value of auto, other vehicles, boat   _____
Market value of household furnishings, appliances,
  personal belongings   _____
Other assets   _____
       TOTAL   _____

LIABILITIES

Current bills   _____
Charge accounts   _____
Installment debts   _____
Auto loan   _____
Taxes   _____
Home mortgage   _____
Other loans   _____
       TOTAL   _____
   NET WORTH (assets minus liabilities)   _____

to see how the unintelligent use of credit can add to the burden of being in debt.

Our two purchases are going to be an automobile and a winter coat. The car is going to cost us $5,000, and we'll be putting $1,000 down on the purchase. The coat will cost $175. We'll shop for bank financing to pay for our car, and try to decide between using our MasterCard or a store credit card for the coat.

There are two important elements to remember when shopping for credit — the finance charge and the annual percentage rate. Under the Truth in Lending Act, the creditor must tell you what these are, in writing and before you sign an agreement. (Of course, whenever you use your bankcards, or your credit cards, it is taken for granted that you've read the terms of your agreement before signing the back of your card.)

Before we tackle our two purchases, let's have a short course in the true cost of credit.

The finance charge is the total dollar amount you pay to use credit. It includes interest costs, and sometimes other costs such as service charges, some credit-related insurance premiums, and appraisal fees. For example, borrowing $100 for a year might cost you $12 in interest. If there was also a service charge of $3, the finance charge would be $15.

The annual percentage rate (APR) is the percentage cost (or relative cost) of credit on a yearly basis. This is a key figure for comparing costs, regardless of the amount of credit or how long you have to repay it. Again, suppose you borrow $100 for one year and pay a finance charge of $15. If you can keep the entire $100 for the whole year and then pay it back all at once, you are paying an APR of 15 percent. *But* if you repay the $100 and the finance charge in twelve monthly installments of $9.50 each, you don't really get to use the $100 for the whole year. In fact, you get to use less and less of that $100 each month. In this case, the APR is closer to 20 percent.

In addition, in the case of open-end credit, creditors must tell you the method of calculating the finance charge. Creditors use a number of different systems to calculate the balance on which they assess finance charges. Some creditors add finance charges after subtracting payments made during the billing period. This is called the adjusted balance method. Others give you no credit for payments made during the billing period. This is called the previous balance method. Under a third method — the average daily balance method — creditors add your balances for each day in the billing period and then divide by the number of days in the billing period.

Here's a sample of the three billing systems:

	ADJUSTED BALANCE	PREVIOUS BALANCE	AVERAGE DAILY BALANCE
Monthly interest rate	1½%	1½%	1½%
Previous balance	$400	$400	$400
Payments	$300	$300	$300
Interest charge	$1.50	$6.00	$3.75
	($100 × 1½%)	($400 × 1½%)	($250 × 1½%)

Additionally, creditors must tell you when finance charges begin on your credit account, so you know how much time you have to pay your bills before a finance charge is added. Some creditors, for example, give you a thirty-day free ride to pay your balance before imposing a finance charge, although that practice is going the way of the horse and buggy, thanks to state legislators.

First, we'll shop for financing for our car. As you can tell from the above descriptions, the actual mathematics of installment borrowing can get very complicated. Here's how to keep your eye on the important details.

Bank A offers loans at 10 percent APR, with 36 months to repay. Bank B offers loans at 12 percent, with 36 to 48 months to repay. Bank C offers loans at 9 percent, with 24 to 48 months to repay. All three offer credit insurance: Bank A and Bank B offer it as an option, at $10 a year, but Bank C requires it, at a cost of $45 a year. Both Bank A and Bank C assess late charges of $10 after ten days of the monthly due date, but Bank C will not accumulate charges over $25. Bank B also charges a service charge of $50 simply for making the loan.

If you want to make your loan for a 36-month period, for $4,000, Bank A seems to be your best bet. The late-charge factor — A's can exceed $25 and C's won't — against the extra $105 (the difference between A's and C's insurance rates) for C's credit insurance weighs heavily in A's favor, and also cancels out C's 1 percent APR advantage. B is clearly out of the running — with its high interest and service charges. (Don't be surprised, though, if a lot of your friends are getting their loans at Bank B. Those extra charges probably pay for B's exhaustive marketing.)

Before you actually make your decision on any large loan, get the *actual cost* in dollars and cents, in writing.

Now, let's go shopping for our coat. We can pay up to $30 a month for the next six months on this coat ($1 a day for warmth isn't bad). Let's calculate how much above the $175 ticket price we'll actually spend.

MasterCard calculates 1-percent-per-month interest on the average daily balance (some of MasterCard's finance charges can vary, depending on the issuing bank). You'd need a computer to specifically average out the $175 over 6 months, so let's simplify by charging 1½ percent per month on the declining balance produced by payments of $30 per month. Over six months, you would pay $9 in interest, providing you paid the last payment before finance charges were due on it.

Another alternative that MasterCard offers is a cash advance for which you are charged 1 percent per month. At that rate, you would pay $6 in interest over six months.

The store card charges 1½ percent per month, but on the previous balance system. On that system, we would pay a total of $9.45 interest.

So, we'll walk down to the bank, pick up a cash advance, and go back and buy our coat. Unless, of course, we feel that the time and effort spent in all that traveling is worth $3, in which case we'll use our MasterCard *or* our store card. Three dollars may not seem like much, but it adds up.

You *can* be fooled by finance charges and annual percentage rates. Many a department store has sold its goods to customers while the goods were on sale and marked down by 25 percent, only to make a healthy profit above and beyond the 25 percent on the interest charged to the customer on the installment purchase.

People who borrow heavily on the "buy now — pay later with inflated dollars" philosophy are betting against odds which, as we have seen, rival the complexity of a physicist's calculations. People who buy that philosophy forget that the purchase of goods, for the normal household, is almost always an expense, never an investment.

Finally, all of this points up to the high cost of being in debt. The further you are indebted to creditors, the more your credit becomes limited because of late payments, exceeding credit limits, and so forth. By losing your freedom of choice between credit plans, you can fall prey to those who lend to high-risk borrowers while charging higher-than-average interest rates.

IN CASE OF EMERGENCY . . .

Facing up to your debts, as we have seen, can involve a complete reassessment of your role as a wage earner, property owner, and borrower. You've seen what you owe and to whom, where your assets lie, and what your obligations are to your creditors. Most likely, you've had a few surprises — I hope that at least a few of them have been pleasant.

In the natural course of things, the next step would be to develop a debt-management program. But the natural course of things doesn't always match the present circumstances. Sometimes emergencies arise — you are threatened with legal action, or are in the midst of it, you are being harassed, your property is going to be repossessed, or some other situation has arisen where time is of the essence.

The next chapter contains a detailed breakdown of those emergency situations, how they can affect you, and what you can do to buy time until you have gained control of the situation and can meet it on your own terms.

Fortunately, most of you are not faced with an emergency. In that case, while the next chapter can provide you with some useful knowledge of what creditors and collectors have in their arsenals, the procedure for making a debt-management plan you can stay with is found in "Making a Plan You Can Stick To."

EMERGENCY SITUATIONS

CONSUMER CREDIT TRANSACTION
IMPORTANT!! YOU ARE BEING SUED!!
THIS IS A COURT PAPER — A SUMMONS.
DON'T THROW IT AWAY!! TALK TO A LAWYER RIGHT AWAY!! PART OF
YOUR PAY CAN BE TAKEN FROM YOU (GARNISHED). IF YOU DO NOT
BRING THIS TO COURT, OR SEE A LAWYER, YOUR PROPERTY CAN BE
TAKEN AND YOUR CREDIT RATING CAN BE HURT!! YOU MAY HAVE TO
PAY OTHER COSTS TOO!! IF YOU CAN'T PAY FOR YOUR OWN LAWYER
BRING THESE PAPERS TO THIS COURT RIGHT AWAY. THE CLERK
(PERSONAL APPEARANCE) WILL HELP YOU!!

— City of New York Summons to Appear for Default Judgment

IF YOU BOUGHT THIS BOOK because you are in desperate need to resolve a threatening situation imposed by a creditor or collector and don't have the time right now to deal with two weeks' worth of planning, the advice in this chapter is designed for you.

If you are in the extremely critical position of having a creditor's remedies immediately imposed on you, you may not realize that you're also in a very strong position. Most companies don't want to repossess your car or your furniture (they'd much rather have your money than used merchandise). Court costs are expensive and erode the profit margins of creditors. What you need to do when you are nearing the point of legal action or repossession, no matter how much you've procrastinated or lied before, is to present yourself immediately as someone who has taken hold of his or her financial situation and needs only a short time to begin to make good on the agreement.

There are two important things to remember. You are most likely going to need outside help at this point, either from a credit counseling service or a lawyer. Don't hesitate to search out this help. The second thing to remember is to put everything in writing. Even when you make a phone call, make notes about the call — the date, who was contacted, and what was discussed.

In the next chapter, I will discuss how to go about finding a credit counselor. It's an important decision, and one that is filled with as many consumer pitfalls as any credit purchase. But at this point, you can't afford to be choosy. You can locate a credit counselor quickly by contacting your local office of consumer affairs, or by asking your creditor to refer you to one. (This second route isn't the most preferable, but time is of the essence.)

If it appears that a credit counselor can't help you — and in some cases they can't and will tell you so — you will have to find a lawyer. Looking for a lawyer when your creditors are on your back is like looking for a doctor when you're bleeding. At the end of the list of emergency situations, I detail how to find a good lawyer quickly.

Putting everything in writing is one of the best things a consumer can do. Most consumers don't know which practices of their creditors and collectors are improper, and the collectors and creditors rely on this ignorance. By sending a letter, you demonstrate that you want your situation changed, and are willing to work for it. Your rights in a consumer credit transaction, and the situations in which they are most often violated, are outlined in the chapter "Can They Do This to Me?" Right now, it's important to know how to write a letter to your creditor that lets him know, in no uncertain terms, that you are part of the small group of consumers who cannot be deceived, defrauded, or bullied. It's an important point — in your favor.

When you send the letter, send it by certified mail. And follow these guidelines, adapted from the consumer handbook *Super Threat* by John M. Striker and Andrew O. Shapiro.

- Be confident. You have to be able to take the matter from the personal level in which the collector or creditor has no doubt placed it. By sending a certified letter outlining the history of your account and any relevant conversations, setting forth your proposals, and recognizing your rights, you take things out of the personal sphere and place them on a business level — where they should have been all along.

- Go for their weak spot: money. They want your money, and have so far been unable to get it. But their success will still be measured by whether or not they get your money, and how much of it they get. In your letter, demonstrate to them that you intend to repay them. Enclose some money now, if at all possible, or show them you have taken serious steps toward getting the money.
- Give them an alternative. Show them what you propose to do, and take their needs into account. Show them that you've been listening to them all these months, and respond to what they've been saying. (You do *not* have to admit to any slanderous charges, of course). Offer them a ray of hope. Remember, they want your money, not you. Prove to them that you are serious.
- Give them a time frame. Tell them with as much precision as possible when you will be taking action, and when they can expect results. Or, tell them when you expect them to take action — or halt the action that you feel is violating your rights.
- Without being abusive or angry, let your creditor know that you are aware of your rights, and are planning on exercising them. Let him know that you are enlisting the help of credit counselors, lawyers, and local officials at the consumer affairs office, the Federal Trade Commission, and any other agency you can think of which might have jurisdiction.

BUYING TIME

Letters of any kind are your best tool. You'll never go wrong by communicating with your creditors. Further: be specific. Tell them about your job. Tell them about your last turn-down for a raise. Tell them about your kid's dentist. Tell them about your Aunt Flora, visiting from Minneapolis, who eats like an army. While you're telling them your troubles, tell them how wonderful they are. Tell them you *knew* they would understand. Tell them you won't leave home without them. Tell them how you love having clout. Tell them that you, like the rest of America, love to shop their store. Creditors are most worried when they don't hear anything from you. Soon, they'll warm up to your letters. Draw the line at dinner invitations, though, whether you extend them, or they do.

THE SIX MOST COMMON EMERGENCIES

1. Dunning Letters

For some consumers, the receipt of a dunning letter is cause for panic. For many others, the long succession of dunning notices is a way of life.

Every creditor differs in the cycle of dunning letters, although they all follow the same general pattern. (Many creditors have tightened up on their procedures since the credit restraints of 1980, and it's safe to assume that whenever the economy gets rough, they'll continue tightening the screws, as the competition for the repayment dollar becomes fiercer.)

According to Tom Lynch, vice-president for consumer credit at Chase Manhattan Bank in New York, their dunning cycle is as follows:

"You receive a bill on the first of the month. If you don't make a payment, on your next bill we make a note. If you still don't pay, ten days after the second bill, we'll send you a note. After sixty days, we'll send a letter, reminding you and telling you that your account is in jeopardy. Our people will then call you to find out why you haven't made your payment. At this point, or at any point after, we can suspend or cancel your account.

"If after ninety days you still haven't made a payment — and we're speaking here of the minimum payment on the account — we will pass it on to our legal department. If they are unable to get a payment from you, and by then your account is usually closed, and we are looking for a new payment arrangement or a complete payment, we will send the account to a legal collection agency after 180 days."

Most creditors I spoke with told me that their highest rate of payments came when a third party entered the collection picture, such as a legal collection agency.

If you feel that you are receiving dunning notices at the tail end of the cycle — meaning that you haven't made a payment in at least 60 to 90 days — then you may have an emergency situation on your hands. If the creditor has set a date for legal action or transfer of your account to a collection agency or attorney, then it is important for you to call them immediately, and then to write to them confirming what was said in your phone conversation.

Tell them you have been having problems paying your bills (which they no doubt suspect anyway) and are working on a complete, comprehensive debt management program. If you have begun talking to a credit counselor, tell them this. (Working with a credit counselor is widely regarded as a very positive sign for any debtor. It can often keep your account from "aging" further — that is, from proceeding to the next step in the collection process.) Above all, you have to be prepared to show them that you are serious about paying back your debts, regardless of what their past experience with you has been. If you are following the debt-management steps in this book, you'll have plenty of ammunition for this.

Give them a date, probably two weeks from your conversation, when you will come back to them with a definite plan for repayment. (They may accept this date — or they may want you to call them earlier; in which case explain to them that you are completely reviewing your finances and need the time to make sure that the answers you give them are honest and reliable, not just something off the top of your head, to which you may not be able to hold.)

Incidentally, there's no need to panic if you receive letters filled with legal jargon. It is illegal for a collector to threaten legal action unless they are absolutely prepared to take it. This does not mean that they cannot refer to "imminent legal action," or some other ambiguous phrase. But it does prohibit their saying "We will take you to court next week," if they are not actually planning to do so. Refer to the chapter "Can They Do This to Me?" for complete details.

2. Harassment

The distinction between what is legal and illegal in contacts between debtors and creditors is not clear to most people, as I said earlier. This holds true not only for debtors, but also for creditors and courts. It's something you can use to your advantage. Once you know your rights and have a solid repayment plan in hand, you can do a great deal to stop harassment. For more about your specific rights, see "Can They Do This to Me?"

3. Legal Action

If the creditor or his lawyer has set a specified time for legal action, there is still room to convince them that you are serious about paying back your debt. *Most accounts get this far because there has been no communication between the debtor and the creditor.* You can step in now and make an arrangement, and many lawyers will drop the action against you. All of this depends, of course, not on the justice of your proposed payment plan, but on how the lawyer is being paid: on retainer, or by the case.

If the lawyer is being paid by the case, as is often done by small lenders, he may be hesitant to accept a payment plan because of the structures of his fee — it may be to his financial interest to get you into court. A lawyer on retainer, on the other hand, gets the same amount of money no matter how the case is settled. In fact, a creditor might find his fee to a lawyer worth it because of the number of clients who come to terms when they receive a lawyer's letter. This is a case of lawyer as dunning service — the lawyer doesn't identify himself as a collector, because he isn't, since you make your payment to the creditor. This type of set-up leaves you a great deal of flexibility — if you can present a fair means of repayment.

In general, the task of delivering the summons is left by the court to the creditor's lawyer. If you have received a summons, and the lawyer won't make an outside arrangement with you, the first thing you should do is determine how long you have to answer it. Usually, the time given to respond to a summons differs according to the method by which the summons was delivered. If it was hand-delivered, the time period is shorter than if it was delivered by mail. In New York City, for example, you have twenty days to respond if the summons was hand delivered, and thirty days if it was delivered by mail. These time spans differ from state to state, but they are usually spelled out in readable English on the summons.

One note: one of the most despicable sidelines in the consumer-credit industry is known as "sewer service." As we will see later, if a consumer does not answer a summons, he will be found in default and the creditor can proceed with his next lawful remedy — usually wage garnishment. Some unscrupulous creditors, in an attempt to get to their money without going through the step of having your side of the story heard in court, will hire summons delivery services who have a reputation for "sewer service" — the summonses are delivered to the sewer (or the garbage can, or whatever) instead of to the defendant. Estimates of the percentage of defaults that are a result of sewer service run as high as 15 percent, according to David Caplovitz in his study *Consumers in Trouble*.

If, within the time limits given on your summons, you have a week or two to go through the budgeting and debt-management steps in this and the next chapter, do so. This will give you a firm base to work from when you contact your creditors, a counseling service, or an attorney.

The purpose of the summons is to have you appear at the court to answer the complaint made by your creditor. You might be asked to appear before a clerk of the court before a certain date. You have three choices at this point: go to the clerk and answer the summons, contact the attorneys for your creditor, or not answer the summons at all.

The worst thing you can do at this point is to ignore the summons. Even if you *haven't* had time to work out a debt-management program — even if you *don't* have a lawyer — *GO*. Your appearance, in itself, is a sign of good faith on your part, and even at this late date some accommodation may be worked out. A "no-show" will almost invariably be taken by the court as an admission that the creditor's claims are valid and cannot be resolved without stern measures.

I'm all for breaking down the Wall of Fear, but there are times when fear can be a healthy motivator, and this is one of them. If you fail to answer the summons, the court will find you in default of the agreement, and make a judgment against you. After this, wage garnishment — either voluntary or involuntary — is only a matter of time, and a short time at that. Your ability to negotiate anything with your creditors will, for the most part, be out of their hands. At this point you'll have to deal with the sheriff's or marshal's office.

You can contact your creditor's lawyers when you receive a summons and, if you are able to reach some kind of arrangement for repayment of the loan, they can cancel the summons. If you obtain such an arrangement, put it in writing and keep checking with the clerk's office of the court to see that the summons has, in fact, been dismissed. Of course, if you fail to live up to the agreement you make with them, they'll jump like sparks to summon you again, and it will be on the court record that this is the second summons. So, it's important to budget properly.

The third alternative is to go down to the court clerk or to the court appearance to plead your case. Again, a solid plan for repayment is your best defense. Be honest. Tell them why you haven't been able to pay your debts, and tell them you plan to make good. Even if you've lied to them before, demonstrate to them — by using the budget worksheets and guidelines provided in this book, for example — that you are now serious. The courts, for the most part, are sympathetic to people who have gotten in over their heads. You will not be found in default if you are able to present a workable repayment plan to the court. On the other hand, the stakes are higher now than ever before.

Court clerks are usually helpful in this area, although they may be overworked and, in fact, underinformed. But, if you go in knowing what your defense is, and how you want to respond to the claim made by your creditor, you can knowledgeably present your case well.

4. Wage Garnishment

If you have been notified of a wage garnishment, try to work out a voluntary plan. This will probably wreak havoc on your budget, but your hands are tied at this point. If your garnishment is involuntary, go to your employer and explain your situation. Tell him that you are seriously trying to manage your debts, and that you would appreciate his cooperation and help during this difficult time. If you are a good employee, your employer might be sympathetic.

Of course, one of the dangers of garnishment is that you may be fired if your employer learns of your indebtedness. Although this is illegal, it is *not* illegal — since it cannot be proven — for an employer to find dissatisfaction with some other part of your job because of their aggravation over your garnishment, or because of the atmosphere of distrust a garnishment might create.

On occasion, someone has found he is subject to garnishment although he never received a summons. The mail, and the clerks, can make mistakes. In this case, or in other cases where you suspect you are the victim of a faulty legal process, get a lawyer. He can vacate the judgment against you, or reopen the judgment. Again, see "Can They Do This to Me?" for more details.

5. Repossession

Your creditor can move to repossess any possession that is security for your loan — such as your car, appliances, or other items for which the loan was expressly made and contracted for — whenever they feel you are in no position to keep up with your payments. Repossession rarely occurs without some kind of strong warning to the consumer, since the creditor would rather have payment than returned goods.

If faced with repossession, sometimes it is worth your peace of mind to surprise the lender and arrange for a simple exchange of goods, especially if there is no way possible for you to make any kind of payment. This leaves your creditor with a better impression of you, and *perhaps* will leave you in better standing in the future, when you wish to regain credit with him.

In most states, by law, when the merchant or lender takes back property, he is obligated to put it up for sale and seek a fair price for it. If he sells the product for more than enough to pay the balance of your account, he is usually obligated to repay the difference. Sometimes, a waiver will be produced after the default judgment, which the creditor will ask you to sign. The waiver will state that the creditor will *not* be subject to repaying the balance of the price obtained in reselling the goods. Of course, you should only sign the waiver if the creditor also includes a clause that states you will not have to pay any unrecovered balance after the sale, if the goods bring less than the money you owe.

There are further details on repossession on page 182.

6. Deficiency Judgment

If your creditor does not receive the full amount owed to him by the resale of your repossessed goods, he can go back to the court and get a deficiency judgment. This means that he can come in and take whatever possessions you own that he feels can be resold to pay off your balance.

Some consumer-credit agreements contain a "deficiency clause." This entitles creditors to the same remedies as a deficiency judgment, without requiring them to go to court.

The emergency situations described in this chapter come about when all communication has broken down between the consumer and the creditor. In most cases, the creditor will make other arrangements with the debtor and, as we have seen, these arrangements can be made even in the midst of an emergency situation if you are able to convince the creditor that you are able to pay your debt through a solid debt-management program. The steps you need to take to begin that program are covered in the next chapter.

MAKING A PLAN
YOU CAN STICK TO

You can't just look at what a person has coming in every month and what they have to pay out at the end of the month if you really want to help them out of debt. You have to take everything into account — their problems with being old, their psychological problems, what's going on in their family, with their boss — or you're not helping them at all.

> — LUTHER GATLING, member of the Federal Reserve Board's Consumer Advisory Council

THE JAPANESE CHARACTER FOR CRISIS is also the character for opportunity. At this point in your debt problems, when you are first realizing the depth of your difficulties, you can turn your crises into opportunities by taking the offensive. You've already taken the first steps by seeing just how deeply in debt you are, and by getting an idea of how long it will take you to meet your obligations.

You are currently in a better position than ever to negotiate your way out of debt. The phenomenal rise in bankruptcies has left creditors reeling, searching for some way to avoid having their assets diminished by people filing for relief in the courts. Until the bankruptcy code is revised (a process that could occur in the next year or two), their one remedy is to work, to the best of their abilities, with their debtors. The threat of bankruptcy, although I advise against stating it explicitly to your creditors, definitely works for the debtor.

Knowing how much you owe and to whom is the first step to getting out of debt. But money, whether owed or owned, is only a medium of exchange for a vast number of goods and services that fulfill our personal needs. For most of us, owing money, making a budget, and paying the money back involve putting our personal resources to work, as well. Often, this extends beyond the family — to counselors, lawyers, and friends.

The next steps you will be taking to get out of debt carry your program from your home to your creditors — with possible stops at credit counselors, family counselors, or lawyers. It's important that you have a firm plan of action, based on the facts of what you are able to repay, not what you wish you could. This chapter will get you moving in that direction.

Whether you decide to work on your own or get help, it's important to know what the process of budgeting, establishing a repayment schedule, and contacting your creditors is all about.

This is the essence of the debt-management program outlined in this book. If you go to a credit-counseling service or a lawyer, you will eventually have to go through a process similar to the one I have developed. But no process you go through will be as complete and thorough as the one in this book — and this debt-management program has one very distinct, very important advantage: you do it all on your own. In this program, you learn firsthand how your budget operates. You develop and tailor your repayment program, maintaining complete control over your personal needs. And *you* negotiate with your creditors, and learn where you stand from what they say to you — not what a counselor or lawyer tells you they're saying.

Not everyone will be able to follow through with this program entirely on his or her own — some people will be personally unable to commit to the debt-management program, and others will find their debts *too* unwieldy to follow it. But everyone owes it to himself to gain the essential information included here. You don't want to hand these jobs over to someone without knowing what's best for you. Also, you won't be able to negotiate intelligently with creditors without having done your homework.

This chapter deals with approaches to creditors, negotiating skills that will come in handy, and calling on other resources for help. The chapter after next will break down, creditor by creditor, what is expected of you by the people to whom you owe money, how each of them differs in the way business is set up, and how each will deal with you.

GETTING THE FAMILY INVOLVED

If you're reading this book, it's safe to assume that what you have coming in doesn't quite meet adequately what you have going out. Using the next worksheet, you can begin to see areas where you can cut back. This is the most detailed budget worksheet of all, and comes from the National Foundation for Consumer Credit, which uses it as a model for all of its Consumer Credit Counseling Services.

It can take several attempts to get this one completely accurate. Perhaps you can fill it out once, then fill it out and revise it on a daily basis, for a week or two. The budget given here is meant to show you the most accurate picture of your everyday expenses. It's the budget-slasher's budget, since it catches almost every penny going through your hands, and really calls for absolute honesty.

Let's take an example of a family that used this worksheet and came up with some surprising figures.

When the O'Neills filled out the monthly expense worksheet in "Facing It," they wrote a figure of $1,500 under clothing, figuring that this was the amount spent every year on new clothing for their family. This broke down to $125 a month. When they completed *this* budget sheet, their $1,500 figure was completely discarded. Mrs. O'Neill, a design consultant, spent close to $29 a month on her dry cleaning alone, and Mr. O'Neill had neglected to add the $100 spent every year on repairs and alterations of his business suits (a frugal measure, given the cost of new suits, but an expense nevertheless). Together with a careful examination of what they *really* spent on new clothes, the new budget sheet brought their clothing expense to $2,000 — another $41 a month.

Before we look at some other items in the O'Neills' budget, let's examine closely just what that $41 means to their budget overall. First, it adds an immediate expense that is not available for debt repayment — but on close examination, that money never had been used to pay back debts in the first place. On the other hand, now that it appears on the budget, the $41 becomes a tangible figure that can be added to or subtracted from consciously.

Discovering where the money is going and then gaining the ability to work with the expenses and obligations of your household are the essential objectives of careful budgeting.

Another example from the O'Neill family budget: since both Mr. and Mrs. O'Neill work, their dinners are often catch-as-catch-can affairs, especially if they both find themselves working late and their eldest child, a teenager, has also come home without time to make dinner. While no member of the family had ever realized that structuring a system — by which dinner would be a planned affair, yet flexible enough to accommodate their schedules — would help to pay debts, an arrangement that accomplished that meal plan was made, and close to $100 a month was salvaged from fast-food expenses and the extra money spent on "quick trips" to the grocery store.

You should begin this worksheet by talking among your family, deciding which items in your budget are necessities and which are luxuries. Don't expect your budget cutting to be a "set in stone" process — it often requires a long series of experiments to see which combination of dollar slashes and penny pinches works best for you.

According to Mildred Tuffield, a family financial counselor in New York, there are two mistakes that most families make when cutting their budgets: they assume that certain things are necessities and others are luxuries based on traditional notions that might not be true; and they underestimate their own ability to bring in extra income.

We are often told, for example, that movies, dinners out, and books and magazines are luxuries. Yet our *real* budget luxuries might be a second car, or where we shop for clothes. It's important to separate the luxuries and necessities based on what they mean to us *now*.

In our society, having a good time usually means spending money. While sometimes the emphasis on spending is too closely linked to enjoyment, you should remember to budget realistically for those small pleasures that keep you and your family going. If you are able to live with a strict budget *because* you can look forward to movies on Saturday night, then the movies just might be worth the money.

The second most overlooked area, says Mildred Tuffield, is your ability to bring in more income. "Most people overlook the fact

RECORD OF EXPENSES

	WEEKLY		MONTHLY	
HOUSING AND HOUSING MAINTENANCE				
1. Rent or house payment				
2. Taxes				
3. Insurance				
4. Electricity				
5. Heat and/or air conditioning				
6. Water and sewer				
7. Trash pick up				
8. Telephone				
9. Repairs and maintenance				
10. Furnishings — furniture, linens, and appliances				
FOOD				
1. Milk delivered to house				
2. Edible food stuff				
3. Nonedibles usually bought with groceries				
4. Pet foods				
5. Snacks, "coffee" breaks, lunches				
6. Restaurants				
TRANSPORTATION				
1. Car payment				
2. Personal property tax and license				
3. Driver's license				
4. Gas and oil				
5. Tires				
6. Repairs				
7. Taxi fares				
8. Bus fare				
9. Insurance				
10. Town tax and/or inspection fee				
CLOTHING				
1. New clothing (including shoes)				
2. Repairs, alterations, etc.				
3. Dry cleaning				
4. Laundry				
MEDICAL				
1. Insurance				
2. Doctors				
3. Dentists				
4. Hospital				
5. Drugs				
6. Treatments				
7. Vitamins				

EXPENSES, *continued*	WEEKLY		MONTHLY	
EDUCATION				
1. Tuition				
2. Books, magazines, and papers				
3. Equipment				
4. School lunches				
EMPLOYMENT				
1. Insurance (income protection)				
2. Union and/or professional dues				
3. Special equipment				
4. Clothing (uniforms, etc.)				
5. Lunch				
CHILD CARE				
1. Nursery school				
2. Baby sitter				
3. Child support				
GIFTS AND DONATIONS				
1. Birthdays				
2. Christmas				
3. Church				
4. Sympathy				
5. All other				
RECREATION AND ENTERTAINMENT				
1. Cigarettes, cigars, etc.				
2. Alcoholic beverages				
3. Movies, plays, etc.				
4. Sports (spectator and participant)				
5. Hobbies and special interests				
6. Vacations				
7. Home parties				
PERSONAL				
1. Toilet articles and cosmetics				
2. Stationery, cards, etc.				
3. Barber and beauty shop				
4. Allowances				
SAVINGS				
1. Savings bonds				
2. Credit union				
3. Payroll deduction				
4. Bank				
5. Other				
MISCELLANEOUS				
1. Alimony				

that they can make money doing things that they already do for fun," she claims. You should take a look at your hobbies and interests. Chances are, any skills or abilities you have can be turned into moneymakers, with a little energy and self-marketing. Most people assume that bringing in extra money means taking on jobs that are dreary and difficult, leaving them exhausted and drained. If you are able to turn your own interests into money, you can avoid this. Consider working for yourself, or for someone on a part-time basis.

Recently, I read of a woman who had left her business career to have children. After their second child, she and her husband began to have some serious money problems. She didn't want to return to full-time work out of her home, since doing so would undo all of the good her genuine commitment to staying home with her children had accomplished. Other part-time work, she found, was uninteresting and difficult. She contacted one of her old business associates, and began doing freelance work from her home for that company. She enjoyed getting back into the rhythms of her profession, and seeing some of her old friends. As she improved her at-home expertise, the company began to ask her to do other assignments, on a more regular basis. Recently, one of her freelance employers offered her a "full-time/part-time" job, complete with benefits, for work she does from her home. "It's better than I could have imagined," she told the magazine interviewer. "I've really got the best of both worlds."

While you may not be able to work out such an ideal situation, you should never underestimate the power of your own enthusiasms and interests to earn real money for you.

I could fill pages with budget suggestions — use coupons when you grocery shop, review your phone service with the telephone company to make sure you aren't paying for more than you need, insulate to save heating costs, keep your car well tuned to save money on gas and repairs — but they'd all boil down to one rule: look at *every* item on your budget and ask if each one of them is necessary. Why do you spend this money? What satisfaction or need is filled by it? Could the same task or need be accomplished or filled more cheaply? Could something substitute for this?

As an example of the give and take involved in this process, one family I spoke with thought they could save $50 a month on haircuts by having one of their daughters cut their hair. The results, despite the daughter's sincere efforts, were disastrous. The family's morale hit an all-time low, and everyone equated their new budget with looking awful. One son complained that the new haircuts were a kind of sackcloth and ashes. "Everyone looks at us," he complained, "and they know we must be poor." The family went back to the drawing board with their budget. Some of the older children decided to put more of their after-school earnings toward haircuts, and the parents provided money for the younger children out of other items in the budget.

The ability to place "real" values on money, rather than just working with numbers and cutting your budget on abstract principles, is a necessity in this process. According to New York psychiatrist Paul Olsen, it is women who excel at this, not men. "As a result of the women's movement," he says, "women have become more involved in family finances and in the business world. We're finding that women are very often more naturally skilled at working with money than men are. They're better able to define it in real terms, rather than just numbers."

Cutting your budget can be a difficult and long process. The process can be eased, and the results will be more successful, if the whole family is involved.

For many families, this is a sensitive matter. Particularly among middle-class families, the taboo of discussing money with children is very strong. But, according to a study done by two stockbrokers, it is precisely the middle-class children who grow up least able to handle money. According to the authors of this study, Tom Taylor, a senior vice-president of Shearson Loeb Rhoades, and Ken Davis, a stockbroker at Morgan Stanley, "Too many parents try to insulate kids from financial pressures. But children should know what the family income is, and how they fit in. They should share in hardship when it exists. Generally, a child's material demands will become excessive only when he's unaware of the family's financial structure. The essential thing is to replace children's financial dependence on their parents with self-reliance, and that means that everything must be brought out in the open."

Parents should decide for themselves how much each child

should be told about their financial situation. While children should not be burdened with financial worries, it is often reassuring for a child to know that they are a part of the family, for better and for worse, and that the family *works* as a place of refuge and strength even in difficult times.

Older teens are particularly helpful in this respect, since they have an idea of what it is to handle money, based on their own experiences. Young children, of course, have a limited understanding of the real value of money, and it should be discussed with them based on the limits of their experience and understanding.

No one, though, should be left out. The process of getting out of debt can sometimes change a family's life-style drastically, and no family can go through this smoothly without first being open and loving with each other about this.

It's important for the husband and wife (or single parent) to decide *before* the family meeting exactly what will be discussed, and in what direction the family will be heading. Knowing themselves and each other well before speaking with the children about money will offer the entire family a sense of security that will help weather emotional squalls.

Of course, in some families it is impossible to discuss finances and debt openly. If you feel that you can manage a strict budget and a solid debt-management program without having such a meeting, you should do so. There may be circumstances, though, where you will need to see a family counselor or get outside help of some other form to help with problems within the family that are either caused by money difficulties, or may in fact have caused these money difficulties.

In the first chapter, I quoted Paul Olsen as saying that money can very often be the psychological battlefield on which a bad marriage is fought. Money can also be the cause of marriages going bad and families falling apart. Very often, the cause of money problems lies deep in the psychological makeup of the family. Or, the cause of the problem might be a psychological complication with one of the family members which drains the family of income. But these are severe cases. Just as often, the cause of money problems lies in external circumstances — medical expenses, the loss of a job, etc. Facing up to debt, then, sometimes means facing up to other, more complex problems as well.

There are many places to turn to for help in times of family crisis, such as Alcoholics Anonymous or Gamblers Anonymous. One such group, Overspenders Anonymous, was founded by a Wisconsin housewife, Jeanne Fioretto. Ms. Fioretto was a spending addict herself, and with the help of a group of financial experts, has developed a twelve-part program to help people control their compulsive spending habits. (For information on how to get a free copy, see the bibliography.)

Sometimes, the psychological complications that create debt are also the factors that inhibit people from looking for help. You may experience low self-esteem, depression, and other difficulties from not being able to pay your bills and from the way creditors and collectors treat you. And very often the guilt engendered by these will prevent you from seeking help. If your situation seems to fit this description, you should really seek advice from a professional counselor. Counselors can help not only with your emotional problems, but can help you begin to straighten out your financial ones, as well.

INFLATION-PROOFING YOUR BUDGET

Once you have reached a figure that will be available for debt repayment every month, you have to take into account the effect inflation will have on that figure. For many people, the repayment plan will last for more than a year, and in that time inflation can completely demolish any budget.

The Consumer Price Index, issued monthly by the Bureau of Labor Statistics, measures the effect that inflation has on consumers. It breaks down the rise in prices for different areas of the country, and for major goods and services. Over the last two years, from 1979 to 1981, the CPI has risen more than 25 percent. If you had begun a debt-management program and a strict budget in 1979, you would have had to find 25¢ more for every dollar in your budget to make it at the end of 1980.

The Bureau of Labor Statistics, reviewing a period of typical growth for the CPI, released this chart, showing the rise in prices from 1978 to their projected cost in 1983:

ITEM	RATE OF RISE	1978 COST	1983 PROJECTED COST
Shopping cart of food	54%	$50	$77
New car	38%	$5,000	$6,875
Day in hospital	79%	$100	$179
Year in college	49%	$5,200	$7,740
Electric bill	58%	$100	$158

Of course, the Bureau of Labor Statistics was almost as shocked as everyone else when inflation drove prices through the roof in 1980 and 1981. Many of their own loosely calculated projections were met in 1981, and by the time we'll reach 1983, the prices will far surpass what is in the above chart.

Your own cost-of-living increase will probably not be the same as the CPI, since it is a national average. To calculate your *own* CPI, follow these steps:

1. From your budget worksheets, find out how much you spent for each of the following major CPI categories: housing, food, transportation, medical, apparel and upkeep, entertainment, all other.

2. Calculate how much "weight" each of these carries in your budget by adding all of the categories, then dividing by the total.

For example — if the total of your major yearly expenses was $20,000, and $5,000 of that was for housing, $2,000 was for apparel and upkeep, $6,000 for food, and $3,000 for transportation, your spending can be evaluated as follows: 25 percent for housing expenses, 10 percent to apparel and upkeep, 30 percent to food, and 15 percent to transportation. When all of the percentages have been totaled, they should equal 100 percent.

3. Call your nearest Bureau of Labor Statistics, which has a phone service for this purpose, to obtain your city's official CPI. Ask for the percentage change from the same month one

year earlier for all items, and for each of the seven categories.

4. Multiply each percent in your budget by the official CPI change in that category.

Following our example, if the Bureau of Labor Statistics had informed us that the CPI for housing had risen 19 percent, food 12 percent, apparel and upkeep 9 percent, and transportation 10 percent, we would multiply each weight by the official change as follows:

HOUSING	$.25 \times .19 =$	.0475
APPAREL AND UPKEEP	$.1 \times .09 =$	.009
FOOD	$.3 \times .12 =$	.036
TRANSPORTATION	$.15 \times .10 =$	.015
		.1075

5. Add these to get your total CPI change — .1075, or 11 percent.

What this means, in short, is that you will have to build in an additional 11 percent of income into your earnings over the next year in order to stay safely on target in your debt-management program. According to your CPI, what had cost $20,000 last year could cost $22,200 next year.

CASH ONLY, PLEASE

At this point, it is time for you and your family to move into a cash-only economy. I don't advocate cutting your credit cards in half — if you've come this far in your program, you know how seriously debt has affected your life, and you have a lesser chance of becoming foolhardy with your credit again. Put the cards away — lock them up if you have to. But keep the cards that are still active accounts. You might need them in an emergency, or to make a major purchase after you are debt-free. Make sure that at least two people in your family, or a friend or relative, have access to the cards to check whether they are safe. You might even want to seal the cards in an envelope so you can tell if they've been used. (If a family member needs a credit card for business purposes, then that account should be completely divorced from the family budget. Don't use it for personal purchases, and don't pay any bills with personal money.)

The cash-only system is the best way I know to keep on a budget in a debt-management program. Everything is paid for in cash or by check. If cash isn't available, the purchase isn't made. Depending on how much of a spendthrift you are, this can be a little painful for a week or two. But you'll get used to it if you've budgeted wisely.

The night before you are paid, the family should have a short meeting (five or ten minutes) to decide how much of the paycheck will be needed for next week's out-of-pocket expenses. In my system, out-of-pocket expenses are everything except bills and monthly obligations. These are paid by check, in order to have an accurate record. Groceries, transportation (gas, train, or carfare, etc.), clothing, entertainment . . . everything else is on a cash basis.

The paycheck goes into the bank, probably into the checking account, as soon as possible. First thing after that, all of the obligations for the week are met. I can't stress enough the importance of putting *all* of your paycheck into the bank. This completely eliminates temptation to spend money that isn't accounted for. The deposit slip doesn't lie — if it shows less than your whole check, you should have a good reason why. Pay the creditors you've agreed to pay on that day, and whatever other bills need to be paid then. What is left is what you will live on for the week (or two weeks, depending on how you are paid). This should be withdrawn from the bank — by check, if you can, so that even the amount of the out-of-pocket expenses will be recorded. Of course, this may not be possible for you to fit into your schedule. But every effort should be made to build a system that is safe and secure.

The responsibility for this system falls into two areas: wise budgeting and careful spending. If you do both, you won't be hit with end-of-the-week crunches. If you haven't budgeted and spent wisely, you may end up borrowing carfare from your daughter!

What about long-term expenses, such as clothing? This is where the second and third worksheets come into play, since they break down these seasonal expenses into monthly and weekly amounts. Make sure that this money is put in the bank so that it does not get spent for other things. (Believe me — if it isn't banked, it *will* be spent.) You might want to establish a separate account in savings for this money.

One reminder: the old saying "an ounce of prevention is worth a pound of cure" is true here. Keep an eye on medical and dental expenses, but don't ignore regular appointments and check-ups that can keep you from much bigger medical bills in the future.

The short weekly sessions will act as a safety catch for bad budgeting. Family members can voice their approval or disapproval of certain budget figures, and everyone can work together to find alternatives.

The cash-only system is the best way possible to teach the real value of money. The first week or two is usually tough, and you find yourself searching for loose change under the sofa cushions to buy the newspaper on Thursday morning, but in the long run it's worth it. You see how much money you have, and where it goes.

Most importantly, it meets your obligations immediately. Whatever worries you have are *completely* yours. No one will call you up at dinnertime to ask if you might run out of pocket money on Wednesday.

There is also a certain amount of flexibility built into this system. I know of one family in which the youngest son had found a way to cut sixty cents a day out of his busfare to school. In a couple of weeks, he had built up a little nest egg, which he discreetly lent to family members when he heard they were running a little short. And he charged interest!!! This just points out how clever anyone can become when it comes to juggling a few dollars from one expense to another.

Finally, there is an interesting psychological advantage to the cash-only economy. Watch what happens when you go into one of your familiar "easy credit" stores and make your first over-$25 purchase completely with cash. Chances are the clerk will do a double-take. Same thing at restaurants. We've become a credit-card society, and no one knows it better than people who use cash. (In a busy Boston department store, one sales clerk was overheard asking a customer "Do you want to charge it, or pay for it?" And a

New Yorker cartoon several years ago showed a maître d' in a fine restaurant removing one customer's cash payment from the table with his nose raised and his hand outstretched, as if the green bills were some kind of offensive matter.)

There's another special feeling that comes when you spend cash for a large purchase — you own it! No one is going to remind you next month what you have bought, and you won't be putting money into something that has outlasted its use long ago.

It all adds up to a healthy dose of self-reliance and independence which, in a very short time, can become the most encouraging part of your road out of debt.

SETTING PRIORITIES

Your main concerns in establishing a repayment plan are (1) getting out of debt as soon as possible, and (2) reestablishing your credit rating as soon as possible.

Establishing a repayment schedule is not as simple as dividing the money you have for repayments among the number of creditors, and then paying it out until everyone is paid off. In the first place, some creditors would not accept the amount of money you would offer to pay them per month. With other creditors, you might end up paying more per month than you have to. And finally, the amount of time you may be in such a plan could extend for years and years.

You set priorities for repayment in two stages. The first stage is described in this chapter, and takes place before you contact your creditors. This step helps you decide whom you want to negotiate with, and on what terms. The second stage occurs *after* you've spoken with or contacted each of your creditors, when you know what terms they will accept and how they view your debt.

The first three sets of questions you should ask of each debt are:

1. Who is this money owed to? Attempt to calculate how your debt affects the creditor, why you incurred this debt, and whether such a need is likely to occur again in the future.

2. How much do you owe? How long was the loan made for?

3. What is the finance charge on this debt? How much will it cost in interest and other charges to place this at a low

priority? Can I pay this debt off earlier and save some money?

If you are like most people in debt, the first time you start to sift through your bills with these questions in mind, it will seem as if *every* bill needs to be paid yesterday and that you need to maintain your credit relationship with everyone on your list.

But examine those debts more closely. In the next chapter of the book, I go through the most common types of lenders and show how their operations work: how they profit from their loans, what they expect from debtors, and how they handle people who can't make regular payments. Reading this should help you answer some of the questions you have about the people to whom you owe money.

Of course, I don't include brothers-in-law in the next chapter. It's my belief that brothers-in-law, doctors on whom you rely, corner grocers, and so on, should be paid first in the debt program. Our debts hurt these people the most.

One more reason to pay off the "little" lenders: you should pay special attention to the high interest rates charged by small, non-financial-institution lenders. Some doctors charge 15 to 20 percent on overdue bills.

When you list small lenders at the top of your priorities list, it doesn't necessarily mean that you will be paying them back completely before the other lenders. It means you are going to talk to them first. In many cases, these people are the most flexible in negotiating a repayment plan, because they'll listen to your problems with some degree of consideration.

After you've listed your "personal" debts, list all remaining obligations, along with the reason the loan was made, what the present monthly payments are, what the current balance is, what the delinquency status is, and whether or not the loan is secured.

Let's look at a typical debtor's priority list:

Michael, a man with two children and a wife who stays at home to take care of the family, owes close to $500 per month to eleven different creditors, with a total of $7,400 in debt. He currently earns $14,000 a year, taking home about $800 per month of that after taxes. After slashing his budget as far as he can, he comes up with $250 a month to pay back his creditors.

TYPE OF LOAN, REASON	PRESENT MONTH-LY PAYMENT	BALANCE	AMOUNT DUE NOW	STATUS	SECURED*	ARRANGED PAYMENT
1. Friend — short on cash one month	$75	$75	$75	Promised to pay ASAP	No	$25
2. ABC Motor Credit (auto loan)	$105	$1,575	$105	Up to date	Yes	$80
3. XYZ Credit Corp. (furniture)	$30	$525	$100	2 mos. behind	Yes	$18
4. Visa	$35	$700	$105	3 mos. behind	No	$23
5. Bank loan (overdraft checking)	$75	$1,200	$150	2 mos. behind	No	$46
6. Department store (clothing)	$25	$250	$50	2 mos. behind	No	$10
7. MasterCard	$70	$1,400	$140	2 mos. behind	No	$38
8. American Express	$40	$400	$400	Not paid for 5 mos., current plan just established	No	$14
9. Dentist	$42	$425	$425	Not paid for one year	No	$15
10. Hospital	$50	$500	$500	Not paid for 6 mos., legal action threatened	No	$18
11. Collection Agency	$25	$350	$350	Legal action threatened	No	$18
Total	$572	$7,400	$1,975			$305

*Guaranteed by a pledge of something valuable, usually the item borrowed for.

For the next three months, Michael will be $55 short, given his present income and because of the payments on his friend's loan. After the loan is paid off, he will be $30 short a month. Both he and his wife feel that they can make up that money by working part-time and moonlighting. They also hold open the possibility that, in the future, she will return to work full-time. It appears that, with commitment and a little luck, they'll be out of debt in three years.

Let's take a look at how Michael went about arranging new payments with his creditors.

1. A loan from his friend. Michael borrowed money from a friend at work one month when he came up short with ten days to go until payday. He promised the friend to pay him back as soon as possible, and it has been six weeks since the loan was made. Although Michael would like to pay his friend back in full immediately, after talking to all of his creditors, he knows that this is impossible. He sat down with his friend, explained the situation to him, and proposed paying $25 a month for the next three months. This was completely agreeable to Michael's friend, who also told Michael that if, for one reason or another, he had to miss a month, it would be fine with him.

2. According to a spokesman for General Motors Acceptance Corporation, almost half of their delinquent loans are brought up to date by a refinancing agreement. "We have a long-standing policy in helping with unexpected financial developments," the spokesman told me, "and we are more than willing to work with a person who has come to us in good faith."

In Michael's case, ABC agreed to refinance the car at a lower payment. Previously, Michael had owed $1,575, to be paid over the next fifteen months. ABC offered to extend the loan to twenty-four months, reducing the payments to $70, but increasing the interest. After talking it over with the finance office, Michael was able to avoid the higher interest by extending the loan for only five additional months, at a rate of $80 a month.

If he and ABC *hadn't* been able to come to workable terms, Michael would have had to pay the full payment in some way, since his car was necessary to get to and from work.

3. Although XYZ's furniture was a secured loan, they clearly

wanted their money a great deal more than used furniture. Michael had some leverage with them because of this, and because he approached them with a well-conceived plan of repayment. He had been two months behind in his payments, without having spoken to his creditors for this time, and at first had to work a little extra at convincing them of his sincerity.

4 and 7. Both Visa and MasterCard were willing to accept reduced payments, provided Michael suspended his account with them. What Michael had to be sure of in this was that his payments would reduce the principal of the loan, and not just meet the interest payments. VISA agreed to suspend interest payments, MasterCard did not.

5. Bank loans are tricky, and call for sensitive handling. In this case, Michael went directly to the local banker who opened the checking account for him. The banker, who knew Michael as a regular customer, placed a call with the accounts receivable department that paved the way for a more sensitive, sane negotiation between the bank and the debtor. The account, though, has been closed until full payment is made.

6. The store told Michael that they wanted 10 percent of the unpaid balance, but was willing to accept the $10 monthly payment for several months, after which Michael would talk to them again to see if a more regular payment schedule could be made.

8, 9, and 10. These three creditors were demanding payment in full. But all three were willing to accept monthly payments, provided they were receiving their full share of the money available.

11. The collection agency was continually harassing Michael, and would not negotiate a payment schedule with him. Michael originally proposed a $10 per month payment, and came up to $18 after a great deal of haggling.

Setting up priorities is a significant step toward gaining control of your financial affairs. By establishing the importance of each creditor to your overall debt-management program, you will have a psychological edge on working with them. Of course, once you begin to negotiate repayments, you'll find — as Michael did —

that some creditors won't settle for their place on the ladder. But the sense of order you've produced by setting these priorities should see you through most problems.

CONTACTING YOUR CREDITORS

The common wisdom states that you should first contact your creditors by phone. I strongly advise against this. Talking to your creditors on the phone is fine after you have made an agreement. But right now you need proof that they have received and noted your intentions — you won't get that in a phone conversation. Your first contact should be by mail. Here is a sample letter:

Address
Date

XYZ Credit Corp.
Central City, U.S.A.

Dear XYZ,

Because of a number of factors [*if there are specific factors, you should mention them here*] I am currently experiencing financial difficulty. I have taken a long, hard look at my situation, and have worked out a very careful budget, along with a repayment schedule for all of my creditors, which I can say with complete assurance is reliable.

In order to provide for my necessary household expenses and the payments I am making to my creditors, I am asking each creditor to accept a reduced payment until I am back on my feet again.

In place of my regular payment of _____, I request that you accept payments of _____ each until the loan is paid back.

I assure you that I will incur no new debt obligations while I am engaged in my debt-management program.

I am enclosing the first of these payments. [*If this is not possible, indicate when the payment will be made.*]

If there is any question about the repayment schedule, please feel free to contact me between the hours of _____ and _____ at _____. Please do not contact me at any other time or place, as such contact is extremely inconvenient to me.

Sincerely,

Although the letter you send will vary with your circumstances, any letter sent to your creditor to establish a repayment plan should accomplish four things:

1. It should state *realistically* what you can pay per month on your debt. (Some creditors won't take your word for it, no matter how you stick to your guns, and you'll have to negotiate with them. See pages 75 and 150.)

2. It should give the creditor information about the reasons for your delinquency and inability to pay, but only the information that the creditor needs to be assured that you are willing to pay your debt and are performing to the best of your ability to do so. If, in the past, you have "bought time" with lies or some other technique, you'll have to work that much harder to prove your good intentions.

3. It should indicate to your creditor that all your creditors are being treated equitably and fairly.

4. It should assure your creditor that you do not intend to create any new credit obligations until your accounts are paid, or at least brought up to a current status.

At this point, your creditor will no doubt contact you, either by letter or phone — one hopes within the hours you have indicated, although you never know.

TIME FOR A PAT ON THE BACK

Before discussing the fine art of negotiating, let's take a few steps backward and reassess the shape you're in.

You've already employed a great deal of clever, intelligent strategy. You've analyzed your situation, you know what your goals and alternatives are. You've done your homework.

You are so many steps ahead of the game right now that you have very little to worry about. The number of people who contact a creditor with as much savvy as you have gained from doing your homework is approximately equal to the number of people who enter a bank with the combination to the safe.

So take a deep breath and relax. While they may pull every trick in the book now, all they *have* is tricks. You've got the game on your side because of your control of the situation. The wall of fear has some very large cracks in it.

NEGOTIATING—PUTTING YOUR MOUTH WHERE YOUR MONEY IS (OR SHOULD BE)

To what extent negotiating is a part of making a debt-management plan you can stick to depends on you and your creditor. Most of the time, if you present your creditor with a reasonable payment arrangement and assure him that it is the best you can do, he will accept it. In many cases, it's best not to try and outfox creditors or collectors — they make a living at negotiating, and are undoubtedly more proficient at it than you. But some collectors and creditors won't accept any plan at face value, and that's where negotiating skills enter the picture.

At this point, you are ready to truly surprise your creditor. He *thinks* he knows you. But he doesn't. He knows debtors who shade the truth, lie, cheat, and can't fulfill their promises. You can. And you can prove it.

Edward Levin, a professional arbitrator, outlines some hints for negotiating in *Levin's Laws: Tactics for Winning Without Intimidation.* Levin's approach is particularly applicable to the debtor, since he doesn't believe in the "hit 'em over the head and leave 'em hurting" school of negotiating. Levin knows that, for most of us, the people we negotiate with are the people we have to live with every day, people on whom we rely for their goodwill. Certainly your creditors fill this description.

Early in his book, Levin breaks down conflicts into three types. Knowing these types is useful in judging the ways in which your creditor is responding to you.

Type A: The Manageable Conflict. Any dispute where you have the power to reach a satisfactory settlement of your differences is a manageable conflict, according to Levin. Spotting one is easy: If the other person has the authority to say yes, no, or give you what you want, then you're in a manageable conflict. Your goal is reachable. If it's not, what you are in for is an exercise in futility.

Type A conflicts can come up when you are dealing with a

creditor or collector who is obviously the person in the office who can approve your repayment plan (not everyone you talk to can — one of the reasons for sending the letter is to reach this person as soon as possible). This person should be willing to listen to what you have to say and take into account the factors influencing your ability to make payments.

Type B: The Veiled Conflict. A squabble where people are talking about one thing and really mean something else cannot be resolved. It's a charade, a phony, a game only a patsy would walk into. You have to strip off the veils. Then you can win.

The veils for collectors and creditors are many. They use labels — "deadbeat" is one of them — to distract. They "create" other alternatives for you to come up with their money — even suggesting that you not pay other creditors so that they can get their money (but God help you if you do the same thing to them!) or suggesting that you go out and get a consolidation loan to pay them off. They might bring up your past behavior in an attempt to discredit any repayment proposal you are currently making.

The goal in a Type B situation is to change it into a Type A. Strip the veils. Bare the issue. In most instances with a collector, the veil comes in the form of a personal slur: "You're a deadbeat anyway, why should we believe you? Pay up right now." You have to "bare the issue." "If I was a real deadbeat," you can reply, "I wouldn't be on the phone with you. Why don't we discuss my payment plan? If I turn out to be a deadbeat, which I assure you I am not, you'll have plenty of time later to get my money out of me your way. Right now, I'm offering it to you . . . [state the plan]."

You have to be persistent in this. Keep testing the veiled conflicts. Try to get past what is preventing the collector from discussing your proposed plan. If this fails, according to Levin, it's time to call in an outsider. Ask to speak to a superior, go to a higher level within the company. If that doesn't work, it may be time to go to a credit counselor or a lawyer.

Type C: The Insoluble Conflict. With collectors, this kind of conflict most often appears as "I don't want to hear about your problems. Pay up the money right now or we sue." There are two things you can do here. First, use the long pause. (They do, all the time.) Count to five, slowly. Then ask, "Is that your final word on the matter?" It probably won't be. If it is, call their bluff. Legal fees are exorbitant, and chances are the collector will settle for your payments rather than incur the extra expense of a lawyer. Just say, "Okay, go ahead with whatever you feel is necessary. In the meantime, I will continue to send you my regular proposed payments." (Of course, if they're not bluffing, you'll find out now, and can switch to the manageable conflicts related to actual legal action.) This conflict also appears in the form of "You'll have to come up with something better than that," when no offer is being made from the creditor.

Finally, the secret of *any* good negotiation is to make the other side feel as though they've won. Tell them, "I'm glad we could come up with a plan you can work with. We're both in good shape this way." End, if possible, on an "up" note.

GETTING HELP FROM A CREDIT COUNSELOR

If you turn to a credit counselor, you are asking for sensitive, responsible assistance in a very complex area of your life. It's important, then, that you know just what to expect, what is going to help you, and what won't help.

If you need help, seek it. Don't be inhibited by feelings of guilt or embarrassment when it comes to your debt problems. Don't feel that because undertaking a debt-management program was too unwieldy for you that turning to a counselor is admitting failure — seeking help from a counselor is an alternative that is, in fact, a legitimate part of any debt-management program.

The most prominent of the credit-counseling services in this country are the Consumer Credit Counseling Services. While CCCS are the most visible, there are many more small, independent credit-counseling services. Taking all of the CCCS offices and all of the independent services into account, a wide variety of services are offered, with an astounding difference in the quality of those services.

Despite the fact that credit counselors can provide an invaluable service, you should be aware of what those services are, and how they are *properly* performed. If you don't have some standards for judging a counseling service, you could find yourself in even deeper trouble than when you began.

(One absolute: stay away from "debt prorating services," which are illegal in many states. In states where they are legal, these businesses will negotiate with your creditors for you and disperse your monthly payments to them, and usually charge a very high fee for the service. In addition, many of these services are fly-by-night operations, taking consumer's money and *not* giving it to creditors.)

In New York City, there are two major credit counselors, CCCS and Budget and Credit Counseling Service (BUCC$). The differences between the two describe the entire range of credit counseling available to consumers.

CCCS is funded, as are all offices under the umbrella of the National Foundation for Consumer Credit, through voluntary, tax-deductible contributions from major credit grantors, corporations, and employers. Approximately 70 percent of these creditors contribute 15 percent of the monies collected from debt-management programs to CCCS. Forty percent of the board members of the organization are from the credit-granting community, and their 1973 incorporation papers were filed by a vice-president of Beneficial Finance Company.

BUCC$ is funded by the Community Service Society of New York, a nonprofit agency serving New York since 1848. Although BUCC$ receives contributions from the credit-granting community at times, they do not rely on these for survival, and they are not under obligation to creditors.

The differences between BUCC$ and CCCS are evident in the first counseling session. I went through both, and felt that the difference was obvious in their approach to my household budget. After tallying up all of my expenses and seeing what was left over to repay my creditors, the CCCS counselor asked me, "How are we going to come up with the rest of the money you owe?" The BUCC$ counselor said, "Let's see if we can get your creditors to work with this amount."

What exactly are the services offered by consumer-credit counselors, and what should you expect when you enter their program? Let's look first at CCCS, and then at a community-funded operation.

The Consumer Credit Counseling Services under NFCC provide the following services:

- Budget counseling. This is a free analysis of an individual's or family's financial situation with the assistance of a trained counselor. This is a confidential counseling session that often includes actual suggestions for budget alternatives and discussion of potential sources of outside income which the consumer may be eligible for.
- Credit counseling. Free advice and guidance for consumers on how to use credit opportunities more wisely and to their best advantage is available. Often, those consumers who seek CCCS for guidance in this area are able to manage paying their bills on time as long as they live within the newly developed budget specifically prepared with them to meet their needs. Further discussion will often lead to a better understanding of the real cost of credit in monthly payments and interest charges, and more effective overall budget discipline.
- Debt management. For those already in financial trouble, trained CCCS counselors work with consumers to develop an alternate repayment schedule that is acceptable to them as well as to their creditors. Debt management is offered to consumers after budget counseling if they indicate they are having difficulties repaying their debts on their own. The initial counseling session is free. If the consumer enters a debt-management program, there is a monthly charge, which should not exceed $12, and is often waived in hardship cases. Participants in this area of the program are asked to return all their credit cards and not incur further debt during the duration of the program. When the debts are reduced to the point where the consumer can again take over that aspect of his or her finances, the program is discontinued by mutual consent.

Robert Gibson of the NFCC cites as the advantage of CCCS the fact that most people can't do this kind of program on their own. They need to reexamine, in depth, their family life-style. "We talk about how they are spending family income, and whether there is any way of gaining additional income. These are the kinds of things that other agencies aren't able to do. Banks and finance companies will help you refinance or consolidate, and that's about it. We have the time to help you. We'll spend one to three hours with each family or couple, hopefully with their older teenagers as well. We get them thinking about changes they can make so this won't happen again. This is another advantage of counseling over straight bankruptcy — we *teach* people something about their spending habits."

The primary difference between the community service and the creditor-oriented service is one of attitude. The main critics of services such as BUCC$ say that they are trying to help people beat the credit system. "We're not here to help people beat the system," says Luther Gatling, director of BUCC$. "We're here to make it work for them, both the creditors and the debtors. They say we're a bankruptcy mill, a friend of the debtor rather than the creditor. Perhaps we are. And some people think they [creditor-oriented agencies] are just a glorified collection agency."

BUCC$ is totally free — there is no monthly debt-management fee, nor is a percentage of their collected funds given back to them. A trained counselor, such as CCCS provides, helps the client evaluate his or her situation and work out a solution. Often BUCC$ counselors will call creditors and get an agreement for repayments of debts over a longer period of time. Sometimes a loan is renegotiated. The client is helped to work out a new, realistic budget and shown where savings are possible. As a last resort, the counselor may help the client go through bankruptcy.

According to David Samuels, of the Department of Consumer Affairs in New York City, a consumer counselor should be an advocate for the consumer. They should be consumer-oriented, give a sense of the entire range of options. They should give consumers an idea of what their status is so that the consumer can make an informed choice about what to do.

The consumer, according to Samuels, should immediately find out who is funding any service he is considering using. If it's creditor-oriented, or has its origins in the credit community, the service may be wearing two hats.

A community-funded agency, on the other hand, doesn't have to satisfy the creditor community, is not getting its money from consumers. It doesn't have a particular interest in terms of what it tells consumers to do.

It's clear that, when you go into credit counseling, you should be absolutely aware of your interests and the service's interests. There are three factors that you should be immediately aware of in judging a counseling service:

1. The degree to which your counseling agency is tied into other community services. We've already seen how money problems can be intertwined with medical, psychological, and other problems. Your counseling service should have a working relationship with other agencies to help you in these areas.

2. You should get the feeling from your counseling agency that you are learning something from the process you are going through, and are not just satisfying your creditors. You should be gaining a familiarity with consumer finance. You should be working more closely as a family unit, and have a better sense of yourself as a part of the debtor-creditor relationship.

3. The length of the proposed program. It should not be longer than 3 to 5 years. Anything over three years, in actuality, might extend the hardship beyond reasonable limits. If the program is going to strap you for a longer period, you should at least seriously examine the option of bankruptcy.

These three factors will ultimately decide whether consumer-credit counseling frees you from your debts or keeps you in the frustrating prison of continued payments.

The National Foundation for Consumer Credit, which is the umbrella office for the 209 Consumer Credit Counseling Services, estimates that of the families who come to them for help, one out of ten can't be helped and is referred for legal assistance. Five out of ten don't really need their help, and are simply counseled in working out a realistic budget. Four out of ten are asked to enter a debt-management program.

The average program at CCCS is 21 months long, although some families have been in programs for up to four years. When I asked an official of NFCC for a more understandable "success ratio," I was told that they keep statistics only on families who have (1) come in for an initial counseling session, and (2) made two payments for dispersal to creditors.

This process involves about 90 days' participation. Of *these* families, 90 percent get out of debt successfully.

"What other agencies do wrong," according to Luther Gatling, "is offer the creditors what is not there. They will divide an $8,000 debt over 36 months, and they'll say to the guy — whatever the figure is — you've gotta pay $175 a month, $200 a month. How the hell is he gonna do it? He's got $60 left over, and he's on a tough budget. What we might do in a case like that, and in that case where there's so much money owed you can't possibly work something out with the creditors, is suggest that the guy go into Chapter 13 bankruptcy. I'd put that $60 into a Chapter 13 plan, then the creditors will get everything the guy *can* pay back."

Whether you use the services of a community-based counseling service or a creditor-oriented one, it's important to know what makes their operations so different. What they offer, basically, is a structure that allows many debtors to accomplish what others can do on their own. The important thing to be judged in any counseling service is whether that structure helps or hinders financial recovery.

CONSOLIDATING AND REFINANCING

As with all credit arrangements, a consolidation loan or a refinancing agreement should be considered carefully. Both *can* provide a viable option in a debt-management program. There are several guidelines, though, that you should follow in judging these as options.

A consolidation loan, simply, is one in which a finance company or, sometimes, a bank offers to pay a number of your bills for you. In turn, you will repay the finance company or the bank by the terms of an agreement, much like any other loan.

Refinancing a loan is a process by which your creditor rearranges the main terms of your present agreement, usually the finance charge and the length of time you have to repay. For example, if you have an auto loan which originally was made for a balance of $4,000, to be repaid over 36 months at 10 percent interest, refinancing that loan at some point — perhaps with 18 months left to go — would allow you to repay the remaining balance of the loan (approximately $2,000) over a longer period of time, at the same or higher interest. The terms may now come out to be repayment over 36 months more at 10, 11, or 12 percent or more. You will benefit from significantly reduced payments, and the creditor will profit from the increased finance charges received.

The first question you have to ask is, "Can I handle this increased debt?" In the case of refinancing a loan, the question can be simply answered, since the main result for you is the lessening of monthly payments. If you can handle the present payments comfortably, there would seem to be no reason to increase the profits of your creditor.

In the case of a consolidation loan, the question is a little more complicated, but can be answered with a little arithmetic.

Using our first worksheet, calculate your income, monthly and annual expenses, and your loan and credit obligations.

Then, remove the debts you wish to consolidate from the loan and credit obligations, and recalculate to see how much money would be made available to pay back a consolidation loan. If you are able to make a loan which covers a major portion of your loan and credit obligations, at a monthly payment equal to or — preferably — less than the money you would normally have to pay, and at an interest rate which seems to you fair in relation to the benefits of a consolidation loan, then you might have a good deal.

Let's take an example: Harry Richards owes a total of $295 to six different creditors every month, for close to $6,000 total debt. A local finance company can give him a loan for $6,000, at 15 percent interest, for a total payment of $190 a month, to be repaid over 36 months. The loan carries a total finance charge of $700, for which Harry can enjoy the benefits of reduced monthly payments and only one creditor to pay every month. Now, he can weigh the disadvantages of a longer period of indebtedness and a high finance charge against what he might be able to do with his own personal resources and a well-conceived debt-management program.

Harry's example points out another important facet of consolidation loans. What if, in fact, Harry owed $295 a month, but could only come up with $190? Although I would advise trying to exercise his own debt-management program, debt consolidation could serve as a sound option.

No one can make an educated choice about consolidation without having already studied the three worksheets in this book. A loan officer would never be able to provide you with the complete, thorough knowledge of your financial affairs that these will give you and, in fact, that is not his job. If you are considering a consolidation loan, my advice is DO YOUR HOMEWORK. That's the only way you'll avoid the considerable pitfalls of consolidation loans.

For the uneducated consumer, consolidation loans can become a way of life. As Luther Gatling, director of BUCC$, described it, "You see people who went into Household Finance to get a $500 loan, and now it's five years later, and they owe $2,500 and they haven't got a nickel. All that money comes from interest, reconsolidation, and constantly rewriting the loan. And these people are rewriting at 30 percent interest, on top of what they already owe."

Without knowing exactly how much money you need, and how you will repay it, a consolidation loan can become a vicious cycle. It's up to you to make a solid, workable agreement — most finance companies will be glad to take you on as a customer, at 15 to 20 percent for life. A spokesman for Household Finance Corporation told me that they had many customers who had been with them, continuously, for ten or fifteen years.

Now you have a plan you can stick to. You know what your debts are and how you want to repay them. You also have some "contingency plans" to offset problems that can arise completely outside of your control.

Most likely, a week or two ago, things looked rather bleak. I'm sure they look a lot better now.

It's time to contact your creditors and present your repayment plans. If you've been having problems, but most of your creditors don't regard your relationship with them as troubled, they will probably meet your plan with surprise. They'll welcome the early call.

If you *have* been contacted by your creditors, or if you've been running from them, you'll be greeted by a different sense of surprise, and probably a degree of mistrust. Don't worry. You've got a solid plan behind you that will eventually win them over.

But before you contact the creditors and collectors, it might be worthwhile to see just how much they really know about you — on your credit report.

YOUR CREDIT REPORT

Thank you for your recent credit application, which we have reviewed carefully. However, we regret that we are unable to extend credit to you at this time because of the information supplied to us from your consumer reporting agency.

You have a right to inspect and receive a copy of the agency report or any additional information about it by contacting the agency at the name and address below.

— A credit turndown from a New York department store

"We are one very large automated filing cabinet."

— A vice-president of CBI, one of the largest credit bureaus in America

THE CREDIT REPORT IS, to many debtors, a mysterious thing. It seems to carry a great deal of weight in judgments of our creditworthiness. Collectors often threaten to ruin our credit rating by reporting bad debts to a credit bureau.

As we will see, for better or worse, creditors rely on credit reports as being the most complete record available of how you got into, and out of, debt. I think it's wise at this point to examine the credit report — what it shows, how information is placed on it, and to whom that information is given.

The credit report is usually provided to your creditor by a credit bureau. This report is only one factor that is taken into account in the decision to give you credit. Most of the major lenders use a credit scoring system — a complex mathematical formula that judges your creditworthiness on the basis of factors with which the creditor has had experience. For example, when you fill out the line on your credit application that states how long you have held your present job, that information is not only judged against your creditor's experience with people who have held jobs as long as you have, but it is placed within a sophisticated set of interlocking circumstances, grouping the length of time you've had your job with where you live, your marital status, how much you earn, credit that you have from other sources, etc. No single factor decides your credit status — it is the total interrelationship within a statistical formula that counts.

According to Ellen Broadman, an attorney for Consumers Union, publisher of *Consumer Reports*, credit scoring systems emerged after the enactment of the Equal Credit Opportunity Act of 1975. Before then, lenders decided who to lend to on the basis of personal judgments. Many lenders discriminated on the basis of such factors as sex, race, marital status, and age. For example, family men were often viewed as better credit risks than single career women. The Equal Credit Opportunity Act prohibited such discrimination. When nondiscriminatory credit scoring systems were developed to identify creditworthy individuals, lenders discovered that many single career women were better credit risks than family men who were overburdened with bills and obligations.

If you are currently overextended, and yet still have a good pattern of repayments and no bad relationships with your creditors, chances are that only the most astute creditor will deny you additional credit. You can get sunk even further in the sea of debt before anyone notices your ship is spouting leaks. On the other hand, if you've begun to experience problems with your creditors — late payments, having your accounts turned over to collectors, or having judgments filed against you — your credit report will show this. At that point, your main concern is to repair your credit rating so that, if you come to a point in the future when you must borrow money, you will be able to.

How important is the credit *report* to the credit-granting process, and credit scoring in particular? According to the credit grantors I spoke with, the report carries a great deal of weight. It is their way of seeing how well you handle credit, and what your current status is.

Creditors look for a number of things in granting credit. But there are five major factors that summarize their concerns:

Character. If you have used credit before, the creditor wants to know if you met your obligations and paid as promised. Your creditor might check to see if you lied on your application. He'll want to know if you paid on time, and if you paid the full amount when due. They'll check to see how long you've been on your job, and how long you've lived in your home. This last factor is particularly strong in judging people who have never had credit before.

Capacity. Earning power and your current credit commitments define your capacity to repay your loan. This is also determined by your past income and obligations.

Capital. How much are you worth? What is the value of your home, life insurance, etc.? The creditor needs to know your financial situation.

Collateral. What do you have of value that can be placed as security for a loan? Long the province of auto loans and mortgages, more and more credit-card companies are becoming interested in establishing collateral for their lending.

Conditions. These are the credit grantor's own considerations, which exist outside your control. What supply of credit do they have on hand? How is the economy? What time of year is it? How willing are they to lend, considering the profit they could make at this time?

Perhaps the first signal you received that you were becoming overburdened with debt was a rejection of a credit application. There are a number of reasons why people are turned down for credit. Among them:

- You may not have held your present job or lived at the same address long enough. Some creditors require residency for two or even three years.
- You might have too much to pay on your present accounts.
- Your purpose in requesting credit might seem unreasonable.
- Your co-signer may not pass their credit scoring.
- Your credit report may contain erroneous information.
- Your creditor may have stricter than usual standards.
- The funds for lending were not available at that time.

There are two ways of finding out exactly why you were turned down for credit. The first is to visit the office where you applied for the loan. Tell them that you have been turned down, and would like to know what you can do to improve your creditworthiness. If your would-be creditor is evasive, you might want to go through the above list with him, to see which items apply to you.

The second way is to obtain a copy of your credit report. You'll find instructions for this later in the chapter, in the section entitled "Reviewing Your Credit Report." *Whenever* you apply for credit, you should review your credit report. You'll probably be surprised by what they do — and don't — have on you.

By the way . . . some agencies advise employers who are considering potential employees, particularly if the employment involves handling money. Those agencies who will not report to prospective employers do not, for the most part, wish to get involved in the complications surrounding career decisions.

CREDIT BUREAUS

In order to understand how a credit bureau operates, let's follow an application made for credit to A&B Sales by Jane Consumer. Jane's general creditworthiness, judged from her application, seems good — she has a solid job, has lived in the same place for several years, and holds several other accounts. Her performance on those accounts, though, will be the basis for A&B's final decision, and so they will request a credit report.

Consumer credit is a basic fact of our day-to-day life in this country. Every day, thousands of consumers apply for some form of credit. In such an environment, it is absolutely essential that a clear picture of a consumer's debt and payment habits be readily available to credit grantors. Credit decisions should be based on objective information, claim the credit bureaus, that reflects the consumer's willingness and ability to repay debts.

There are close to two thousand credit bureaus in America. The five largest are Equifax (which owns CBI, a consumer reporting agency, and is located in Atlanta), TRW (Los Angeles), Transunion (Chicago), Chilton (Dallas), and Pinger (Houston). They hold, among them, a total of 150 million credit records. Estimates are that the consumer credit reporting industry earns over $200 million a year in revenues.

I looked at two of the largest credit-reporting agencies in the country — TRW, which provides its services under the name

Credit Data, and the Credit Bureau Inc., CBI, which provides its services under the name Acrofile.

Let's trace Jane Consumer's credit file through these large credit bureaus, and see just what kind of credit history she has.

TRW has in its files information on more than 80 million consumers, and supplies this information to 24,000 subscribers — the term they apply to those lenders which both supply information to and receive information from TRW. CBI has approximately 14 million consumers on file.

The basic, day-to-day operations of TRW and CBI are fairly similar. Both receive information from their subscribers on a monthly basis. The credit department, computer services department, financial department, or some similar office, supplies the information on an electronic tape. (In some instances, the information is filed manually.) The information provided is a copy of the accounts receivable file of the subscriber. The credit bureau does not receive "unsolicited information" about consumers, meaning information from sources other than legitimate credit grantors with whom you do business, and who subscribe to their service. Your landlord, your attorney, or a credit grantor to whom you have only applied for credit, for example, cannot supply information to a credit bureau about you, unless it is a matter of public record that has been entered into a court of law.

Looking at Jane's credit report from TRW, then, we see the same kind of information she has received on her credit card and charge account bills: her account number, the status of her account, the balance, and her payment profile.

Both TRW and CBI ask that subscribers give them the most accurate information they have, directly from their own records. The different credit grantors, by the nature of their business, give different information. Banks give the credit-reporting agencies details on their bankcards, their home installment sales, and auto loans, but most banks and savings and loans do not report mortgage information. Federally charted credit unions use reports but, because of federal privacy laws, they usually do not provide *their* account information to credit-reporting agencies.

Other information on your credit status is provided from public records, which are gathered directly from court records and

TRW CREDIT DATA — UPDATED CREDIT PROFILE — CONFIDENTIAL

TCR2

INQUIRY INFORMATION

DFD2 9999999ABC CONSUMER JANE Q.., 1825 H 90027, P-2234 W 92667,
S-548926847, M-1825 HILL STREET?LOS ANGELES CA 90027

PAGE 1	DATE 09-11-80	TIME 15:19:14	PORT AL11	H/V A14	CONSUMER			02-999999/99

JANE Q CONSUMER
1825 HILL STREET
LOS ANGELES, CA 90027

2-80 A & B SALES
1350 4TH STREET
LOS ANGELES, CA 90067
3388338

SS# 548926847

YOB-1952

ACCOUNT PROFILE			SUBSCRIBER NAME/COURT NAME			SUBSCRIBER # COURT CODE	ASSN CODE	AMOUNT	BALANCE	ACCOUNT NUMBER/DOCKET		PAYMENT PROFILE NUMBER OF MONTHS PRIOR TO BALANCE DATE
POS	NDN	BES	STATUS COMMENT	DATE REPORTED INQUIRY	DATE OPENED	TYPE	TERMS			BALANCE DATE	AMOUNT PAST DUE	1 2 3 4 5 6 7 8 9 10 11 12
A			SPNB CURR ACCT	7-80	6-77	3900900 CRC	1 REV	$1000	$242	40245566789 7-15-80		CCCCCCCCCCCC
A			CITIBANK PAID SATIS	1-80	1-77	3900900 AUT	1 36	$5000		892939495969		CCCCC
A			SEARS CURR ACCT	7-80	3-75	3647586 CHG	2 REV	$500	$0	8384858687777 7-28-80		CCCCCCCCCCCC
A			JC PENNEY CURR ACCT	7-80	2-79	3494959 CHG	1 REV	$200	$149	59697989493922 7-21-80		CCCCCCCCCCCC
A			MAY CO CURR ACCT	6-80	2-80	3388338 CHG	2 REV	$200	$0	770004112233333 6-28-80		CCCCCCCCCCCC
	M		MAY CO INQUIRY	2-09-80		3388338						
	M		B OF A INQUIRY	9-21-80		3892212 CHG	REV					

© TRW INC. 1971, 1978

converted to a computerized format and entered into the system in the same manner as credit information from credit grantors.

Whether or not A&B Sales actually grants Jane Q. Consumer the credit she has applied for is the function of their credit scoring system. But the credit report has provided them with a picture of someone who has a good history of repayment, and appears to have experience with a variety of types of credit.

WHAT'S ON MY CREDIT REPORT?

- Credit account information. This includes the name of the company reporting the account, the date the information was reported, the date the account was opened, the type of account, terms, the original balance or credit limit, the current account balance, and the status of the account, such as "current account" or "30 days delinquent." (More about this later.)
- Public record information. If you have been to court over bankruptcy, taxes, a judgment, or a wage assignment, this information may be on the report. It includes the location and the name of the court from which the data was obtained, a description of the item such as "judgment," or "state tax lien," the docket number or page number where the listing can be found, and the status of the items, such as "judgment satisfied."
- Inquiries. Where a request has been made by a creditor for a copy of the report, that request or "inquiry" is automatically recorded on the profile and is retained for a period of one year.

  An inquiry doesn't really mean anything on your credit report. But, if you have applied for credit to a number of places in the course of a year, and there is no subsequent account listed in the report, your creditor may wonder why, in fact, an inquiry was made but no credit was granted.
- Identifying information. The consumer's full name, including generation (such as Jr. or Sr.), addresses over the last five years, social security number, age or year of birth, and spouse's initial. The consumer's place of employment, as indicated by the consumer on a credit application, may also be included in the report.
- Consumer statement. All consumer credit reporting agencies, in compliance with the Fair Credit Reporting Act of 1971, allow the consumer the opportunity to include a statement of 100 words or less regarding any item which they have reinvestigated and with which the consumer is still dissatisfied.

Information not in your file includes: checking and savings accounts, race, religion, sex, salary, personal life-style, or criminal records. A series of "status codes" designed by the credit bureau conveys in shorthand the current standing of your account. Among the status codes used by TRW are:

BK ADJ PLN	Debt included in or completed through Bankruptcy Chapter 13
BK LIQ REQ	Debt included in or discharged through Bankruptcy Chapter 7
CLOS INAC	Closed inactive account
CLOS NP AA	Credit line closed / not paying as agreed
COLL ACCT	Account seriously past due / account assigned to attorney, collection agency, or credit grantor's internal collection department
CO NOW PAY	Now paying, was a charge-off
CR CD LOST	Credit card was lost or stolen
CR LN CLOS	Credit line closed / reason unknown or by consumer request / there may be a balance due
CR LN RST	Account now available for use and is in good standing. Was a closed account.
CURR ACCT	This is either an open or closed account in good standing. If the account is a credit card or charge account, it should be available for use and there may be a balance due. If the account is closed, there were no past due amounts reported and it was paid.
CUR WAS 30	Current account was 30 days past due (this status continues into CUR WAS 30–2, meaning that the account was 30 days past due twice, CUR WAS 30–3, 4, 5, +6; CUR WAS 60, CUR WAS 90, CUR WAS 120, 150, 180, etc.)
DELINQ 60	Account delinquent 60 days (variations include DELINQ 90, 120, etc.)
DELINQ WAS 90	Account was delinquent 90 days / now 30 or 60 days delinquent
PAID ACCT	Closed account / zero balance / not rated by credit grantor

NOT PD AA	Account not being paid as agreed
PD CHG OFF	Paid account / was a charge-off
PD WAS 30	Paid account / was past due 30 days (this has the same variations as CUR WAS 30)
SCNL	Credit grantor cannot locate consumer
SETTLED	Account legally paid in full for less than the full balance

There are quite a few other codes (some of the others convey matters of public record). What is important to note here is that there is a status designation for practically any position your account is in.

If you "read between the lines" you can see how difficult it would be to "clear" your credit report. Paying an account that had been charged off (closed and sent into a collection procedure) doesn't appear on your credit report simply as a paid account — it is listed as "PD CHG OFF," giving the exact disposition of your account.

There are, by the way, status codes employed by the major credit bureaus to indicate the successful completion of a credit-counseling debt-management program. Most creditors, though, will only report an account with this code *after* the program is completed. Until that time, the account is listed by its regular code. The theory behind this is that if you are currently in a debt-management program, you shouldn't be worrying about your credit rating anyway.

In addition, TRW provides designations and payment profiles. The designations, which are assigned to each item of credit or public record information on the report, generally signal a "positive," "negative," or "nonevaluated" nature on the status of an account or public record item. For example, a paid satisfactory account would be designated as "positive." The designations are formulated in conjunction with the credit grantors. Lenders will often skim the designations if they don't have time to review the entire report.

The payment profile provides credit grantors with a comprehensive picture of the last twelve months' payment history. By its nature, the payment profile stresses, to the consumer, the importance of paying installment loans on time. For example, an account that has been current for the past twelve months would be indicated by a series of C's, the signal for current. A 30-day, or one month, delinquency would show on the profile as a 1.

Both TRW and CBI deny that they issue "credit ratings." According to a vice-president of CBI, "Our bureau's role is compiling information. The user decides. There's no such thing as a credit rating. It's all part of a finely tuned control mechanism that helps the consumer as much as the creditor."

Exactly how the subscribers to credit bureaus use a report is still something of a mystery. We know for a fact that the assessment of the items on your report weigh strongly in the credit scoring system, but creditors will not reveal on what basis that assessment is made. Some creditors just skim the credit report, looking for negative status comments. Others, I assume, study it more carefully.

The information about you provided on a credit report makes it possible for a creditor to grant credit. The methods of obtaining information and providing it to creditors define the way in which creditors see borrowers. In that sense, the influence of the credit bureaus is pervasive. It is very important for you to know what is on that report, how you can influence what creditors place on the report, and what your rights are for correcting the information you feel is wrong or misleading.

OTHER USES OF YOUR CREDIT REPORT

Both TRW and CBI provide creditors with other services related to the information on your credit report. Among these services are collections, billings, and a variety of "early warning" systems to alert creditors to possible problems with their accounts.

CBI has over sixty offices throughout the United States and Canada, which combine the local CBI collection agency with a nationwide network of offices through the facilities of their data base. As a result, they claim to offer their subscribers "a single-source agency for your recovery needs on a local, regional and national level."

CBI Billing Services offers a complete billing service through CBI's computer, and also makes available a series of up-to-date pre-collection letters that are issued on CBI letterhead.

TRW has three techniques for what it terms "Asset Control," which go under the names "Quest," "Signal," and "Search."

To understand how these services can affect you, particularly if you are having problems with your creditors, let's look at the consumer credit file of Jane Q. Consumer's brother, John.

Imagine, if you will, that you are a subscriber to TRW's Quest System, and a credit officer of the Mountain Bank. Quest is a system that monitors the credit files of TRW and provides a full updated credit profile on any account which meets a pre-selected criteria. As a credit officer you may, for example, ask to see a profile on anyone who falls 90 days delinquent in one of their other accounts.

This service is designed to assist credit grantors in periodic renewal decisions, or in the decision to raise or lower a credit line. Also with Quest, a creditor can review an account holder's overall payment history to tell whether missed payments are an isolated incident related to that credit grantor, or if there is an overall trend.

One day, TRW sends Mountain Bank a Quest alert form for John Q. Consumer. Earlier this year, John had been a little behind on his payments, but things seemed to be fine now. Quest tells you that he is delinquent 90 days with the Garden Finance Company. As an intelligent credit officer, you can also tell from the profile that John has a habit of "juggling" his payments when times get hard, and has been 60 to 90 days delinquent on two other accounts. All of that adds up to trouble, but there's another side of the coin — John has just about paid off the $4,200 he owed Mountain Bank, and he has a good credit history with the bank and Wisteria Finance. You might wonder, though, why the Revolving Credit Corporation and the Grove Credit Union haven't extended him any credit.

On the whole, as an officer of the bank, you might think that it would be a good idea to keep a close watch on John Q. Don't give him any 30- or 60-day grace periods. If he misses a payment, get

TRW CREDIT DATA

QUEST
UPDATED CREDIT PROFILE

CONFIDENTIAL

INQUIRY INFORMATION

QUEST

1122250 CONSUMER JOH QS., 10655 B 30720, M-123456789 QUEST 2 641

PAGE	DATE	TIME	PORT	HIV
1	08-19-80	19:19:40	A999	B14

ACCOUNT PROFILE			SUBSCRIBER NAME/COURT NAME			SUBSCRIBER #/COURT CODE	ASSO CODE			ACCOUNT NUMBER/DOCKET		PAYMENT PROFILE NUMBER OF MONTHS PRIOR TO BALANCE DATE
NO	NON		STATUS COMMENT	DATE REPORTED	DATE OPENED	TYPE	TERMS	AMOUNT	BALANCE	BALANCE DATE	AMOUNT PAST DUE	1 2 3 4 5 6 7 8 9 10 11 12
E			FILE IDENT: JOH QS./CUR—10655 B 30720/SS#—548603388/YOB—1944									
			4-79 SELF									
			JOHN Q CONSUMER / 10456 A / BOLTON GA 30721									
	A		MOUNTAIN BK			1131035	2			3562401973		
			CUR WAS 30-2	2-80	8-78	SEC	36	$4200	$933	8-1-80		C C C C C C 1 C C 1 C C
A			HILLSIDE BK			1140018	1			29144508119		
			CURR ACCT	8-80	12-79	AUT	48	$5300	$4748	8-15-80		C C C C C C C
	A		HEMLOCKS			1306601	2			986543184026		
			CUR WAS 90	1-80	6-77	CHG	REV	$600	$437	8-12-80		C C C C C C C 3 2 1 C C
	A		BAY CO			1336090	1			46812391013		
			CUR WAS 60	4-80	10-Y	CHG	REV	$300	$206	8-11-80		C C C C 2 C C C C C C C
A			BOWERS			1365771	0			212250		
			CURR ACCT	9-77	8-77	CHG	REV	–$100				
		A	GARDEN FIN			1500132	1			241870		
			DELINQ 90	8-80	7-79	UNS	12	$500	$49	8-15-80	$49	2 1 C C C C C C C C C C
M			WISTERIA FIN			1542240	0			5238610		
			PAID SATIS	7-77	6-76	SEC	12	$500				
	A		HILLSIDE BK			1140018						
			INQUIRY	7-16-80		AUT	48	$5300				
	M		REVOLVING CREDIT CORP			1600829						
			INQUIRY	2-27-80		ISC	24	$800				
	A		GROVE CREDIT UNION			1784340						
			INQUIRY	4-3-80		H/I	12	$500				
			END									

© TRW INC. 1971, 1979, 1980

him on the phone. It's best to keep a sharp eye on these troubled accounts.

Now, let's say that you're a subscriber to TRW's Alert system. Alert is a system that tells credit grantors when certain conditions exist in a consumer's account with a different creditor. For example, if the Mountain Bank wishes to be alerted when their customers are more than 60 days delinquent anywhere, they can do so.

The bank might receive a monthly rundown of these cases, or TRW can send individual bulletins. (Both are pictured here.) Either way, as a banker, you can probably draw the same conclusions about John Q. Consumer, although you won't have all the facts in front of you.

A concerned credit officer *can* get all the facts, and the benefit of having information singled out with the Signal system. Signal also offers a variety of classifications for early warning. Signal reviews payment practices of customers, much in the same way as Alert, but in a different breakdown for use by the creditor.

CBI offers similar services under the Account Review Service Program.

What these systems mean to the debtor is that if you are having trouble with one or two creditors, they may all know about it. It's important to know this when you are negotiating a repayment plan. (Many creditors whom I asked about this system said that they didn't use it, so it's hard to say just how many, and which particular types of, creditors subscribe to them.)

The people who are the customers of CBI and TRW must meet strict standards for "legitimate purposes" when they have access to your files. "For example," a TRW spokesperson told me, "we don't provide access to our files to lawyers who are also credit grantors because we have no way of controlling whether or not that information is actually going to be used for credit granting." In most cases, state and federal licenses for the business must be provided to the credit bureau, and an on-site investigation of the business is usually conducted.

All credit-reporting agencies have provisions for automatically purging credit files. Usually, adverse information is deleted by the computer after seven years from satisfaction of the debt.

MOUNTAIN BANK
123 MAIN STREET
ANYTOWN, NEW YORK

TRW
ALERT

SUBSCRIBER NO. 1131035 ACCOUNT TYPE 00

ALERT CODE	ACCOUNT NUMBER	TRIGGER SUB	TRIGGER STATUS COMMENT	ALERT NOTICE DATE
X	12345678	1160615	DELINQ 60	08 21 80

CONSUMER INQUIRY IDENTIFICATION

SURNAME	GEN	ZIP	SOCIAL SECURITY NO	ITEM NUMBER
1234	B	21412	123-45-6789	123456789

CONSUMER NAME

TRW INC. 1980

MOUNTAIN BANK
123 MAIN STREET
ANYTOWN, NEW YORK

TRW
ALERT

SUBSCRIBER NO. 1131035 ACCOUNT TYPE 00

ALERT CODE	ACCOUNT NUMBER	TRIGGER SUB	TRIGGER STATUS COMMENT	ALERT NOTICE DATE
X	12345679	1230173	CO NOW PAY	08 21 80

CONSUMER INQUIRY IDENTIFICATION

SURNAME	GEN	ZIP	SOCIAL SECURITY NO	ITEM NUMBER
4567	B	21412	000-00-0000	001234567

CONSUMER NAME

TRW INC. 1980

MOUNTAIN BANK
123 MAIN STREET
ANYTOWN, NEW YORK

TRW
ALERT

SUBSCRIBER NO. 1131035 ACCOUNT TYPE 00

ALERT CODE	ACCOUNT NUMBER	TRIGGER SUB	TRIGGER STATUS COMMENT	ALERT NOTICE DATE
X	12345693	1510702	REPO	08 21 80

CONSUMER INQUIRY IDENTIFICATION

SURNAME	GEN	ZIP	SOCIAL SECURITY NO	ITEM NUMBER
5678	F	21412	000-00-0000	445678901

CONSUMER NAME

TRW INC. 1980

MOUNTAIN BANK
123 MAIN STREET
ANYTOWN, NEW YORK

TRW
ALERT

SUBSCRIBER NO. 1131035 ACCOUNT TYPE 00

ALERT CODE	ACCOUNT NUMBER	TRIGGER SUB	TRIGGER STATUS COMMENT	ALERT NOTICE DATE
X	123456790	1180225	DELINQ 90	08 21 80

CONSUMER INQUIRY IDENTIFICATION

SURNAME	GEN	ZIP	SOCIAL SECURITY NO	ITEM NUMBER
5678	C	21468	000-00-0000	223456789

CONSUMER NAME

TRW INC. 1980

MOUNTAIN BANK
123 MAIN STREET
ANYTOWN, NEW YORK

TRW
ALERT

SUBSCRIBER NO. 1131035 ACCOUNT TYPE 00

ALERT CODE	ACCOUNT NUMBER	TRIGGER SUB	TRIGGER STATUS COMMENT	ALERT NOTICE DATE
X	123456792	1370430	COLL ACCT	08 21 80

CONSUMER INQUIRY IDENTIFICATION

SURNAME	GEN	ZIP	SOCIAL SECURITY NO	ITEM NUMBER
1234	C	21412	000-00-0000	334567890

CONSUMER NAME

TRW INC. 1980

MOUNTAIN BANK
123 MAIN STREET
ANYTOWN, NEW YORK

TRW
ALERT

SUBSCRIBER NO. 1131035 ACCOUNT TYPE 00

ALERT CODE	ACCOUNT NUMBER	TRIGGER SUB	TRIGGER STATUS COMMENT	ALERT NOTICE DATE
X	123456794	1610209	JUDGMENT	08 21 80

CONSUMER INQUIRY IDENTIFICATION

SURNAME	GEN	ZIP	SOCIAL SECURITY NO	ITEM NUMBER
6789	Z	21412	000-00-0000	556789012

CONSUMER NAME

TRW INC. 1980

MOUNTAIN BANK
123 MAIN ST
ANYTOWN, N.Y.

SUBSCRIBER NO. 1131035   ACCOUNT TYPE 00

TRW CREDIT DATA

ALERT

ALERT CODE			ACCOUNT NUMBER	CONSUMER INQUIRY IDENTIFICATION									TRIGGER SUBSCRIBER NO	TRIGGER STATUS COMMENT	
				SURNAME				ZIP	SOCIAL SECURITY NO.			ITEM NUMBER			
X			123456789	CONSUMER NAME	1234	B		21412	123	42	1927	123456789	1160615	DELINQ 60	78
X			123456790	CONSUMER NAME	5678	C		21468	000	00	0000	223456789	1180225	DELINQ 90	79
	X		123456791	CONSUMER NAME	4567	B		21412	000	00	0000	001234567	1230173	CO NOW PAY	86
		X	123456792	CONSUMER NAME	1234	C		21412	000	00	0000	334567890	1370430	COLL ACCT	93
	X		123456793	CONSUMER NAME	5678	F		21412	000	00	0000	445678901	1510702	REPO	96
		X	123456794	CONSUMER NAME	6789	Z		21412	000	00	0000	556789012	1610209	JUDGMENT	

SIGNAL

TGA1 MST 1131035   CONSUMER JOH QS., 10655 B 30720, M-1 1500132 3562401973

INQUIRY INFORMATION

PAGE	DATE	TIME		
1	08-19-80	16:49:46	A999	B11

FILE IDENT: SS# IS 548603388, MID INIT IS Q. YOB IS 1944
JOHN Q. CONSUMER
10655 BIRCH ST.
BOLTON GA 30720

8-80 AJAX HARDWARE

ACCOUNT PROFILE	SUBSCRIBER NAME/COURT NAME / STATUS COMMENT	DATE REPORTED/INQUIRY	DATE OPENED	SUBSCRIBER#/COURT TYPE	ASSN TERMS	AMOUNT	BALANCE	ACCOUNT NUMBER/DOCKET BALANCE DATE	AMOUNT PAST DUE	PAYMENT PROFILE
A	MOUNTAIN BK — CUR WAS 30-2	2-80	8-78	1131035 SEC	2 36	$4200	$933	3562401973 8-1-80		CCCCCC1CC1CC
A	HILLSIDE BK — CURR ACCT	8-80	12-79	1140018 AUT	1 48	$5300	$4748	29144508119 8-15-80		CCCCCCC
A	HEMLOCKS — CUR WAS 90	1-80	6-77	1306601 CHG	2 REV	$600	$437	986543184026 8-12-80		CCCCCCC321CC
A	BAY CO — CUR WAS 60	4-80	10-Y	1336090 CHG	1 REV	$300	$206	46812391013 8-11-80		CCCC2CCCCCCC
A	BOWERS — CURR ACCT	9-77	8-77	1365771 CHG	0 REV	-$100		212250		

●●●●●●●●●●●●●●●●●●●●●●●●●●●●●●●●●●●● ACCOUNT SIGNAL CLASS 1 ●●●●●●●●●●●●●●●●●●●●●●●●●●●●●●●●●●●●

| A | GARDEN FIN — DELINQ 90 | 8-80 | 7-79 | 1500132 UNS | 1 12 | $500 | $49 | 241870 8-15-80 | $49 | 21CCCCCCCCCCC |

●●

M	WISTERIA FIN — PAID SATIS	7-77	6-76	1542240 SEC	0 12	$500		5238610		
A	HILLSIDE BK — INQUIRY	7-18-80		1140018 AUT	48	$5300				
M	REVOLVING CREDIT CORP — INQUIRY	2-27-80		1600829 ISC	24	$800				
A	GROVE CREDIT UNION — INQUIRY	4-3-80		1784340 H/I	12	$500				

END

©TRW INC. 1971, 1978, 1980

Many credit-reporting agencies keep business credit reports as well as consumer reports. Your business and personal reports may overlap if you have taken personal loans that you will use for business, or if you haven't explicitly identified the purpose of the loan.

THE INVESTIGATIVE REPORT

The consumer credit report, then, is pretty much a nuts-and-bolts record of your credit history. But there is another kind of report, known as an investigative report, which can contain a good deal of damaging information. (The investigative report is not gathered by all credit bureaus — TRW, for example, doesn't do them, although it does pull together special credit reports for some clients which entail talking with creditors on a one-to-one basis about certain consumers.)

The investigative report is usually compiled at the request of someone who has a more extensive interest in you than the average creditor — an insurance company or a bank from whom you are borrowing a large sum. Sometimes executive "headhunters" will employ them. The report will include details of your life-style, your character, and your reputation. When the report is done responsibly, an interviewer will speak with former employers, neighbors, and any references you have given on your application. Some investigators might talk to references you've given on old applications, as well.

What this means, then, is that when your employer-to-be, say, has elected to run an investigative report, someone outside his office, who may in fact have no direct knowledge of the job you will perform or the talents needed, could be talking to references you've given on your application.

The Fair Credit Reporting Act requires users of these reports to notify you that they may request an investigation and that you have the right to know what they turn up. The notice might be on the application, or sent to you separately. According to the Federal Trade Commission, the notice should be something like this:

This is to inform you that as part of our procedure for processing your application, an investigative consumer report may be prepared whereby information is obtained through personal interviews with your neighbors, friends, or others with whom you are acquainted. This inquiry includes information as to your character, general reputation, personal characteristics, and mode of living. You have the right to make a written request within a reasonable period of time to receive additional, detailed information about the nature and scope of this investigation.

There are two difficulties that arise with the investigative report. The FCRA applies only to third-party companies, not to the staff or employees of the company which is granting you credit. Thus, if your creditors decide to run their own check on you, they are "entitled" to whatever information they receive, however they get it.

The other problem is that you may, in your application, have signed a waiver of confidentiality that would allow your creditor or employer to search into records and areas deemed illegal by the FCRA.

REVIEWING YOUR CREDIT REPORT

The Fair Credit Reporting Act says that you may examine information in your credit file and have any mistakes corrected. As I've said previously, if you are having trouble with your creditors, it's a good idea to know which of your problems are showing up in your credit report and under what "status" they are being filed. As you proceed to repay your debts and repair your credit, you'll want to check periodically to see that this is showing up on your report, as well.

If a lender has refused you credit because of unfavorable information on your credit report, you have the right to the name and address of the agency that keeps your report. Then, you may either request information from the credit bureau by mail or in person. You may not get an exact copy of the file, but you will at least get a summary of it. The law also says that the credit bureau must help you interpret the data. If you are challenging a credit refusal made within the past 30 days, the bureau may not charge a fee for giving you information.

Any important error that you find must be investigated by the credit bureau with the creditor who supplied the data. The bureau must also check any public record information which you dispute. The bureau will remove from your credit file any errors the creditor admits are there. If you disagree with the findings, you can file a short statement in your record, totaling 100 words, giving your side of the story. Future reports to creditors must include this statement or a summary of it.

If you haven't been turned down and are curious, you may wish to review your file by mail. You must properly identify yourself to the agency by providing your full name, including generation (Jr., Sr., etc.), your addresses for the past five years, your social security number, your year of birth, and your signature. TRW and CBI, and all other credit bureaus, have complete procedures to review your credit file with you. CBI asks that you include your current accounts and numbers. Both agencies charge a fee for reviewing your file if you have not been turned down for credit in the past 30 days. A phone call to the office will ascertain this fee.

It's safe to assume that most of the major credit bureaus in the country have a file on you, particularly if they have an office in your area. Look them up in the phone book, and ask what their particular procedures are for obtaining a copy of your file.

If you wish to make a visit to the office of the credit bureau during business hours to review your report, an appointment must be made. Trained interviewers will go over the file with you and help you with any dispute, or with a consumer statement. These statements, of 100 words or less, can contain anything you wish, provided it is not slanderous or libelous. A TRW spokesperson told me of a man who wished to include the fact that he had not paid his creditors for two years because he had been in jail. When advised by the interviewer that this kind of information might prejudice future creditors, he still insisted on having it included.

There are limits placed by the FCRA on the length of time certain information can be kept in your file: bankruptcies must be removed from your credit history after ten years; suits, judgments, tax liens, arrest records, and most other kinds of unfavorable information must usually be removed after seven years.

Another important aspect of the law states that you may withhold your credit record from anyone who does not have a legitimate need for it.

Other rights guaranteed by the FCRA, including rights pertaining to billing errors, are covered in "Can They Do This to Me?"

ISSUES SURROUNDING CREDIT REPORTING

A variety of controversial issues currently surround the credit-reporting industry. Among these are:

- Privacy. The FCRA has taken a number of critical steps toward insuring the consumer's privacy. Access to credit reports is limited to businesses having a legitimate need for the information in connection with a business transaction. Government agencies, unless they are credit-granting agencies such as the Guaranteed Student Loan Program, can only verify your name, present and former addresses, and places of employment unless a court order is obtained. As with investigative reports, consumers must be notified when such investigations are going to be undertaken.
- Accuracy. Incorrect information, disseminated as it can be through a Kafkaesque web of computers, provides the largest difficulty in the credit-reporting industry. At present, incorrect information usually comes to light only when a consumer has been turned down for credit. Consumer groups, though, are currently attempting to make credit reports more available to consumers and hold the creditors as responsible for the inaccurate information as the reporting agency.
- Use of credit information systems for debt collection. As I said in the opening of this chapter, collectors often threaten to ruin a credit rating by reporting a bad debt to a credit bureau. With some credit-reporting agencies diversifying into collection activities, the consumer finds himself under even more pressure.

  There are a number of problems that arise in this connection. Not all debts claimed by a creditor are actually owed. Some are in dispute by the consumer. Currently, most debts that are legitimately in dispute during the collection process do not find their way onto the credit report. When the reporting agency serves as the collector, this is not so, and the consumer finds himself cut off from other sources of credit based on the derogatory information in his report.

  Second, as we have seen, paying off a debt doesn't wipe it off the credit report. When the credit bureau acts as the collector, it is more likely that the information listed will be more pointedly damaging.

Currently, legislation is pending in the House and the Senate to give consumers more control over their credit reports. These bills require the consumer of information to inform you, soon after you apply for a loan, of the kind of information that will be gathered, and who will be gathering it. The entire file, not just the "nature and substance of the file" now required, will have to be shown to you. You will be notified, if these bills pass, of the specific reasons for adverse decisions on your creditworthiness. And the bills authorize civil actions for violations of the Fair Credit Reporting Act.

One of the most succinct comments on the issues surrounding the credit reporting industry was made by James Traub in the July 21, 1979 issue of *The Saturday Review*. I quote:

The recent Harris poll found that fully one-third of the public feels that we are very close to, or have already reached, the state of affairs described by George Orwell in *1984*. This may be, as information industry executives claim, an opinion founded on ignorance. It is surely a melodramatization. But it does indicate a sense of constriction in the world's most open society, a feeling of close barriers, and above all, a fear of powerlessness before the vast institutions that shape our lives, and seem to know more about us than we do ourselves.

YOUR CREDITORS:
WHO THEY ARE, HOW THEY WORK, AND HOW TO DEAL WITH THEM

"We're a society that lives on credit. To say that someone shouldn't have been living on credit, shouldn't have gotten in over their heads, is oversimplifying things. You're encouraged on one hand, then when you get behind, they come at you with the other hand."

— A New York consumer advocate

THERE ARE AS MANY WAYS of managing the repayment of your debts as there are creditors. The principles of the preceding chapters apply to negotiating with all your creditors, but each lender has a different set of goals and a different style when working with debtors. Each creditor has a reason for doing business with you, and if you can work with that rationale, you can tap into the best way of negotiating with them.

A retail store, for example, wants to keep selling you goods, and making money on selling you credit is not their main reason for doing business. Therefore, they push their accounts a little less and are a little more flexible than, say, a bank, whose sole purpose for doing business with you was lending you money. For the bank, your relationship is already damaged if you are severely delinquent, and they probably won't be interested in "repairing" the lender-borrower relationship in the near future.

This chapter will tell you what you need to know to be a savvy negotiator with each creditor. You'll find out how each of them perceives his relationship with his customers, what each expects from you, and what the procedures are for collecting delinquent accounts. In some cases, I'll tell you how these creditors might be able to help you in your debt-management program. In the next chapter, I'll discuss collection agencies — how they do business, and how to tell if you'll be able to work with them.

The competition for collecting on delinquent accounts in the past few years has increased enormously. The recession has seen a tremendous rise in the number of accounts being turned over to collection agencies, and the threat of bankruptcy by their debtors has forced creditors into a position of sending accounts into collection earlier and earlier. Industry estimates say that there are seven creditors clamoring for every delinquent dollar — meaning that the average creditor imagines himself in competition with six others for the money you owe him.

Two billion dollars was lost from personal bankruptcy filings alone in 1980. The lending institutions claim that this has done much to increase their *already* sizable losses on consumer credit. The Bank of America, the nation's largest consumer lender, reported at the end of 1980 that its losses on consumer loans were up 40 percent from 1979. Citibank, the second largest, said losses on its consumer loans rose 56 percent in 1980, to almost $200 million, from $125 million in 1979. In 1980, Citibank loaned $2.3 billion to consumers, bringing their total consumer loan total to $15.7 billion. (In 1975, to offer a contrast, Citibank's losses totaled a relatively small $68 million.) Beneficial Finance reported losses increased by 54 percent in 1980, to $109 million. And Sears, Roebuck, the largest issuer of credit cards in the country, reported that losses from personal bankruptcies in the first eleven months of 1980 rose 124 percent, to $40 million.

In 1980, major credit-card operations experienced their most unsettling year since the recession of 1974–75. Dee W. Hock, president of Visa, estimated that their losses in 1980 would reach one billion dollars — other industry sources say Hock was being conservative, and the losses would come closer to $1.2 billion. Major New York banks alone estimated that together they would lose $500 million on their Visa and MasterCard operations.

Obviously, banks didn't get into the credit-card business to lose money, and 1980 was the first year that they experienced any kind of significant losses. According to credit-card industry watcher Spencer Nilson, in 1978 the average U.S. bankcard operation had a net profit of $22 per $1,000 charge volume. The average cost of money then was 8 percent. In 1979, money costs rose to 11 percent and reduced the profit margin to a near break-even point, at $1.40 per $1000. The first half of 1980 saw the average bankcard *losing* from $30 to $50 on every $1,000 in charge volume, due to higher rates on the cost of *their* money and low usury ceilings, which kept many banks from passing their expenses on to the consumer. By repricing their services, most of those banks were narrowly able to climb into the black again at the end of the year.

These tremendous losses are changing the face of consumer credit in America. The banks have gotten wise from their experience, and have manned a full-scale attack on the enemy of their profit margins — the legal limitations placed on their earnings. Across the country, bankers have successfully lobbied in state legislatures and on the federal level to raise or eliminate usury ceilings. In addition, the banks have ferreted out restrictions on their ability to tack on extra finance charges — such as transaction fees and annual membership dues — which might have existed in state laws. They've lobbied, successfully in many cases, to wipe these out, too.

In other words, there were laws on the state books which said that the banks could only charge you so much for using their money. The banks argued that the laws were unrealistic, and pointed out that many of them had been made before or shortly after the Depression. To be fair, the laws did not reflect current economic conditions. But the banks received too much of a good thing when state legislatures either removed interest rate ceilings completely (as they did in New Mexico and Pennsylvania, for example) or allowed banks to tack on extra charges which, in effect, raise the charge to you. (More about how banks are gearing up for the 1980s in "Can They Do This to Me?")

Banks are also tightening their credit scoring standards, and reducing the availability of credit, particularly on unsecured loans. In fact, some industry experts forecast the end of unsecured loans in the near future. Even your credit card will be secured by something — and if the banks have their way, that something will be your home.

Credit-card lenders have, in the decade or so since they began to "mass market" their services, made a tremendous impact on our lives. Credit cards are a part of our culture and, for many of us, affect the way we feel about ourselves. Have you ever noticed the pride and almost self-righteousness with which some people announce "I pay all of my credit-card bills in full every month"? This simple act has become, for many, a means of self-assertion. The selling of credit to Americans entails more than getting us to use cards. Those who sell us credit invite us to participate in a genuinely defined segment of American life. What few of us realize, when the ball is rolling along smoothly, is that it is the sellers who are defining that life. It is the creditors who call the shots, who decide the values and philosophies of the credit-card society.

Because their system is so large, because they are so intent on pervading every possible aspect of American life, the creditors also find themselves suffering their share of failures. One can't look at the pattern created by heavy lender loss and the rising number of people in serious debt without considering whether the creditor had some part in it. "Business as usual" for them might, by the nature of their business, spell out overburdening debt and the loss of financial control for many others.

As Ellen Broadman, Consumers Union attorney, states, "Lenders have an obligation to determine whether or not they think the individual can carry further debt before extending credit to them. Creditors should not let customers get in over their heads."

Many creditors promote credit like crazy. One member of the Fed's Consumer Advisory Council told a story about a woman who earned under $10,000 and who had tens of thousands of dollars in credit outstanding. He claimed that she just walked into the bank on the right day.

There's a great deal of pressure in our society on people to have things, to show the world their success. All of the ads encourage people to consume more. Because of that, the creditors are able to say, "Come on in, arrange credit, it's a good deal, low prices." They use their vast barrage of marketing techniques to get people to come in and buy on credit. Unless the lenders assume some responsibility, people will continue to get sucked in.

In my interviews, I heard many consumer advocates express, with a degree of despair, the same sentiment: "They think they can string people along. They offer more and more incentives to get people to use credit, even though the people are just barely making it, just as long as their default rates aren't cutting into their profit margins."

Jim Boyle, director of Consumers Federation, calls the overextended debtor "the lender's best customer. They've got them for life. They keep refinancing them, making new payment arrangements, rolling them over, and they don't have to go out and drum up new business."

Of course, bankers feel very differently about this matter. As one vice-president of a major New York bank told me, "We can't double-check on people all the time. If they ask us for credit we have to assume — unless something tells us otherwise — they can pay us back." Whether or not that "live and let live" attitude is good or bad is a point of controversy between lending institutions and consumer groups.

One of the most damning pieces of evidence against the major lenders is Ralph Nader's study group report on the First National City Bank, entitled *Citibank*. Consumer loans, the authors wrote, "are merely a product to be sold. The unfortunate fact, however, is that Citibank sells its product to thousands of people who simply cannot afford to pay."

For instance, in 1977 Citibank sent out millions of unsolicited credit-card applications. Five million people who used the cards from that mailing didn't pay the bills they had run up. As David Samuels, deputy counsel of the New York Department of Consumer Affairs, states, "There couldn't possibly have been a careful screening of those loan applications."

It seems that creditors may have been making plans to continue leading their debt-ridden lambs to slaughter until 1980. Then, the new realities of credit in America began to take hold — high interest rates, the credit crunch, and the recession. Instead of taking a more responsible attitude toward credit, though, they merely increased its cost to the consumer. Again, it's you and I who pay the price. And again, the real obligation to be responsible is on our shoulders.

Of course, lenders have a very different picture of things. In the course of my interviews for this book, I asked one simple question of every creditor and collector I spoke with: "Why don't people pay their bills?" After hearing their answers, I began to form the impression that many creditors keep little lists in their heads to categorize their difficult accounts. It might read something like this:

1. They didn't like my product. (This headache particularly plagues bankcards and retail creditors.)
2. They stuck the bill in a drawer somewhere and forgot to pay me.
3. They figure I won't go after them for the money.
4. They're waiting for me to go after them.
5. They're paying someone else instead of me.
6. They can't pay me — they're ill, sick, etc.
7. They don't like me.
8. They're deadbeats and I'm going after them.

Every day, the average creditor or collector in this country is caught up in a difficult and complex psychological game. His experience is that, while most people would like to pay their bills, many can't. Experience also tells creditors that, while many can't pay their bills, very few will admit it. Before the average person will tell a collector that he can't pay what he owes, he'll lie, cheat, and even abuse the collector. The pattern of collection becomes one of pursuit, intimidation, and then rejection.

There are two basic laws in the collection industry: (1) keep the debtor on the defensive, and (2) the collector who works the hardest gets paid first.

How they keep you on the defensive, how they work, and what strategies you can employ to meet them head-on are what this and the next chapter are all about. In this chapter, I'll break down all the major types of creditors you might owe money to, and tell you how to negotiate with them on *your* terms, using your debt-management program. In the next chapter, I'll show how to deal with that singular creature, the collection agent. You'll learn how to talk with him, what his point of view is, and how to defuse his threats and intimidations. This chapter will also be helpful to you if you're dealing with collectors for bankcards and retail stores. In both chapters, you'll learn the principles *they* operate under, and what signals you'll want to give them.

BANKCARDS

The American Bankers Association defines a bankcard as "any card issued by any bank which accesses the customer's financial resources." Of all bankcards, credit cards are the most common. Basically, a credit card extends a line of credit to a customer and, in fact, many banks make the majority of their small loans through their credit card "lines of credit." The maximum amount that may be owed on any card at any given time is normally set by the bank at the time of credit approval. Lines typically range from $400 to $5,000, and some go as high as $15,000.

More than 123 million Americans had bank credit cards at the end of 1979, and used them to obtain more than $60.6 billion in goods, services, and cash advances.

Normally, if you pay your bill within 25 days from the billing date, there is no interest charged on the money you borrow. (And the banks make no money, a situation they're trying to remedy by charging a yearly fee to people who pay their balances in full every month.) If a customer doesn't pay the balance in full, finance charges are applied on the next bill. These charges vary according to the laws of the state in which the institution issuing the card is located. Charges typically run around 18 percent a year. There are also, as I've said before, a variety of charges — transaction fees, late charges, annual "dues" — that can be added on to a card. Credit cards allow the customer to make a minimum monthly payment on the balance — say $10 or 1/36 of the balance.

Bank credit cards can also be used for cash advances, obtained at any participating bank. There may be a service charge for each advance, and the interest is charged from the day the advance is posted to the account.

Here's what happens when you use your bankcard. Let's say Sally goes into a clothing store. The clerk records the sale on a sales ticket, which is provided to the store by the bankcard. If her purchase is more than the store's limit, the clerk telephones the bank for an authorization. Sally is then given a copy of the ticket as a receipt. The original ticket is deposited at the bank with which the clothing store has contracted for card service (this is typically the store's regular bank). The bank immediately credits the store's account for the amount of the purchase, after taking out a fee. If Sally's card has been issued from the same bank as the store's, the bank immediately bills Sally's card account for the amount of the sale.

(The fee charged to the store by the bank for bankcard transactions has caused some stores to offer customers discounts for paying cash, usually equal to the bank's fee. The store might advertise this, or you might have to ask. If you're making a large purchase with cash, it's worth trying to bargain for such a discount. It *is* illegal, though, for a store to charge more if you are using a credit card. In May of 1981, Exxon announced that it was proposing a 3¢-per-gallon reduction on their gasoline for people who paid cash, pending the approval of their station owners.)

If Sally's card is issued in Chicago and the store is in Omaha, the pertinent data from the sales ticket must be transferred to the Chicago bank, and the accounts of the store and Sally's credit card are settled between the banks. Bankcard plans such as Visa and MasterCard have enormous processing and authorization centers throughout the world to handle this work.

Recently, a new kind of bankcard has made an appearance on the scene. It's called a debit card, and is more like a pre-authorized check than a credit card. When you use a debit card, the amount of your purchase is deducted from your checking account. When the sales slip reaches a bank and is posted, the amount is instantly deducted from an account instead of being posted on a bill. New technology allows the transaction to be almost instantaneous if an electronic terminal is used at the point where the sale is made. The merchants pay the bankers to participate in the plan, and some debit cards require an annual fee from the cardholder. Industry experts estimate that the debit card won't be a mainstay of the credit-card scene until 1985, at the earliest. One of the major blocks to the growth of the debit card is that its advantages have yet to be clearly spelled out to consumers by the banks.

The most significant development in bank credit cards over the last year has been the change in pricing structures — what the banks can charge their customers for their various credit services and products. As consumers are quickly learning, credit is going to cost more in the future. In addition, more and more banks are shifting to systems under which new purchases will start accumulating interest immediately if you carry a balance over from the previous month. Higher minimum monthly payments, higher transaction fees, and higher interest on cash advances, increased charges for paying late and for exceeding your credit limit are all part of the scene now. As if that weren't enough, most banks are also raising their fees for merchants accepting their cards — you can bet that cost will be passed on to the consumer, as well.

The outcome of all these extra fees and charges is that, before using credit, the wise consumer should total all these extra fees and charges to evaluate the real cost of a particular item. He may find he could be paying 50 to 60 percent interest on the money used with a credit card. (Hypothetically, the charges could reach that high, with difficult circumstances. A $40 charge, for example, at 18 percent interest, might also carry a $2 transaction fee, represent $5 of a $35 yearly fee [if the card is used only seven times a year], receive a $3 late fee, and be charged $3 for exceeding the credit limit — a total of $20.20 in finance charges — 50 percent!)

Especially for the consumer in trouble, or getting out of recent trouble, the situation is not good. As I said before, card debt losses in the last year were staggering, and the banks are holding grudges. It's harder than ever for the person who has had debt problems to get new credit, and close to impossible for someone who has gone through bankruptcy. The bank's attitude does change, though, when the consumer has worked intelligently with the lender. Many lenders told me that a consumer who had worked out a solid plan for repayment and who stuck with the plan could often renew their credit arrangement when a debt had been paid off, although usually with a lower credit line.

For most banks, the first sign of a customer in trouble is a late payment, although an official of Citibank informed me that they used the TRW Alert and Signal systems as well. A second recognized sign of trouble is a quick rise in the balance due on the account, especially if it exceeds the credit limit. Still another sign of trouble can come when one bank contacts another to see if the irregular repayment pattern of an account is being repeated at the other institution. (Although some bankers mentioned this practice to me, I was unable to learn how widespread it is, or if it was routine.) In this kind of situation, by law, banks can only deny or confirm repayment patterns. They can't provide what would, in essence, be a credit report.

Only occasionally do consumers contact the banks to notify them of a problem before these signs of trouble appear. That's all the more reason to take the offensive by contacting your creditor with the details of your debt-management program in hand.

Almost all of the banks with accounts over $100 million (that includes almost all of the major card issuers) have an automated procedure for handling delinquent accounts. A collector will call you when you are 70 to 90 days past due on your payments, or if the computer has notified the collection department that you've gone substantially over your credit limit, say by more than $300.

One collector at a major New York bank described this call to me as "an educational, counseling process. The amount over the credit line is due immediately, and an attempt is made to determine if there is a problem, if perhaps the card is stolen or missing. We often have to remind consumers of what their credit line is."

What follows is the typical collection process of a bankcard account. Let's look at the basic time schedule and then see how to deal with your creditors at various points in the collection cycle.

Let's say you charge up a storm at Christmastime. Since your cycle closes on the nineteenth of the month, most of the charges don't appear on your January bill, posted on January 1, but do appear on the February bill (a good argument for last-minute Christmas shopping, if that's your billing cycle). For whatever reason, you aren't able to make a payment that month. On the tenth of March, or 40 days from the billing, you are sent a note from the bank. It's usually a short reminder, asking if you have forgotten to pay, and telling you to call them if there is a problem.

If you don't make a payment, when you get your April bill, there is usually a stern reminder on it. If no payment is received after 70 days (counting from the February 1 bill), the collection process begins. The first step, usually, is to suspend the account. (By the way, your card number may have appeared on the card company's "hot list" before this point, or the card's authorization center may have turned down a merchant's request for authorization because of your delinquency.)

The primary goal of the collection department at 70 days is to bring your account current. They want the last two minimum payments, period. They'll try to find out if you have a problem, and from this point on they'll keep every communication you have with them on record. The collector will enter into his computer or into your file (most of them sit in front of video display terminals), when the call was made, to whom he spoke, why payment hasn't been made, what was said, and when the payment or another call was promised. When he calls the next time, whether it's the same collector or not, he'll have a very good memory of what you've said before.

Most bank collection departments are structured by the age of the delinquency. There are 70-, 90-, 110-day collectors, and a great deal of competition goes on among the collectors to bring payments up to date at their particular "age." (Some collection departments have blackboards and bulletin boards that list the number of accounts brought current by each "age" level.)

Somewhere between 90 and 120 days, your account will be handed over to the bank's legal department. At this point, the bank will ask for payment of the account in full — you will no longer be able to settle the account by paying the last two or three months' payments.

Most banks have a staff counsel, and when your account has been handed over to the legal department you will be sent a letter over that department head's signature. By this time, the account will have been canceled, and with most banks there's a good chance that they won't reinstate it for several years unless you give them good reason to believe you've repaired your debt situation.

The attorney letter, one collector told me, is the most effective technique they have for "turning" delinquent accounts. The impact of a third party entering the picture is very strong, and between day 110 and 120 of the debt a tremendous amount of money comes into the bank.

After 180 days, the bank writes your account off, and usually turns it over to an external collection agency. These agencies will be discussed more completely in the next chapter.

(When an account is deemed as uncollectable, it is charged off, and transferred on the bank's accounting ledgers to a "suspense" or "profit and loss" account. By doing this, the bank recognizes, through its accounting practices, that they're not getting any more back from a borrower than they already have. Most banks have a profit and loss reserve, which they keep to cover their losses on anticipated charge-offs.)

According to one banker, who is in charge of the collection department of a major New York bank's Visa operation, the collection effort is "a cat-and-mouse game. It's psychological warfare. Sometimes being aggressive, sometimes being nice works.

"You try to trust the people first," he told me, "but if they break two promises to you, you know they're not good for the money, and you accelerate the account to charge-off."

The time schedule for collection procedures is only a guideline. If at any point in the collection process a collector feels that further effort will produce no results, he will immediately "accelerate" the account into charge-off. One collector estimated that 25 percent of the charge-offs in every month are accelerated accounts.

Your biggest worries about dealing with your creditors come at the tail end of the dunning cycle — 90 to 120 days. Until that time, they merely want to "get you back in line," as one collector put it. After 90 days, you'll have the problem of overcoming your lack of credibility for having allowed your account to slide for three months or more.

I can't stress enough the importance of being prepared to negotiate with your creditors with a good idea of how you will repay them — the essence of the debt-management program.

It's important to remember these time schedules can be bent in your favor. Although the dates for suspension and cancellation of an account are fairly hard and fast, a payment or good working arrangement with a creditor will save the account from going to the next step in the process, or from going to legal collection.

What should you expect when you call a bankcard collection department? "Our first goal," according to Tom Lynch, vice-president in charge of Visa at Chase Manhattan, "is to get the debtors to admit that they do owe us money. Get them to recognize that we do expect to be paid, and are willing to assist the debtor in any way to get our payment.

"The collector wants to keep the person talking. He wants to get them to make a commitment. The collector is conscious of the fact that you only get so many shots at a debtor."

What happens if you call and say, "I just don't have the money?"

According to Lynch, "When you tell us you don't have money, we try and convince you that you do. We have people who are trained to counsel you via the phone, who can help you look through your budget. Don't forget that, in most cases, we are just looking for a minimum payment to hold the account.

"Collectors realize that the more specific they are, the more the person on the other end will build in their mind an obligation about the debt."

If, after all of that talking, you still are unable to make a payment, the account will usually be charged off, and an outside collector will have the responsibility of getting you to pay. Most bankcard collection departments will mention to you the option of going into consumer credit counseling, and most will take your participation in such a program as a positive sign for your account.

It's important, then, to contact the bankcard as soon as you realize you have a problem with your account, and have formulated a plan for handling your problem. Usually, the number to call is printed on the statement. When you begin negotiating, it's important to request that your account stay with the same collector, or with his supervisor, so that you'll be able to talk to the same person every time you call back.

As one creditor put it, "It's the way you handle paying your debts that makes a difference to us, not just that you paid them off. If you made an agreement with us, and were able to live up to that agreement, that shows good faith. And if, after you've finally paid off the debt, you want an extension of credit, it's a strong possibility. But you have to expect that nobody's going to lend you any more than what you were able to pay back in your agreement."

The major thing to think about in proposing a plan to a bankcard is that the plan must be "reasonable" to them. Most banks want to be paid back in two to three years.

There are two important points to remember in negotiating terms with your creditors, especially with the bankcards. First, ask them to cancel any future interest and finance charges on your account. As a negotiating point, you might mention that they would do this automatically if a consumer credit counselor were making the new arrangement, and by dealing directly with you, they save the 15 percent fee that might go to the counseling service.

Second, if they have begun any kind of legal proceeding, get a written guarantee that the proceedings have been canceled and removed from the public record. If you don't, you may find yourself being sued even after negotiating a new repayment schedule. At the very least, the legal action could find its way to your credit report, where it will stay for seven years, unless you can convince your creditor to go back and change it — not an easy task.

CHARGE CARDS

In a customer brochure, American Express terms bank credit cards "Buy Now, Pay Later" cards. They call their own plastic "Pay As You Go" cards. Long known as "T&E" cards (for travel and entertainment, the province of the business world that comprises the majority of their users), companies such as American Express, Diners Club, and Carte Blanche — the three major issuers — now refer to their credit instruments as charge cards. The main reason for this is that the cards now offer a much wider variety of services, at a greater number of locations, than they did in the past. Especially in their penetration into the retail world, charge cards have achieved their goal of becoming a much more predominant fixture on the credit scene.

Charge cards have far fewer users than bankcards. At the end of 1978, the bankcards had more than 135 million cardholders, while the top three charge cards totaled just over 13 million. And yet, in the bust year of 1980, the *Nilson Report*, a newsletter for credit-card executives, placed American Express as the only truly profitable credit-card operation in the country. In many ways, this can be attributed to the charge-card company's careful screening, high standards, and the self-discipline imposed on borrowers by the pay-as-you-go method. (The banks certainly feel that the charge cards are worthy profit centers. Citicorp owns Carte Blanche, and at this writing Chase Manhattan is trying to buy Diners. Both banks hope to use the basic T&E format to turn Diners and Carte Blanche into profit centers as strong as American Express. Along the same lines, Visa and MasterCard are, as I write this, developing plans to market their own cards aimed at "prestige" users.)

For most of us, there is only one difference between a charge card and a credit card — when you use a charge card, you have to pay the bill in full every month. The cost of the card, in the long run, can be much cheaper because of this — there are no interest charges on outstanding balances because there are no outstanding balances. There is a once-a-year annual fee, but it is not much more than the fee now charged by the bankcards. However, if your bill does become seriously delinquent, late charges will be imposed on the card and your account will most likely be canceled sooner than the bankcards normally would cancel you.

The collection process for the charge cards is very much like that for the bankcards. Let's take a look at one major card, American Express.

The first sign American Express has that you are in trouble is if your payment is 60 days delinquent or if there is extraordinarily high charging on the card. Prior to that 60-day limit, you will only receive a reminder notice at approximately 45 days past due, in addition to the reminder on your bill. At 60 days, you will receive a notice that you are seriously delinquent. According to the card member agreement, if a seriously delinquent account is not paid by the closing date on the statement sent to you after you are notified that the charges are seriously delinquent, American Express will add to that statement a delinquency charge of 2½ percent. The 2½ percent is calculated monthly only on the amount that is seriously delinquent — if you've made any new charges, they won't be considered delinquent until you haven't paid them for 60 days.

At any point in the collection process, if American Express feels that you aren't going to pay up, they'll cancel your card. They'll also get on the phone to you rather early in the process — probably within 45 to 60 days — to find out what your problem is, although that depends very much on the credit history of the delinquent cardholder.

When the collector contacts you, he has a much different goal than a bankcard collector does when he calls. While the bankcard collector wishes mainly to bring your account current by collecting any past-due minimum payments, the charge-card collector wants the bill in full — and for some people that 60- to 90-day bill can be a whopper, since charge cards carry no pre-set spending limit.

The collectors who work with the charge-card companies are fairly flexible in working out an arrangement with the cardholder, and if you can convince them that your setback is only temporary, you might be able to have the card suspended, rather than canceled, during the time you pay your bill. This is especially true if you've had the card for several years, with few previous problems. The collectors know that their cardholders are, for the most part, economically "upscale," and they keep this in mind when talking to debtors.

Once you do come to an agreement, you will probably be asked to sign a promissory note on this new payment plan. Make sure that it contains none of the clauses mentioned in "Facing It," which would limit your legal remedies in case of default.

Once the collection department feels that the account is uncollectable — and there is no set date for this determination — it goes to an outside agency. In American Express's case, the accounts go to collection agencies and not lawyers, since it already has a large staff of collection lawyers on the staff who handle those accounts they feel should be brought to court. Carte Blanche, on the other hand, uses a number of attorney-operated collection agencies to settle their accounts.

According to the American Express agreement, court costs plus attorney fees equaling 15 percent of the unpaid balance may be added to your account if they refer it to an attorney for collection. This generally holds true for all of the charge cards.

SINGLE-PURPOSE CARDS

Single-purpose cards are those issued by department stores, oil companies, and retail establishments. There are three types of single-purpose credit. The first is the charge account, for which billings are totaled at the month's end and paid on or before a specified date of the following month. No interest charge or penalty is paid on this plan. The second kind of credit is the revolving charge. Under this plan, the customer is given a limit against which he can charge. Payments of 5 to 10 percent of the balance must be made monthly. Interest is charged on the unpaid balance. The third form is the time-payment or installment plan, and is generally used on large items such as furniture and appliances. Credit for this kind of plan generally is carried over and above the revolving-charge limit, and payment can be spaced out for over a 36-month period. Interest rates and annual percentage rates are set at the time of the purchase.

At the end of 1979, retail stores still controlled over half the total credit cards outstanding in this country. Retail stores and oil companies issued cards to 149 million people, while bankcards and T&E companies issued a little over 72 million cards. The top ten card issuers in the country are single-purpose cards — Sears, Penneys, Wards, Texaco, Federated Stores, Mobil, Amoco, Gulf, Shell, and Exxon.

While the oil companies had a brief fling with accepting MasterCard and Visa on a company-wide basis, they now leave that decision up to their individual station owners, since the headache of processing the charges was too much for them. The bankcards have been making significant inroads on the retail scene, though, with major stores such as Penneys and Sears experimenting with various plans to incorporate the bankcards into their credit operation.

The intrusion of third-party cards, though, doesn't change the initial purpose behind the in-store card. Single-purpose issuers give you a card because they want you as a customer. The logic is that if you have their card, you will shop with them instead of their competitors. Likewise, if you fall behind on your payments and get into debt with them, it is your relationship with the creditor as a customer that is their first consideration. While a bank or finance company sells you money — and your falling behind is enough to damage your relationship permanently — a store or oil company is in the business of selling you goods and services. When you fall behind with an oil company or department store, while they want you to clear up your bill as soon as possible, they also want to keep you as a customer. Their margin of profit is hurt less than a money-seller's by bad debts since the cost of their goods is less than the "face value" of their loan to you.

The largest credit-card issuer in the country is Sears, Roebuck, with 80 million cards, 40 million accounts, and an annual volume of over $9 billion. According to Sears's vice-president of consumer credit, Linden Wheeler, the store is in a "unique position. We feel a kind of responsibility to our customers. We have an ongoing relationship with them that we want to preserve. Our collection people are trained to work with our customers. We tell them that if the customer can't come up with the money, then work out a plan with them that they can stick to. We make sure that our customers can work with our collection people. We put the same collector on the customer's file until the bill is paid up. Our main advice to the customer is 'tell us the truth.' " (Sears was one of the founding organizations behind NFCC, the umbrella organization for Consumer Credit Counseling Services across the country, and Linden Wheeler has served on the board of NFCC.)

For most single-purpose card companies, a missed payment is the first sign of trouble. From there, the approach to the debtor varies.

According to Linden Wheeler, "We contact the customer at about 40 days. We try to establish some sense of what is going on. After that, there's no set schedule, since we don't use external collection agencies and only go to our lawyers when we have to. We leave it up to the collector to decide if the customer genuinely wants to pay what they owe us."

Sears's approach is quite different from Exxon's. A company spokesman for the oil company told me that their collection procedure was "well-prescribed and fully automated." After the bill is delinquent for 30 days, a "low-key" message is included in the next statement. After 45 days, the company follows up with a letter or phone call, depending on the account's past history and how much money is involved. The caller will try to determine what the problem is caused by, and will begin to work on some kind of arrangement with the customer if the amount due is not immediately forthcoming. "In some cases where the customer is in some kind of financial difficulty," the spokesman told me, "we'll work something out. But the first thing the customer has to do is level with us — be straightforward."

Arranging a repayment plan with a single-purpose card company is usually a straightforward process. The company will usually close your account and ask you not to use your card while repaying. After you've completely paid off your debt, most single-purpose cards will reconsider opening your account. That decision is most often based on the circumstances surrounding the debt — illness, family problems, etc. — and your past history with the creditor. Basically, if they haven't lost money on you, and you appear to be sincere in asking for new credit, they'll reopen your account.

The standard for large, automated, single-purpose lenders is for them to keep their collection efforts within the company for the first four to six months, and then turn the account over to an external collection agency.

Once the collection agencies *do* get the account, though, there is a decisive change in attitude. Jerry Taylor, a collection manager in New York, told me that he felt retail stores were extraordinarily lax on their accounts, that they didn't work them hard enough, and that this made it tougher for the collection agency when they took the account over. "The retailer knows that, if you're strapped, you're going to pay him last. You'll pay your landlord, your utilities, your bankcards because you can use them everywhere, and then you'll pay the retailers. And they also know that you'll pay the general department stores before you pay the specialized stores because you can use your account for more at the big stores.

"The idea behind the collection departments is to bring your account current so they can get you into the store to shop again.

Period. It's hard to convince the management of these companies to do otherwise, because collecting on delinquent accounts doesn't figure into the big profit picture for them."

You have a great deal of leverage when you're negotiating a repayment plan with a single-purpose-card issuer. They want you as a customer, they want your money, and your bad debt doesn't hurt them as much as it hurts the money-sellers. Another point to keep in mind is, if you pay them back to their satisfaction, it will be easier to reopen or keep your account with a single-purpose lender than almost any other credit grantor.

SAVINGS AND LOANS

A few years ago, it would have been unnecessary to include this section in the chapter. At that time, except for mortgages and home-improvement loans, the only way you could borrow from a bank was by using your passbook as collateral. The Depository Institutions Deregulation and Monetary Control Act of 1980 has changed all of that. Thrift institutions (the financial term for savings and loans, cooperatives, and other institutions for savings) can now make up to 20 percent of their total loans with consumer lending and corporate bonds. They are also permitted to offer credit cards and trust services.

Negotiating a payment plan with a savings and loan is pretty much the same as with a commercial bank, with one important difference. Savings and loans, for the most part, are smaller, and they are newer to the collection experience. According to industry estimates, the savings and loans haven't geared up to full collection efforts on their consumer loans yet, since these loans are still rather new. If you do get into trouble with loans from a thrift institution, you can expect the same standards as from a commercial bank, but with a more personalized approach. (For more about loans from thrifts, see this chapter's section "Mortgage Loans.")

UTILITIES

Gas, electricity, oil, water, and phone service — all of these are essentials of life for which you are extended credit, in the sense that you use the product before you pay for it. We rarely think of utilities as credit items, but they are — and can often cause problems in a debt-management program if you don't budget for them properly, or if you don't make intelligent arrangements for repaying overdue bills.

You have two things going for you if you are having serious debt problems with utilities. First, most utilities do not want to "terminate your service" (as they call it). Second, the public service commissions of almost every state have now declared that "moratorium" periods must be honored during which essential utility services such as light and water cannot be cut off. This insures that low-income families, especially in the northern states, will not suffer from extreme cold.

There are two basic types of utilities — large corporations, such as the phone company and the power and light company; and small suppliers, such as heating oil distributors.

According to a spokesman for Consolidated Edison of New York, they have a strictly prescribed cycle for people who get behind in their payments. Thirty days after a bill has come due, a "good customer" (one who has no outstanding history of payment problems) will receive a reminder notice on his bill. After 60 days, a note will be sent to the customer, saying that he risks disconnection or a deposit if the bill is not paid. After 90 days, a notice is sent to the customer, stating that the bill must be paid, and a deposit made, within 8 to 10 days. If the bill is still not paid, the service will be disconnected.

It is fairly easy to "intercept" this prescribed cycle and come up with an alternative payment arrangement with utilities. In some instances, they will help you to locate state and federal energy assistance programs that can aid you in paying your bill. You can contact the customer service representative of your utility by calling the number printed on your bill. The most common arrangement is for the current month's bill to be paid in full, and the back bill to be paid over a period of a few months.

According to the Edison Electric Institute, a national organization of power and public service companies, there are a variety of assistance programs available to consumers having trouble with their utility bills. For reasons of privacy, the consumer must tell the customer service representative that they feel they might be eligible for one of these programs — the representative cannot ask. Among these are Senior citizen relief programs, third-party notification programs (in which a designated person receives a notice if someone is in danger of being disconnected), and community-funded programs for assisting people who cannot pay their bills. Your utility will be able to tell you which programs are available in your area, and how to qualify for them.

The Bell System also has a fairly strict procedure for people who do not pay their bills and do not communicate with the company. Depending on your past record with the phone company they will first put a reminder on your bill, then they will try to get in touch with you to discuss your delinquency and alternative payment arrangements. If they are unable to get in touch with you, they will notify you by mail of an intent to disconnect your service.

Having your phone disconnected generally occurs in two steps. First, your outgoing service is cut off, and you are not able to make phone calls. After that, your incoming service is cut off, and you cannot receive calls. Once your service is terminated, you must pay your bill in full, and also pay a charge for reconnection and a deposit.

The phone company is flexible in making repayment arrangements, and a spokesman told me that their biggest problem is with people who ignore their notices and do not try to get in touch with them. A reasonable attempt on the customer's part, I was told, will almost always get a positive response.

Small suppliers, on the other hand, do not have the generous profit margins and cash flow that the large utilities enjoy. While they want very much to keep good relations with their customers, for the most part they cannot afford to keep accounts for more than 30 days or so.

In order to minimize the number of "bad" accounts they may get, most oil and gas distributors attempt to carefully screen prospective customers. In most cities, there is a central clearing house which lists customers who have attempted to skip from one distributor to another without paying their bills. Distributors make use of these listings, as well as the usual references for job, bank accounts, etc. Most customers, after paying cash on their first delivery, pay a monthly statement — a process which is carefully watched for the first few months. Customers who fall behind on their payments are usually switched to a "cash on delivery" basis.

Both the large utilities and the small distributors offer budget plans for periods of peak consumption. In the northern states, for example, heating oil distributors and the gas utilities will offer plans that stretch the large bills for the cold winter months over a 10 to 12 month period. In the southern states, the peak period might take place in the summer because of high air-conditioning bills. Any overpayment or underpayment is usually adjusted in the twelfth month.

For a person on a debt-management program, these budget plans can be extremely useful. They allow you to count on a specific payment every month, thus keeping your budget under control, especially during periods of peak use.

THE SMALL LENDER

As I said in "Making a Plan You Can Stick To," the small lender — such as your doctor or corner grocer — is someone who should come high in your repayment priorities.

Small lenders realize that the longer an account goes uncollected, the harder it will be to get the money. Most of them employ some kind of collection procedure. Few of them go so far as to employ collection agencies, although one new development in the collection field has changed that somewhat. Some collection agencies are offering their dunning services for hire, at a flat rate per account. The collection agent, for a fee, will send out letters to the delinquent account under the agency's letterhead. In some cases, the letter will instruct you to send the payment to the agency, but most often you will be instructed to pay the small lender directly.

The step-by-step approach employed by most small lenders begins with a note to the debtor. Usually the note will be rather personal, and appeal to your sense of fair play. In fact, the bad debt hurts the small businessman more than an impersonal corporation. The friendly and sympathetic letter will turn into a "flexible" letter after about a month or so, and then become firm and short.

Basically, the usual small businessman would like to avoid a confrontation. That's what you have going for you. More than any other creditor, the small businessman will appreciate the concern and effort of a solid repayment plan.

PERSONAL LOANS, STUDENT LOANS, AUTO LOANS, ETC.

For the purposes of this chapter, I will deal with these large personal loans both as they are handled by commercial banks and as lent by the dealer (for example, auto loans, or large appliance loans financed by the manufacturer). Consumer-finance companies and other lenders that handle large personal loans are dealt with later in the chapter.

The large single-purpose loan is the preferred loan for the commercial bank dealing with retail banking, for a number of reasons. The two most prominent reasons are that these loans are most often secured (and secured by the item for which the loan was made), and the purpose for the loan is usually stated in the application and thus gives the bank an idea of how seriously you'll take your obligation to repay.

Whether its purpose is the purchase of an auto, home improvement, tuition payment, or some other large-ticket item or service, this type of loan is the mainstream of the commercial lender. Often, collateral or security is required for these loans — in an auto loan, for example, the car you have purchased is most often the security. For another kind of loan, you might place your house as security, or something else of value in your possession. The repayment schedule and interest rates vary according to the purpose of the loan, and are determined when the loan is made.

When a personal loan is overdue, the collection procedures employed by a bank are much the same as their bankcard procedures — in many cases, the same collection department is used. In others, such as at Citibank in New York, each loan area has its own collection department. The performance of the debtor is carefully monitored. The bank employs credit bureau early warning systems. According to a spokesman for Citibank, the enormous rise in bankruptcies has put the bank in a position of being much more strict about delinquencies, and a great deal more effort is spent staying on top of the accounts. Citibank gives its accounts over to its own collectors after 90 days, and works those accounts with a great deal of determination.

One option you have with a personal loan which you do not have with a bankcard is the possibility of refinancing. Especially with a secured loan, this option can prove to be a life-saver, and will more eagerly be responded to than a new repayment arrangement.

Refinancing is particularly applicable to auto loans. According to General Motors Acceptance Corporation, the largest auto-loan maker in America, almost half of their seriously delinquent accounts are settled by refinancing the loan. Seven hundred and twenty thousand loans were refinanced in 1979.

As I explained in "Making a Plan You Can Stick To," refinancing is a process by which your creditor rearranges the main terms of your present agreement, usually the finance charge and the length of time you have to repay. Thus, a loan of $4,000 for 36 months, with 18 months and $2,000 left to repay, might be refinanced to extend the repayment period for another year, at increased interest. For a more complete discussion of refinancing and consolidation, see that chapter.

The spokesman for GMAC told me that they encourage debtors with trouble "to contact us as soon as it happens. We have a longstanding policy in helping with unexpected financial problems."

Secured loans can give rise to the most difficult of debtor's problems — repossession. If this is looming on the horizon for you, see "Emergency Situations" for immediate help.

CREDIT UNIONS

No longer the little room in the back of the shop, credit unions have really come into their own as financial institutions. But their purpose and their means of operation have not changed — they still are in the business of making loans, and they still work in a closely knit, cooperative fashion.

A Federal Reserve pamphlet defines credit unions as "A group of people + a common interest + pooled savings + loans to each other." The total assets of U.S. credit unions, as of June 30, 1981, amounted to $74 billion. There are close to 22,000 credit unions in the country, serving over 45,700,000 members. The average member has $1,397 in their credit union.

Since you can get loans at a credit union, you can get into debt trouble with them. But more often, you can get a helping hand in getting out of debt. We'll discuss both instances in this section.

Of all the financial institutions discussed in this chapter, the credit union offers the most hope and the most help for the indebted.

A credit union is a cooperative, self-help thrift and loan society composed of individuals bound together by some tie, such as a common employer, membership in the same union, or residence in a well-defined geographic area. The Navy has a credit union, as does the Pentagon and Fort Knox. There is a credit union for owners of Appaloosa horses, and one for employees of the MGM Grand Hotel.

Membership in a credit union comes from owning shares in it, which are priced by the union and are purchased in the same way as you would make a savings account deposit. Members receive one vote in the union, no matter how many shares they own. Dividends are paid on the shares from the profits the credit union makes by lending and investing the money it collects. Deposits are protected by Federal Share Insurance and by participation in the Central Liquidity Facility, a kind of Federal Reserve Bank for credit unions.

Credit unions make most of their money through loans, which account for three-fourths of their assets, or more. Mostly, these are consumer loans, but where permitted many state associations are moderately active real-estate lenders, as well.

An example of a credit union as lender is provided by Phil Isenberg, who runs the Graphic Arts Federal Credit Union in New York City. "We've done thousands of consolidation loans," he says, "and the loans are not always made from the financial standpoint of whether or not they are good for us. As opposed to most financial institutions, we're not in the business of selling money by indebtedness. We naturally want to make loans, but we also want our people to have a manageable level of indebtedness."

Delinquency rates at federal credit unions, as of the end of 1979, were at 4.1 percent, and close to 3 percent of their loans were delinquent for two months or more. On the whole, credit unions suffer a lower rate of delinquencies than banks. An industry source told me that their delinquency rate rose significantly, by a point or two, in the recessionary year of 1980, especially in the areas of the country where there was heavy union employment.

When someone gets behind in his or her payments, the usual procedure for credit unions is to send a notice to the debtor, asking him or her to come into the credit union office and discuss the problem. "We sit down and figure out what the problem is," says Phil Isenberg. "We might start to accept a smaller payment. We might defer the interest, or discontinue it altogether in an unusual case."

The difficult economy of 1980 was not kind to credit unions. Interest rates battered smaller credit unions, closing their margin between the cost of money, the return on their investments, and the profit on loans. The recession cut down on saving, too, and led many depositors' funds out of the credit unions and into money markets. Some credit unions were left strapped for funds, and their only relief came when the federal credit union board allowed the unions to begin charging 15 percent interest on loans.

Credit unions are also meeting with competition in the financial market. The 1970s saw them entering a number of "full service" areas such as share draft checking. As well, many smaller credit unions are suffering growing pains, straining to maintain their cooperative nature while becoming more bureaucratic.

Most financial analysts say that credit unions will survive these crises and prosper in the coming decade. The quality of their services, and the friendliness of their operations, credit union leaders feel, will make all the difference for the consumer.

FINANCE COMPANIES

The consumer-finance industry, characterized by companies such as Beneficial, Household Finance, and AVCO, does business in over 25,000 offices throughout the United States.

At the end of 1979, $68.4 billion in consumer installment credit held by finance companies consisted of $30.7 billion in personal loans (45 percent), $26.8 billion in retail automobile loans (39 percent), $3.4 billion in mobile homes (5.5 percent), and $7.5 million in other forms of consumer installment credit.

The typical image of finance companies as high-risk, high-cost lenders is rapidly changing in the large consumer-loan marketplace. Smart consumer shoppers found in 1980 that the consumer-finance companies often were providing personal loans at the same rate as banks, and with comparable arrangements. In addition, the finance companies were in a better position to make consolidation loans, not having been subjected to the "tight money" reserve requirements that the banks had been. In 1979, their delinquency rate reached 2.64 percent, and they charged-off 4.47 percent of their accounts. Nineteen eighty rates were not available at the time of this writing, but industry estimates were that they were not significantly high, since many delinquencies were covered by refinancing loans. The average amount of a loan for consolidation in 1980 ranged from $1,500 to $5,400.

The largest area for growth for finance companies has been second mortgages. Basically, a second mortgage — also known as a home equity loan, junior mortgage, homeowner loan, or second trust deed — is a way of tapping the equity on your home, without refinancing your mortgage completely. Second mortgages use the equity on your home — the difference between what you owe on your first mortgage and what your home is worth on the market today — as collateral. You pay an interest rate comparable to the current rate on secured personal loans, and make your monthly payment on the second mortgage at the same time you make payments on the first. For the time it takes to repay the second mortgage loan, it seems to many borrowers as though they have two mortgages. Once the money is repaid, the homeowner is left with the regular mortgage payment.

A spokesman for one of the largest finance companies told me that he felt that the secured second mortgage was going to be their biggest form of transaction in the eighties. (The rapid increase in real-estate prices and the consequent increase in the dollar value of the homeowner's equity have been one of the few "positive" sides of inflation.)

There are definite advantages and disadvantages to consolidation with a finance company. A well-made consolidation loan can help by reducing your obligations and spreading them out over a period of time, lowering the total monthly payment so that you can match the amount you have to pay with the amount you owe. The price of all this, of course, is the interest rate. Many times the interest can be higher than the actual loan. The largest disadvantage is that if you lack the discipline to handle money properly, you may find yourself with the same problem again.

The managers of finance company offices go through a great deal of training, some of which is centered on financial counseling. But it should be remembered that their goal is always to sell money, and their financial counseling may just be a sales pitch for a loan.

According to Jack Downing, a vice-president at Household Finance Corporation, "Sometimes additional money or another loan will help the customer. Again, we will work out a way of stretching their obligations out over a long period. We think that this is a valid solution. On the other hand, if the customer just doesn't have the means to pay, obviously more loans won't solve the problem."

(For more about consolidation and its pros and cons, see "Making a Plan You Can Stick To.")

If you want to contact the loan office to work out a new repayment plan, the best way is to go to them personally. Sit down with the manager and have a firm plan in mind so you can accurately state what your obligations are, how much you have monthly to repay them, and what kind of consolidation arrangement you feel will be satisfactory.

Most finance companies cooperate with nonprofit counseling services.

If you're in debt to a finance company, it might be easier to make an arrangement, but you may end up paying for it, since they may push for their plan rather than accepting yours.

MORTGAGE LOANS

Unlike the other major creditors covered in this chapter, serious delinquency with a mortgage is not usually a simple matter of negotiation. More than anything else, the inability to meet monthly mortgage payments is the sign of *serious* indebtedness. Although we're not in the days of being thrown out into the street anymore, you can lose your home if you mishandle your mortgage.

One financial counselor I spoke with told me that if a debtor found he couldn't meet his mortgage payments more than two months in a row, he should consult a lawyer immediately, either to talk about bankruptcy or to approach the lender about a new mortgage contract.

I have also been told, by a banker, that speaking with the mortgage lender can sometimes yield results. In cases where you have a good past record of payment, it might be possible to work out an arrangement where you will make current payments on your mortgage, and pay the past due payments over a period of several months.

If you've owned your home long enough for it to have increased substantially in worth, it might be possible to work out a new mortgage agreement or a second mortgage. If your home is relatively new and a new agreement is not a possibility, you and your lawyer may have to come to some kind of arrangement with your bank.

BORROWING FROM YOUR LIFE INSURANCE OR PENSION/PROFIT-SHARING PLAN

In a sense, it is impossible to get into serious debt when you borrow from your insurance policy or from the cash value of your profit-sharing plan or pension. But such borrowing carries the heavy risk of reducing the value of your investment in the future.

Life insurance companies make single or partial payment loans, based on the cash value of your life insurance policy. There is no date or penalty on repayment, and if you die the amount owed will be deducted from the value of the policy. Insurance companies have rates that are much lower than most lenders because they take no risk, pay no collection costs, and secure your loan with your policy. Commonly, the loan will run between five and eight percent interest, and the rate will be stated in your policy.

Borrowing from your pension plan or profit-sharing plan at work varies with each employer or union. Check with your personnel department for details.

Borrowing on your life insurance *can* be a way of alleviating some of your debt problems, but you should carefully weigh that benefit against the risk of losing your investment in the policy. The temptation will also be to make no attempt to repay the loan, since there is no obligation to repay even the interest.

If you do decide to borrow, the actual procedures are simple — you file a loan agreement at a company office, requesting an immediate payment of a named amount of the current cash value of your policy. The application is forwarded to the home office, and your loan can be approved in a few days, when you'll receive your check.

PAWNSHOPS

Pawnshops generally operate the same way all over the country. As one pawnshop owner told me, "We make short-term loans based on portable collateral. If you can carry your security in here, we're in business. You've got six months to come back and get what you've left behind, paying us what we gave you for it, and a 3-percent-per-month interest."

According to my small survey of pawnshops in New York City, 80 percent of the people who pawn items reclaim them. If you can't pay off your loan, there is a way to hold your pawned items. As one broker told me, "People come in, sometimes every day, to pay off their interest, get a ticket for the next day, trying to hold something over."

What the pawnshop owner gives you for your item of collateral is usually shockingly less than what you think it's worth. His biggest profit is made on reselling the item if you don't reclaim it.

He then keeps what was due him, plus costs (which are usually stated on the ticket you sign when you pawn), and is supposed to return any other money he receives to you.

If you are absolutely desperate for a relatively small, short-term loan, a pawnshop could be the place to help you. But you run several risks. In a rare case, your item won't be at the pawnshop when you come to claim it, or it will be damaged. The interest rates are high, and if the item means something to you emotionally, losing it can be a double trauma.

LOANSHARKS

Loansharks are *not* legitimate lenders, and so they really don't belong in this section, but millions of people are in debt to loansharks — some of them for a few hundred dollars, some for thousands, and some owing full interest in their business. Because loansharking represents such a large segment of debt in our country — it is organized crime's second largest source of income — I felt that it would be worthwhile to discuss who they are and how to deal with them. If you already owe money to a shark, you'll find some helpful advice here. If you don't, you'll find plenty of reasons to *stay away*.

I wanted very much to interview a loanshark for this chapter, but was unable to do so. I tried contacting a shark through several acquaintances, even through a private investigator. But no luck. I guess that when it comes to sharks, they're more interested in people who make book, not write one.

But up in the Bronx, in the district attorney's office, I met the assistant D.A., John Tartaglia, who specializes in dealing with loansharking as a facet of underworld crime, and who explained how a shark works.

"He asks you what you need, you tell him; then he gives you the rate. Smaller amounts, under fifteen or twenty-five thousand dollars, the rate might be four or five points [percent] a week. Big money, one hundred to two hundred thousand, they knock the points down one or two. But they'll keep a closer watch on you."

Loansharks have as their typical customers people with cash

flow problems, usually small businessmen and people who need money quickly. There's a lot of sharking in the garment district of a city, where businessmen need a quick loan for goods, and may not have a line of credit or a credit rating.

"Basically," according to Tartaglia, "loansharking is a recycling industry. The money comes from narcotics, gambling. They put it on the street for three purposes — laundering the money, extending their influence in legitimate business, and most of all to realize an incredible return on their investment."

Loansharks and their money suppliers are not as rough-hewn and financially unsophisticated as you might suppose. In fact, they adapt incredibly well to shifting economic winds. "Any time there's a credit crunch," Charles Rogovin, a Temple University law school expert on organized crime, told the *Wall Street Journal*, "you're going to drive more people to the sharks." Before the credit crunch hit in the spring of 1980, according to a *New York* magazine article, the loansharks did just what the other lenders eventually did: they raised the rate to 6 points and reduced the supply of credit. They started knocking on doors, asking for more principal. "We're businessmen too," one member of the kneecap set claimed. "We could see what was happening. In fact, I think Carter got the idea from us."

What happens when you can't make payments to a loanshark?

In the old days, according to Tartaglia, "They'd make an example of one of their victims in front of all the other customers, or in a way that all of the other victims would know. There would be brutal killings. Today, there's a more businesslike approach. They want to give you the opportunity to give them your business.

"There are less examples made now. They don't need the actual violence now, they rely on the fact that you know what they could do if they wanted to. They've got an 'aura' about them, largely derived from the media."

What should a person do if he is in trouble with a shark? Tartaglia told me, "As a prosecutor, I'd like to recommend that they come forward. But being realistic, it's extremely difficult to come forward. A lot can be done for you if you encounter a good prosecutor, a good group of detectives. It's hard to disappear after you're done. These people tend to find you. There's really no answer. You have to pay them, some way or another. There's no way out."

As I said, loansharks have very little to commend them to the average borrower. But they do share one common characteristic with even the best of creditors — they have to be repaid.

Creditors, for the most part, believe in the sincerity of their borrowers — even if their actions don't seem to show it. But they're not in the business of trusting people (come to think of it, who is?) and their faith in mankind tends to be shaky. So they put up a front — the Wall of Fear. We've seen behind that wall now, and while the emperor *is* wearing clothes, it's your basic business suit and not black armor that he has on.

Dealing directly with your creditors is the most straightforward, and the most preferable way of making your debt-management program work. But many people find that they have to deal with a third party, particularly if they've been out of touch with their creditor for some time. That third party is the collection agency, the subject of our next chapter.

COLLECTION AGENCIES

48 HOUR NOTICE
TAKE NOTICE . . . That your creditor alleges that you are justly
indebted in the amount listed with us for collection. Further, we have
been authorized to proceed with any necessary lawful action to effect
such collection. Therefore you have *48 HOURS* in which to pay the
amount indicated above.
TIME IS OF THE ESSENCE!
IF YOU REMIT WITHIN *48 HOURS*, NO ACTION WILL BE
TAKEN

— A standard collection letter

JUST WHAT DOES THAT LETTER MEAN? Although the reference to "necessary lawful action," *sounds* rather ominous, it really doesn't say anything. And while no action will be taken within 48 hours if you "remit," chances are that no action will be taken after 48 hours, either — until it's time for the collection agency to send you another letter.

Collection agencies are hired because they will "work" their accounts with greater diligence and persistence than most creditors will. While creditors will follow up on their collection procedure according to plan, a collection agency (to borrow a phrase from Muhammad Ali) "floats like a butterfly and stings like a bee." They jab, poke, prod, and wheedle until they get their money from you. They try every tactic they know, and when they hit a live vein, they go for blood.

Collection agencies vary, from the sophisticated and law-abiding to the roughshod and abusive. Some collectors believe in the old adage that "you'll get more flies with honey than with vinegar," while others long for the good old days of the baseball bat.

In fact, according to the May 1981 issue of *Entrepreneur*

magazine, anyone with as little as $750 and the desire to "make money being an S.O.B." can start their own collection agency. *Entrepreneur* trades in success stories of America's independent small businessmen, and the article on collectors featured one couple, husband-and-wife owners of a Michigan agency, who started five years ago, "out of a spare bedroom, and [who] told us they expect to *net* $150,000 a year from an operation with five separate offices."

I know what you're thinking — I thought the same thing when I read that — "With everything I know about collections from all those phone calls and letters I've seen, I could open my *own* business."

Entrepreneur's opinion of collection agencies as prospective lucrative businesses stated, "Our country's economic climate is expected to stay about the same for at least the next year. That makes it an ideal time to enter the collection business and be on solid ground with established clients when the economy improves. Obviously this business does better during recessions, but the drop during boom periods usually is less than 20%. Proper planning and control of overhead in this high-profit business will make it worthwhile under any economic condition."

Collection agencies are businesses. They make their money — a third to half of what they collect — by succeeding where others have failed. In this case, the creditors are the failures. Most of the collectors I talked with felt that creditors fail to collect because they don't work their accounts hard enough. And for many collectors, "working" an account includes every tactic of intimidation — legal and illegal — known to man.

The Fair Debt Collection Practices Act, passed in 1978, has done a great deal to correct the abusive and destructive behavior once associated with collectors. In addition, the act has created a wave of industry self-regulation, particularly among consumer-finance companies and others not covered by the act. (The FDCPA covers only third-party collectors — agencies hired by creditors to collect debts — and not creditors collecting their own bills, a fact that dismays many consumer advocates.) But the collection of delinquent accounts, by its very nature, invites the use of threats, both implied and stated, and many of the abuses continue.

The next chapter, "Can They Do This to Me?," will go fully into the abuses and practices covered in the FDCPA. This chapter deals with how collection agencies are set up, how collectors are trained, and what you need to know to negotiate payment arrangements with them.

INSIDE THE COLLECTION INDUSTRY

In 1980, the volume of new accounts turned over for collection exceeded $3 billion in the U.S. and Canada. A great deal of this increase came from creditors who were referring accounts to collection earlier because of the rise in delinquencies caused by the economic downturn. According to credit-card industry watcher Spencer Nilson, "The ratio of amounts placed for collection to the amount of dollars actually recovered ran as high as 34 percent ten years ago, and dropped to 25 percent after the FDCPA, went as low as 20 percent in February of 1980. Many card issuers who rely heavily on their cash flow were paying as high as 50 percent of the amount collected to keep their collections current."

In addition, the collectors experienced a real slowdown in the payment of bills by their customers. In a survey taken by the *Wall Street Journal* in the spring of 1980, credit managers complained of bad checks, broken promises, and a general feeling that, in many cases, people were already so squeezed that it didn't make any difference how hard you pressed for money. Eighty percent of the credit managers surveyed said that slow-paying customers were a severe or moderate problem, and nearly 90 percent said that they expected more bankruptcies in the coming year. Their response to this syndrome was stepped-up collection activity and a general sense of bearing down on accounts.

There are about six thousand collection agencies in the country, ranging from fly-by-night offices to legal collection agencies headed by attorneys. According to the American Collectors Association, the average collection agency received about 1,400 new accounts per month in 1980, with an average payment on each account both new and previous coming to $50. In any given month, the average collection agency takes in close to $40,000.

When a creditor hires a collection agency, there are a number of very basic considerations. If the creditor is a large, publicly visible company, they will be concerned with the number of complaints that may have been filed with local consumer offices or with the Federal Trade Commission, since legally the creditor is responsible for what their collectors do. Creditors will most often contact others doing business in the same area to see who they use, and what the performance record has been.

Many creditors choose large collectors because of their capacity for handling collections nationwide, without farming out their business to other, smaller firms, about whom the creditor may have no knowledge.

Five of the largest and most commonly used collection agencies are Payco American Corporation in Chicago, G.C. Services in Houston, American Creditor's Bureau in Phoenix, Capital Credit in Washington, D.C., and Central Adjustment Bureau in Dallas.

In working with a collection agency, the creditor takes great pains to assure that his accounts are properly and actively pursued. All of the documents that the creditor has on file are made available to the collection agency, although the average collector works on the phone with a simplified listing of your records. Frequent reports are made on the account status, and especially of the amount of money paid on the account.

With all of this going on between the collector and the creditor, much of it coming out of economic necessities, the debtor is finding that more and more collection agencies have become more sound, professional, and competent — if the collector feels that he will have some degree of success with the debtor. That's good news for you, since you're prepared to work with your collectors in a reasonable, responsible way.

FIRST IMPRESSIONS

A collection agency has more clout than a creditor does in collecting an account. Consumers know that a collector will have the immediate power of the summons on his side.

According to Bernard Sennet, senior partner of Sennet & Krumholz, a legal collection firm with offices in New York and California, the collection agency gets the account somewhere between 120 and 150 days of delinquency. Generally, they have a good idea of how the creditor has worked the account, and which of the agency's methods they'll have to begin with.

The collector usually has your name, address, and your account history. Some companies give the collector a copy of your credit application, and the entire "work card" from their collection department. Some agencies, though, work on a tape-to-tape basis, and the collector will employ this computerized system to obtain only the information on your monthly bill.

The first thing a collection agency will do will be to send out a letter. Most collection agencies today are automated, and this letter is usually sent by computer. The letter will tell the debtor that the collection agency has been authorized by the creditor to collect the account, and ask the debtor to pay the account at this time. As well, the letter will offer the debtor the chance to dispute the debt within 30 days. If the collection agency doesn't hear from the debtor after that period, they will assume the debt is valid. (There are a number of intricate points of law surrounding the first contact by the collection agency, which are covered in the next chapter.)

At Sennet & Krumholz, the computer that sends out the letters also has several other important functions. It creates a file for the debtor, and makes a 3×5 card for the agency's central file. Thus, the agency can use it to see if the same debtor has other accounts in collection with their office. By law, the agency must remit any payments it receives from the debtor to the account the debtor specifies. This card also helps the agency "skip trace" delinquent debtors who may have left town with some unpaid bills and developed some new bills in their new home. Almost all of the large collection agencies go through this process.

After two weeks, the agency will send another letter if they haven't heard from the debtor. Then they will begin calling the debtor.

There is very little about a collection agency's offices to distinguish them from any other type of business. The tools of the trade are pretty much the same: telephones, files, rows of desks — and in the more modern offices, video display terminals. Once in a while, though, something will appear to tell you what kind of office you're in.

At the American Creditor's Bureau in New York, the walls are covered with posters and signs admonishing their agents in certain practices. There are also blackboards on which are listed the collectors with high totals for the week. One of the signs says, "If you don't want to hear it on tape, don't say it." Another outlines the nine points of a collection call. These are:

1. Identify yourself and your firm.
2. Identify the problem.
3. Pause.
4. Use fact-finding.
5. Make a bridge to the payment plan.
6. Settle on a payment plan.
7. Negotiation — problem solving.
8. Get a promise.
9. Let the customer hang up first.

"A good collector's approach," says Jerry Taylor, a manager of the American Creditor's Bureau office in New York, "should be to convince the customer to pay the account. Convince the customer that's the way it *should* be."

DIALING FOR DOLLARS

Both Bernard Sennet and Jerry Taylor offered me a chance to listen to their collectors at work. Although you may have had your fill of experience with collectors on the phone, here's an idealized version of how those nine points work in a collector's call:

☐ COLLECTOR: Hello, Mr. Jones, this is Mr. Shears from the Acme Collection Agency. I'm calling about your account with Big Bank BankCard. You have an outstanding balance of $1,300, and we haven't received a payment from you in three months. You

[2] haven't responded to our letters, and I'd like to know what the problem is.

[3] JONES: (*long pause*) I've been having a hard time lately. I haven't been able to get the money together to pay you.

4 COLLECTOR: Have you been paying your other accounts?

JONES: My wife has been sick.

COLLECTOR: How long has your wife been sick? Is it serious?

JONES: No. She's been sick a couple of weeks, though.

5 COLLECTOR: We haven't received a payment from you in three months, Mr. Jones. Your account has been canceled, and we have already begun collection proceedings. If you don't send us a payment, we'll have to move you much higher up in the collection cycle.

JONES: I don't know what I can send you.

COLLECTOR: Could you send me half the balance, Mr. Jones?

JONES: Oh, no. Maybe I could send you $10 on Friday.

COLLECTOR: Mr. Jones, I'm asking for $650 and you are offering $10. You'll have to do better than that.

JONES: I don't know. I really haven't got it.

6 COLLECTOR: Could you send us $100? Could you find a place in your budget to come up with that, and then we can discuss a regular payment plan?

JONES: No, I don't have that much, either.

7 COLLECTOR: *(pause)* Mr. Jones, I'm willing to work with you on this. Other collectors would be coming on much harder than I am. But you have to work with me, too. What do you have?

JONES: I might be able to send you $25.

COLLECTOR: They won't take that. I'll need at least $50.

JONES: No, really. I don't even know where the $25 is coming from.

COLLECTOR: Well, I might be able to take that *this* week, but next week I'll need another $25, and then $25 a week for the next two weeks. That will give us that $100 we talked about, and then we can work out a better payment plan after that.

JONES: No, I can't promise that. I might be able to send you $15, $25 a month.

8 COLLECTOR: Then you'll be sending me $25 a month on this account, which you'll put in the mail to me on Friday, and which I'll receive Monday or Tuesday. Then I'll be receiving $25 a month from you until you get back on your feet, and then we can work out a better arrangement. I'm doing this because I want to

work with you on this, Mr. Jones, because — believe me — I don't know if they're going to accept it.

JONES: Well, uh . . .

COLLECTOR: I'll tell you what. I might be able to get this plan through, but you'll have to come in here and sign some papers. Can you do that?

JONES: No. I'm not anywhere near your office.

COLLECTOR: I'll put them in the mail, then, but you'll need to return them to me, signed, immediately.

JONES: Okay.

9 COLLECTOR: I'll be talking to you Tuesday, Mr. Jones.

Those nine points looked pretty innocent, didn't they? Well, look again. If you've ever had a hardworking collector on the line, you'll know what this is like. Afterward, you find yourself wondering, "Who are *they*, who won't accept my payments? Who mentioned a hundred dollars a month? What does he mean by moving me farther up in the collection process? Would other collectors really be harder than this guy? And why do I have to sign those papers? Is there anything wrong with them?"

Of course, no conversation proceeds directly along the lines given to collectors. Both they and the debtors they speak with are subject to subtle, complex, human factors. There's an "art" to good collecting, many agents told me. In the Spring 1981 issue of *The Credit World* magazine, a former president of the International Consumer Credit Association wrote of the "romance" of collections. "Romance, as applied to collections, is the feeling you get in your blood," he wrote, "when you locate or break a delinquent account; it never leaves you. It becomes a part of you, and you are proud of it."

At times, you may get the feeling that the collector on the phone bears some resemblance to a pushy salesman — in fact, the techniques he employs have a great deal in common with those used by people who make their living by getting you to comply with their wishes.

Robert Cialdini, a psychologist at Arizona State University, has made a study of high-pressure salesmen, fund-raisers, charity organizations, advertising agencies, and the like. His book on the subject, *Weapons of Influence: The Psychology of Compliance,* outlines the results of his research. I spoke with him about the similarities that collection agents have with high-pressure salesmen.

"The amazing thing about the majority of compliance professionals," he told me, "is that they don't feel any guilt about the way they operate. Within their mystique is the universal sense that what they are doing is right, in the long run, for America. They feel they are enlightening these other people."

If that sounds an awful lot like the "romance of collections," read on . . .

"One of the main ways people use to get you to comply is to create a sense of obligation, and then play upon it," Cialdini told me. "Some professionals arrange this kind of debt by giving out free samples."

The collector has a head start on the professionals, since the debtor has, in a sense, already received his "free sample." As we saw in the above conversation, there is also the sense of obligation created by many collection agents that they are doing you a great favor by making payment arrangements with you.

The effect that the collector attempts to achieve is pretty much the same as the salesman's: to alter your perception of the obligation you have, and to convince you that you really don't have any decision in the matter being discussed.

"The perception of control is very important in any transaction," Cialdini says. "Tied into that control is the self-esteem of the persons being manipulated. The less of a sense of self-esteem they have, the more liable they are to the powers of persuasion. A collector may try very hard to cause the debtors to view themselves in negative terms, and thus remove their sense of being in control."

What can a debtor do to defy this subversive thrust to compliance? According to Robert Cialdini, you have to stop thinking the way they are telling you to. "Change your cognitive set about the situation, and your rights in that situation. If you are being told you have an obligation to fulfill, remember that what you were given was not a gift."

In the case of the collection agent, then, it's important to remember that the money you owe was loaned to you as a business proposition — which you intend to fulfill, on your own terms.

FIGHTING BACK

Of course, most debtors could tell you about the romance and adventure of dodging collectors, too. Let's take a look at how you can turn the tables on collectors, and perhaps cause a few broken hearts among the romantics.

Most people don't know how to talk to collectors. And they don't realize that talking to collectors works. As an antidote to the nine points of collector's calls, here are the eight points of debtor's calls:

1. Identify yourself, your account number, and why you're calling.
2. Present your plan in a calm, rational manner.
3. Keep talking.
4. Negotiate. If they won't deal with you in a businesslike way, ask for a supervisor.
5. Don't let them change the subject in order to intimidate you. It's your dime — you call the tune.
6. Call their bluff if they threaten you. Remember that it's your *money* they want, not you.
7. Be prepared to "give in" a little when they show they're willing to talk seriously.
8. Money talks. When all is said and done, you can close any conversation with a promise of cold, hard cash. The big difference between being called by a collector and calling him is the debt-management program. It's a powerful tool for working seriously with any collector.

Mr. Jones, of course, would have been in a completely different position if he had worked out a repayment plan and then called the collector to propose it. Then the conversation wouldn't have followed *their* nine points, but *his* eight:

1 JONES: Hello, Mr. Shears, this is Mr. Jones calling about my Big Bank BankCard account. I've been notified by your letter

that you are authorized to collect this account, and I wish to propose a repayment plan to you.

COLLECTOR: Uh, let me get my file.

JONES: I can't hold too long. I'm in the middle of a busy day. Could you hurry?

COLLECTOR: *(after he finds his file, regains his composure)* Well, Mr. Jones, when are we going to start seeing some money from you? How do you expect us to believe you've got some kind of plan when you're six months behind, and you've been sending us little dribs and drabs . . .

[2] JONES: I've carefully gone over my entire financial situation, and all of my obligations, and have a complete debt-management program under way. You have, I know, no reason to believe me. But I think you have many reasons to give me a chance. I'll be sending you a check for $15 on Friday. Before you tell me that this isn't enough, I'd like to tell you how I came to this figure. I owe eight creditors close to $450 a month, due to excessive debt burdens. I've carefully gone over my budget, and I've trimmed everywhere humanly possible so that I can meet these obliga-

[3] tions. Every creditor has received the same fair treatment —you're not being shorted here. I'm proposing a plan I can stick to. You can set your calendar by my payments in the future, and if my situation improves before the debt is paid off, you will be in line, as will my other creditors, to receive an increase in payments.

COLLECTOR: That's all well and good, Mr. Jones, but $15 is really too small. I'm afraid they won't accept that.

JONES: Who, may I ask, are they?

COLLECTOR: My supervisors and the creditors.

[4] JONES: Well, since you aren't authorized to approve my payment plan, would you please connect me with someone who is?

COLLECTOR: I need $50 a month from you, at least.

JONES: I'm afraid not.

COLLECTOR: Then I'll have to sue you.

JONES: Are you authorized to do that? I'm still waiting to hear if you can accept my payment plan after we are finished negotiating it.

COLLECTOR: Who said anything about negotiating?

JONES: I don't want to argue with you, and I don't mean to sound disrespectful, but that *is* what we're doing right now.

5 COLLECTOR: We'll see about that. Are you willing to go to court about this, Mr. Jones? I want $50 a month to keep you out of court.

6 JONES: Is that your last word on the matter?

COLLECTOR: What do you expect me to say?

JONES: That you'll accept a little less.

COLLECTOR: I need $35 a month.

7 JONES: Let's be honest with each other. What do you really need to hold this account? I'm prepared to go a little higher.

COLLECTOR: Thirty.

JONES: Look, since we're leveling with each other now, I'll tell you that I have $25 budgeted here for you. I knew we'd have to negotiate a little, so I came in with $15. But $25 is really top dollar.

COLLECTOR: Thirty.

8 JONES: I'm sorry. I'm really telling you the truth here. I'll send you the $25 on Friday, and you'll probably receive it in Monday or Tuesday's mail. I'll call you on Wednesday to see if it arrived. Don't call me at my home or office, because it is extremely uncomfortable for me to be contacted there. I'll also send you a letter with the entire payment plan outlined for you.

WHEN YOU HIT A BRICK WALL

What if you get a collector who just won't negotiate?

Practically every collector in the business is flexible and will work with their accounts. They have to — that's how they stay in business. "There's a feel in a good collector," Bernard Sennet told me, "he knows, he has a gut feeling if the debtor is being sincere."

And what if you get a tough, harassing collector? Says Jerry Taylor, "Ask for the supervisor. The last thing the collector wants is for this account to go to his supervisor — the last thing the supervisor wants is to get on the phone. He's probably worked for five years to get a promotion so he can get off the phone."

Asking for the supervisor, of course, will get you a different voice on the line, but there is really no way of knowing if that person is, in actuality, the supervisor.

Just how flexible are collectors? It depends on who you're talking to, and when. At first, collectors always come on strong, and push for the entire balance. For the most part, this tactic is a gamble for them, and one collector admitted to me that it was hard for him to say how well this approach worked. "If the person on the other end is responsive and talking, we'll make a reasonable arrangement for payment," he told me. "But collectors all know that the person who is toughest gets paid fastest."

FINAL PAYMENTS

After you make a payment arrangement with a collector, you'll be asked to sign a promissory note outlining the terms of your agreement. (A sample is shown on page 154.) Again, read it very carefully.

When a payment is made, the collection agency deposits it, minus their commission, in a separate escrow account for the creditor.

There is no point in sending the money to the original creditor at this time. They've already listed your account as having gone into collection, and have paid some fee to the agency to take your account on. In addition, the amount of time it takes for the original creditor to credit your payment and notify the collector that it was received could leave you vulnerable to further collection activities.

Collectors have a pretty good idea of just how flexible debtors can be, too. "We know," says Bernard Sennet, "that the real frauds, the real deadbeats, aren't going to get on the phone with us. Ninety-five percent of all debtors have good intentions to pay back."

On the other hand, Sennet says, they know when they're getting stalled. "If a debtor gets on the telephone — and about 20 percent of them do this — and says, 'I'm not gonna pay,' we'll sue him right away. If someone breaks their agreement with us, we'll give them another chance, but if they're not playing fair, we'll take them to court."

RE:
ACCT No.:

This is in accordance with our conversation of today's date.
Kindly sign the original and return in the enclosed envelope, retaining the copy for your records.

Very truly yours,

Legal Collection Agency

It is agreed that I will pay the debt as shown below to the office of the Legal Collection Agency, as attorneys for the above noted creditor, at 15 S. 15th St., Their Town, U.S.A., as follows:

Payment of the sum of $_____ on _____ 19_____ and the balance of $_____ in equal weekly installments of $_____ on or before the _____ day of each and every successive month thereafter until the above sum is fully paid.

It is my understanding that pending the above payments, and in accordance with the above terms, no lawsuit to recover this indebtedness will be commenced.

After trying to collect your account for five months, if the collection agency has been unable to establish repayment with you, they'll turn your account either back to the creditor — who may give it to a secondary or tertiary collector — or to a lawyer. They will, of course, do this sooner if they feel they're getting nowhere with you.

There are problems with collectors, as both Taylor and Sennet agree. "My biggest problem," says Sennet, "is collectors on my staff who call and claim they're lawyers. I have to fire them right away. Sometimes my collectors get a little too tough on the accounts, but the accounts really abuse the collectors sometimes. These guys get the most vile abuse hurled at them all day. Especially if they are women, they get abuse. I tell them to hang up the phone."

Although letters are a main part of the collector's battery, they prefer to get you on the phone. For the most part, letters are a technique to get you on the phone and have very little to do with actual negotiating with collectors. But the letters offer a wide array of methods and madness. While the abusive, threatening letter was once one of the collection agency's main techniques, the FDCPA has drastically reduced instances of abuse, since letters offer their own evidence of wrongdoing, and phone calls do not. The next chapter will tell you what is legal and what is not in a collection letter.

Whatever arrangements you make with your collector, whatever promises they make to you — PUT IT IN WRITING. That's evidence you'll need if they decide to change the rules and put more pressure on you later, whether through lawyers or through court summonses.

The steps of the collection process are calculated to bring in money. That's why collectors have made a practice of them. Most collectors agree that it wouldn't be fair to rush people into court. The system, as Bernard Sennet says, is built around human factors.

"CAN THEY DO THIS TO ME?"

"Consumers are generally ignorant of their rights. People who are in debt, who owe money, or who even just need a loan, are in a very vulnerable position — something the collection people, and even the creditors, take advantage of. They're embarrassed, they feel guilty, and this keeps them from exercising their rights. All of this is reflected in the way creditors and collectors do business."

— A Washington, D.C., consumer advocate

In 1974, two *Chicago Tribune* reporters went to work for a number of Chicago collection agencies. The resulting series of articles shocked and amazed *Tribune* readers. For a week, details of collectors threatening violence, inducing fear, and creating emotional distress filled the paper. In one story, one of the reporters was told to call a man at his job less than 24 hours after his house was nearly destroyed by fire and his five-year-old son had been hospitalized for severe smoke inhalation.

"No matter what an S.O.B. you are to this guy, no matter how hard you hit him, you can't possibly make him feel any worse than he feels right now," the boss collector told the reporter. "We'll make a hardhearted collector out of you yet."

"We didn't find one agency that we looked at that wasn't engaging in the tactics we described in the series," the reporters commented. Among the practices they found were collection agencies that harassed people for bills which, in fact, the people didn't owe; adding exorbitant interest charges to amounts in collection; phoning people at their jobs until the victims were literally fired for creating a nuisance; and in one case hounding an elderly woman to the point where she was hospitalized — and then dropping the case when the collector found out that he had the wrong woman all along.

The collection industry has undergone a tremendous amount of reform since then, much of it because of the 1978 Fair Debt Collection Practices Act, which regulates third-party collectors (those hired by creditors to settle overdue accounts — in-house collection efforts and attorney-collectors are not regulated by the act). The act brought a certain amount of awareness of consumer rights to the collection industry and, in some cases, inspired a degree of industry self-regulation.

When I interviewed collectors for this book, I asked them if there were certain practices they avoided as a general rule, outside of their obligation to follow the FDCPA. I was told that collectors, for the most part, will not use threats of violence or other forms of extortion, will not embarrass people publicly, and are careful not to state directly or even imply that debtors are criminals. Collectors know from experience that it doesn't pay — as a rule — to lose their temper or get into an angry conversation with a debtor. In addition, collectors are warned not to misrepresent themselves as lawyers, particularly if they are in the employ of an attorney-collection agency.

The heightened awareness brought about by new legislation has had an effect in other areas of the credit industry, as well. Earlier in the book I discussed how the Equal Credit Opportunity Act got creditors to take a closer look at the assumptions they had about women as borrowers — resulting in the raising of single career women to one of the more creditworthy positions. The consumer credit laws have, by their sweep and comprehensive quality, changed enormously every aspect of the creditor–borrower relationship.

Despite these changes, consumers remain uneducated about their rights. Almost every creditor I interviewed for this book told me that consumers didn't know their rights and didn't know where they could go to defend their rights. A deputy assistant attorney general of New York State told me that his office receives about eight to ten calls a day about collections, and if consumers knew their rights and knew where to complain, they'd probably receive three or four times as many.

There is a great deal you can do to educate yourself about your rights as a debtor. The entire area of consumer credit law is vast, and I couldn't hope to cover it in one chapter. There are several good books on the subject, which you'll find listed in the bibliography.

What this chapter will do is explain those rights which directly affect you if you are in debt, the laws that will help you negotiate with creditors and collectors, and the laws which protect your rights to an accurate credit report and a fair assessment of your creditworthiness. Of particular importance in this chapter are questions about the rights of women as guaranteed by the Fair Credit Reporting and Equal Credit Opportunity laws. In addition, if you have received a summons or are afraid of your creditor's next step, this chapter will offer some help and will also arm you with some remedies of your own. Finally, I'll offer some pointers on how and when to find a lawyer.

In order to make it easier for you to pinpoint specific problems covered by these laws, I've divided each section into a general introduction and a question-and-answer format.

THE FAIR DEBT COLLECTION PRACTICES ACT

The Fair Debt Collection Practices Act, passed by Congress in 1977, covers a wide area of collection agency activities. It covers collection of any debt incurred for purposes of personal, family or household use. The act applies to any person in the business of collecting debts owed to others; any creditor who, collecting from his own debtors, uses a name other than his own; anyone who regularly collects or attempts to collect debts for another. *Not all debt collectors are subject to the act.* It does not apply to banks, other lenders, or businesses which collect their own accounts using their own name. The best thing to do to be sure of whether or not your collector is covered by the act is to call the local office of the Federal Trade Commission.

Collectors covered by the act may *not* contact you at an inconvenient or unusual time (the hours between 8 A.M. and 9 P.M. are considered to be convenient); at an inconvenient place; at your place of employment if it is known that the employer prohibits such contact; if an attorney is known to represent you (in which case the attorney would be contacted).

The law prohibits harassing, oppressing, or abusive conduct in connection with the collection of a debt. This includes, but is not limited to, the use of threat of violence or harm to the person, his reputation, or his property; use of obscene language; publicizing the debt; annoying or repetitive phone calls; anonymous phone calls; false, deceptive, or misleading representations as to the collector's identity; false representations of the status of the debt and the consequences of nonpayment; failure to adequately disclose the reason for contacting the consumer; collecting an additional fee not authorized by law or the terms of the debt agreement; accepting a check postdated by more than five days except under specified written conditions; charging the debtor with collect calls or telegram fees; communicating by post card.

In addition to these restrictions, there is one very important provision to the act which tends to trip up most unscrupulous collectors. Within five days after contacting you about paying your debt, the collector must send you a written notice telling you the amount of the debt, the name of the creditor, that the debt will be assumed valid unless disputed within 30 days, that if disputed the collector will verify it and send a copy of the verification or of a judgment against you.

Armed with a thorough knowledge of your rights as a debtor, you have the ability to write to your collector and complain. First, you can stop a collector from calling you at work or anywhere else by telling him that the place is inconvenient for you. You may wish to signify a certain place or time as being convenient, or you can be difficult and tell him that you don't wish to be contacted over the phone at all. In that case, the only further phone contact that can be made is to explain to you the possible consequences of a failure of communication.

If you present the collector with a plan of repayments, and then tell him not to contact you except in writing, most collectors will cooperate. If they don't, you have firm grounds for a strong consumer complaint against them, and you should contact the Federal Trade Commission in your area, and your local office of consumer protection.

In the case of collectors, complaining can actually do some good. The FTC and local consumer protection offices are particularly sensitive to collection complaints, and keep a very up-to-date file of who is guilty of what, and who has been complained about. Collection agencies with a number of violations and complaints can find it hard to drum up business, since many major creditors want nothing to do with them.

Another very efficient way of complaining about harassment is through the phone company. Since Ma Bell appreciates the fact that we all have some of her instruments in our homes, she feels it is her obligation to make sure that we don't have any particularly bad feelings attached to her instruments. Collectors who abuse the phone make us feel less than benign about Ma Bell, and she has instituted an annoyance complaint bureau in most of her business offices to handle these problems. Although Bell has no legal authority, they can and have disconnected the service of some collectors who have been the object of complaints, and they pass your complaint on to the proper local authorities. At the least, they will contact your collector to verify the complaint, putting him on notice that you aren't the type to take this lying down.

Q: If I don't dispute the debt, does that mean I'm admitting that it is valid?
A: Even if you don't dispute the validity of the debt in the initial 30-day period, this still doesn't mean that you have admitted any legal liability.

Q: If I feel I don't owe the money, can they still try to collect from me?
A: The collector may not contact you if you send a letter (within 30 days after you are first contacted) saying you dispute the debt itself or the amount claimed. A sample of this letter is shown here.

However, once the collector sends you proof of the debt, such as a copy of the bill, he can begin collection activities. (For further information on this, see questions in the section of the Fair Credit Billing Act.)

Q: What, by law, is harassment?
A: Harassment, by definition, means "to annoy continually."

Using obscene language, threatening violence, or calling the debtor several times in one day is generally considered as harassment, as is advertising a debt or notifying others that the debtor owes money.

While some things a collector may do might seem harassing to you — such as calling you twice a week about a debt — the law states explicitly that a collector has a right to do that. But there are many things about which the law is not so explicit, and consumer affairs offices and consumer advocates will usually side with the debtor in deciding whether or not harassment is actually taking place. (*One* phone call to you, if it is severe enough, can constitute harassment.) If the case goes to court, there is a precedent for deciding whether or not harassment took place by placing it "in the eyes of the beholder" — the beholder being, of course, the average, reasonable debtor.

SAMPLE LETTER FOR REQUESTING VERIFICATION FROM A COLLECTOR OF A DISPUTED DEBT

> Your Address
> Town, State, Zip
> Date

Name and Address
of Collection Agency

Dear Sir/Madam,

I recently received a notice from you in which you state I owe [amount] to [name of creditor].

I dispute the validity of this debt because [the debt was not incurred; the goods were not received; the goods were damaged; the amount claimed is incorrect, etc.].

Pursuant to Section 809(b) of the Federal Fair Debt Collection Practices Act, I request that you provide me with verification of this debt. Until this verification is provided to me, you are prohibited from taking any further actions to collect the debt.

Your compliance with this federal law is expected.

> Very truly yours,
>
> Your Name

Q: Can a collector come to my house?

A: A collector can visit you personally, provided he doesn't disturb the peace. Personal visits which carry with them the threat of violence are strictly prohibited.

Q: Can I tell them to stop contacting me?

A: By law, yes. If you write the collection agency, telling them to cease further communications with you, they must do so, except to advise you that a lawsuit or other legal remedy will be initiated. You should send a certified letter when asserting this right. (A sample of this letter is shown here.)

Obviously, some collectors are in the business of regularly taking debtors to court and will often accelerate the process of getting a judgment once a consumer has closed the door to them. Thus, unless you're prepared to have your next contact be in court, common sense dictates some caution here. (This only applies to those states in which collection agencies are authorized to sue. Your local state attorney general's office can tell you if your state is one of these.)

SAMPLE LETTER DEMANDING THAT A COLLECTION AGENCY CEASE ALL COMMUNICATIONS

> Your Address
> Town, State, Zip
> Date

Name and Address
of Collection Agency

Dear Sir/Madam,

Your company has been attempting to collect a debt in the amount of [amount] which you state I owe to [name of creditor].

As I have advised your employees on the numerous telephone calls they have made to collect this money, I do not owe this debt.

Therefore, pursuant to Section 805(c) of the Federal Fair Debt Collection Practices Act, I direct you to cease all further communications with me of any kind. Your failure to comply with this federal law will result in my report to the appropriate government agencies.

> Very truly yours,
>
> Your Name

Q: The other day, I told the collector on the phone that I felt he had violated my rights according to the federal law. He said that our state law gave him the right to do what he was doing. Under which law am I covered?

A: *Everyone* is covered by the federal law. Most states have consumer credit laws as well — some of them more protective of consumers than the federal law, and under which you have additional rights; some less protective, under which you still have your federal rights, but the collector may be given some other rights which do not conflict with federal law.

Also, most municipalities and counties have consumer laws. If you're really confused, call your local department of consumer affairs or the state attorney general's office.

Q: The collector says I have to pay my bill in 10 days. Do I have to?

A: According to James Fishman of the New York State Attorney General's Office, "There's nothing in the law that says you have to pay by the date set by a collection agency. That's just what they want you to believe." This is not only true in New York, but all over the country. However, this does not prohibit them from starting legal action at the end of a specified period, if that's what they claim they will do.

Q: How is a collector authorized to accept my payment?

A: The collector must post your payment in the account of the creditor promptly. He cannot charge interest on the debt or collection fees not already authorized by your credit agreement.

Q: The collector told me to give him a series of postdated checks to pay my debt. Is this legal?

A: It is not illegal to accept a postdated check or checks for payment of a debt, as long as the collector has no intentions of cashing them before the date on the check and then filing criminal charges against you. In addition, you must be informed in writing three days before one of your postdated checks is to be cashed.

Q: I have the feeling that the collector I'm dealing with is a liar. What are the most common deceptions they use?

A: The FDCPA includes a number of strict prohibitions against deceptive and misleading practices.

One favorite trick of collectors, especially in small agencies, is to use several pseudonyms. It is not illegal for a collector to use one pseudonym (and only one), but that must be the name by which he does business regularly. (One New York City consumer advocate told me how he had once called a small collection agency about a complaint he had received. The agency had only two employees, but in the course of working through their various pseudonyms he spoke to at least six "people.")

Another practice is for a collector to state falsely that he is an attorney, or that he is connected with any government body. This is illegal. It's also against the law for them to state falsely or lead you to believe that a written communication originated from, or was approved by, any court or official agency. The collector also cannot falsely state the character, amount, or legal status of a debt.

A collector cannot tell you that he will take you to court for nonpayment, unless a collector is in the regular practice of doing so. He also cannot falsely state that the result of nonpayment will be arrest, imprisonment, seizure of property, or garnishment, unless such action is actually called for under the law, and unless the collector actually intends to take that action.

A collector cannot state that you have committed a crime by not paying your debt.

He also can't tell you that he works for a credit bureau and will "ruin your credit rating" by reporting you directly to creditors when, in fact, he does not work for such a credit bureau/collection agency. He can, however, report nonpayment to a credit-reporting agency, and they may or may not use this information. (See "Your Credit Report" for more on this.)

Q: I've been sent a form that *looks* legal, but I don't think it is. What can I do? (Sample is shown on pages 166–167.)
A: The use of phony legal documents has dropped off considerably since its heyday in the late 1960s. One reason for this is that it's very easy to prove that sending these documents is the usual practice of a collection agency, thus making prosecution of the offense that much easier.

One of the ironies of the new consumer legislation is that some of the actual summonses for court appearances look less legal than the legal-appearing papers issued by collection agencies.

The first thing you should do when you receive what you believe to be a summons is to call the court named on the paper. There isn't any court? Then you've got a phony. Chances are, if the court and the index number of your case are listed, the summons is real. (For information on what happens when you answer a summons, see "Emergency Situations," and the section in this chapter on "Creditor's Remedies.")

If the document you've been sent isn't legal, go to your local consumer affairs office, or to the state attorney general's office. A criminal complaint against the collector can be filed if the offense is a major one.

Q: Recently, a collector told me that his agency regularly reports "deadbeats" to other creditors. Is this legal?

A: The FDCPA prohibits a debt collector from disclosing your debt to other creditors or collection agencies. If a collector were to report your bad debts to other creditors, this would in essence make him a consumer reporting agency. As we have seen, only licensed consumer reporting agencies can issue reports on your credit activities to creditors.

Q: If one of my creditors contacts another one of my creditors, what kind of information can they exchange?

A: When one creditor *does* contact another for information about common accounts, by law their information has to confine itself to whether or not a person has an account with the creditor. Unfortunately, this is very often not the case, but it is hard to prove in court that two creditors have discussed your delinquencies with one another.

Q: What about the credit-reporting agencies that also operate debt collection offices?

A: There is no law which states that these reporting agencies (such as CBI, as I discussed in "Your Credit Report") can't place your activities with their collection agents in their credit files, and subsequently report them to creditors.

Q: Can he tell my employer about my debts?

A: Not unless you give the collection agency permission to — something they can be very tricky about. Be careful what you say to collectors, or about signing any documents for them. Very often

FINAL NOTICE BEFORE SUIT

In the matter of the claim of $\Big\{$

....
vs.

........................÷.........

TO THE ABOVE NAMED DEBTOR:

Please take notice that ....
has a valid claim against you for services rendered, amounting to ......
.... Dollars, an affidavit supporting said
account being herein below annexed.

The said debt is now overdue, and, although demand for payment has
been repeatedly made, nothing has been received on account of same,
except .... Dollars.

That unless remittance is made to the undersigned at ....,
State of ...., on or before the .... day of
..................., 19......., steps will be necessary to enforce
payment of this claim together with interest and costs of said suit.

Dated at ...., State of ...., this ....day of
..................., 19........

AFFIDAVIT OF ACCOUNT

STATE OF ....$\Big\}$
County of ....

On this .... day of ...., 19......., before me, a Notary
Public, within and for said County of ...., personally
appeared ....
who, being by me duly sworn on his oath, says that the above account is
correct and true, to the best of his knowledge and belief.

....

Subscribed and sworn to before me, this ....
day of ...., 19........

My commission expires:

....

....

FNS-1   Notary Public

No.

FINAL NOTICE BEFORE SUIT

_____ CREDITOR

VS.

_____ DEBTOR

FINAL NOTICE TO DEBTOR

Amount ....$ _____

Interest ....$ _____

Total ....$ _____

they will try to get permission from you to contact your employer, and they'll use this as leverage.

One trick that collectors use is to send you a dunning letter that indicates a copy has been sent to your employer. It's mainly ^   :re tactic, since it is illegal to contact your employer in the firs; place.

Q: Can a collector discuss my debt with others?
A: If the other person is an attorney retained by you to handle your debt problems, or a credit-reporting agency, yes. Otherwise, no.

The FDCPA prohibits any communication, without your prior consent, to others, including your family, employer, or friends.

Q: When can a collector contact a third party about my debt?
A: A collector can call a third party only to obtain "location information" about you — your residence, phone number, and your place of employment. In obtaining this information, the collector must identify himself but may not identify his employer unless requested. He may not discuss the debt, speak with the third party more than once, or speak with anyone *but* your attorney once he knows you have one.

Q: If a collector has several debts of mine to collect, can I control what he does with the checks I give him?
A: Yes. If you owe several debts, any payment you make must be applied as you choose. And a debt collector cannot apply a payment to any debt you feel you do not owe.

Q: What can I do if the collector has broken the law?
A: You have the right to sue a debt collector in state or federal court within one year from the date the law was violated. You may recover money for the damage you suffered, but you are still liable for your debt. Court costs and attorney fees can also be recovered.

A group of people can sue a debt collector and recover money for damages up to $500,000, in a class action suit. Consumer affairs offices, in their "protective" capacity, can assist groups of private citizens in preparing class action suits, and very often do. These class action suits against collectors are appearing through consumer affairs all over the country, and are a good reason to complain when you feel the law has been broken, since your evidence may be just what they need to act upon after watching an offending collector.

For further information about exercising your rights, see the section in this chapter called "Debtor's Remedies."

THE FAIR CREDIT BILLING ACT

The Fair Credit Billing Act establishes procedures for correcting billing mistakes, for withholding payments on defective goods and services, and for guaranteeing that your payments are promptly credited. Knowing the rights guaranteed you by the FCBA can help you keep a creditor from listing you as a debtor while you are in the midst of a billing dispute.

The great value of the FCBA is that it allows your relationship with your creditor to remain stable during billing disputes. If you're in debt, the provisions of the FCBA are sometimes effective "stopgaps" to keep a creditor at bay.

Among the high costs of credit levied on consumers every year are millions of dollars in billing errors. Most people catch these, and most know how to complain and receive satisfaction in having the bill corrected. But, for those who don't, here are the steps.

You have a billing error if:

1. Your bill lists a charge for something you didn't buy.
2. Your bill lists a wrong price for something you bought.
3. The goods or services listed on the bill were not accepted by you, or by a person that you designated to receive them.
4. Your bill lists a charge and you can't figure out what it refers to or what it means. In a situation like this, you can also ask the company to send you whatever "documentary evidence" it has concerning the charges, such as a copy of the charge slip.
5. The goods or services were not delivered to you according to your agreement with the company. For example:
   — delivery was made to the wrong address;
   — delivery was made late;
   — the wrong quantity was delivered;
   — the goods or services delivered were different from those described in your agreement with the company.
6. You made a payment or returned goods and your account was not properly credited.
7. A mistake in arithmetic was made in figuring out your bill.

8. Your billing statement was not mailed or delivered to your current address (as long as you informed the company of any new address at least 10 days before the closing date of the billing cycle for which the bill was incorrectly mailed or delivered).

If you think that you have a billing error, here is how you go about having it corrected:

1. You have 60 days from the date you receive the statement from the creditor to write to that company telling it you think there is a mistake on your bill, or that you have a dispute. A telephone call will not protect your rights under this law. If you do call, send a letter to the company. (A model letter is shown here.) The address of the company will be found either on the billing statement or on the notice you received when you opened the account, and which you are required to be sent twice a year.

SAMPLE LETTER INFORMING CREDITOR OF A BILLING ERROR

> Your Address
> Town, State, Zip
> Date

Address Found on Statement or Notice

Dear Billing Department,

I am writing to inform you that the billing statement which you sent me dated August 19, 1981, contains a billing error in the amount of $12.54. The suit which I bought had a total cost of $100.00, but on my bill the cost is listed as $112.54. I would appreciate it if you would correct this mistake.

My account number with your company is 00-000-0000-0.

> Sincerely,
>
> Your Name

2. Be sure to make a copy of your letter so you have a record of what you wrote. If your billing dispute involves a large sum of money, you should send your letter by certified mail, "return receipt requested." You will be sure then that the company has received your letter and you will have a record of its delivery.

3. Include a copy of the bill, and circle the error on it.
4. Within 30 days after receiving your letter, the company must send you an acknowledgment that it has received your letter. It may also include its decision concerning the possible error at this time. The company may also let you know of its decision on a later billing statement if it clearly identifies the amount it has credited to your account in response to your letter.
5. If the company has not included its decision along with its acknowledgment of your letter, it has two billing periods (or a maximum of 90 days) after it receives your letter to tell you of its decision. The company is required either: (a) to correct your billing statement; or (b) to conduct an investigation and send you a written notice giving you the reason why it believes there has been no billing error.

The Fair Credit Billing Act insures the consumer certain rights while this whole process is going on. The act states that:

1. You *don't* have to pay the amount in dispute.
2. You don't have to pay any finance charges based on the amount of money in dispute. The company can, though, use the disputed charge in deciding whether or not you have reached your credit limit. In other words, if you have $700 in legitimate charges, a $150 disputed charge, and your credit limit is $800, the creditor can decide that you are over your limit and refuse you further credit.
3. The company may not close your account because you refuse to pay the amount in dispute.
4. The company may not threaten to harm your credit rating or credit standing because you fail to pay the amount in dispute.
5. If the company doesn't agree that there has been an error and sends you its reasons why it believes there has been no mistake, you have at least 10 days to pay the amount before the company can report your account delinquent to anyone, such as a credit bureau. Sometimes your credit agreement gives you a longer period of time to pay. If you normally pay your bill on an account within 30 days of receipt, then you have 30 days to pay a formerly disputed amount.
6. If a creditor fails to reply to your letter within the time periods above, or violates any of the other rights you have, he forfeits the amount of money in dispute, together with any finance charges

computed on that amount, to a maximum of $50. This happens whether or not there was an actual billing error.

Q: What if I dispute the charge, and they respond and say that there is no mistake, or don't respond at all, but I still feel that I don't owe them the money?
A: You should write a second letter. Although the company is allowed to try to collect the amount you disputed, you gain several important advantages when you write a second letter:

1. The company can't report you to a credit bureau unless it also tells them that you believe you don't owe the money.

2. The company must report to you the names and addresses of everyone who receives a report of your delinquency.

3. If the company later clears up your dispute, it must tell everyone to whom the disputed delinquency was reported that the dispute has been settled.

As above, if the company doesn't follow through on these rights, it forfeits the money — up to $50.

Q: What if the goods I purchased with a credit card were defective?
A: The FBCA provides that you may withhold payment on any damaged or shoddy goods or poor quality services purchased with a credit card as long as you have made a real attempt to solve the problem with the merchant.

This right must be limited if the card was a bank or charge card, or any card *not* issued by the store where you made your purchase. In that case, the sale must have been for more than $50 and must have taken place within your home state or within 100 miles of your residence.

In the case of defective merchandise or services, a legal action may result to determine the validity of your claim.

Q: If I have a bank credit card, is the bank allowed to use money in my bank account to cover the amounts I owe?
A: Yes, under certain circumstances. It can do this if:
— it first obtains a court order permitting it to do so; or
— you gave the bank permission to make such deductions,

which might have been included in your credit agreement. If this is the case, you have 16 days to dispute this transfer of funds.

Q: What if I've made a major credit purchase, using my home for security, and then change my mind? Am I without hope?

A: The FCBA gives you 3 business days to think about any transaction involving your home as security. The creditor must give you a written notice of your right to cancel, and if you decide to cancel, you must notify the creditor in writing within the 3-day period. If you have made a credit arrangement for a service such as home repairs, no contractor may start work on your home, and no lender may pay you or the contractor, until the 3 days are up. If you want work started immediately for health or safety reasons, you may give up your right to cancel by providing a written explanation of the circumstances.

THE FAIR CREDIT REPORTING ACT

Under the Fair Credit Reporting Act, all consumers have the right to know what is in their credit files. (For a complete listing of the information in your file, see "Your Credit Report," page 92.) The act also provides for specific procedures to be followed so that the consumer can correct errors in the file, and holds credit-reporting agencies responsible for the information in their files.

With the exception of bankruptcies, credit bureaus can only report unfavorable information which is no older than 7 years. Unfavorable information includes items such as past lawsuits, judgments, tax liens which you have had to satisfy, unpaid accounts, arrest records, indictments and convictions of crime. Bankruptcies which occurred up to 10 years ago may be reported by the credit bureau.

However, these time limits do not apply if the credit report is to be used in connection with a credit transaction involving $50,000 or more; life insurance with a face amount of $50,000 or more; or employment at an annual salary of $20,000 or more.

Q: How can billing mistakes compound themselves in my credit history?

A: After you've sent a second letter of dispute to a creditor (see the section in this chapter on FCBA) the creditor can report you as delinquent on your account and begin collection proceedings. If this is done, the creditor must also report that you challenge the bill, and you must be provided in writing with the name and address of each person to whom your credit information has been given. When the matter has been settled, the creditor must report the outcome to each person who received information about you.

So what's the problem? Computers. All of these letters and explanations don't fit neatly into their program. So beware — and get a copy of your credit report after any series of billing disputes.

Q: I've been refused credit for reasons other than what was in my credit report. What does the creditor have to tell me about my rejection?

A: If you were refused credit on the basis of information obtained from a person other than a credit bureau, you have 60 days to write requesting the reasons for credit denial. The creditor must disclose the nature of the information to you within a reasonable period of time. It is illegal, under the Equal Credit Opportunity Act, for the creditor to consider information pertaining to your sex, age or race. (A sample letter requesting information is shown here.)

SAMPLE LETTER FOR REQUESTING CREDIT INFORMATION OTHER
THAN OBTAINED FROM A CREDIT BUREAU

> Your Address
> Town, State, Zip
> Date

Creditor's Name
and Address

Dear Sir/Madam,
    On [date] I was refused credit by your company based on information received from a source other than a credit bureau. A copy of the letter is included. I would like to learn the nature of the information provided to you in this matter, and would appreciate it if you would provide this information in writing.

> Sincerely,
>
> Your Name

Q: Although I haven't actually been refused credit, I am going to have to pay a higher interest rate because of information on my credit report. Do I have the same rights to find out what information they used?

A: Absolutely. You must be informed of the name and address of the credit bureau which made the report or, if the information was obtained elsewhere, the creditor must give you a reason why you have to pay more money. However, he only has to give you the reasons if you write to him and ask for them within 60 days after you learn of his unfavorable action.

Q: Can an employer see my credit report? If he asks for permission to do so, what should I do?

A: Employers *can* ask for a copy of your credit report, and often do when your job entails the handling of money. In order for your employer to receive a copy of your report, you will be asked to sign a paper permitting the reporting agency to release your file to your employer. Sometimes this release is part of your employee application, and depending on how the release is worded, your employer may have the right to periodically check your report.

Whether or not you should give permission to your employer to see your credit report is a difficult decision. If your credit report has no negative information on it your only reservations may be ethical ones. If, though, you have negative information on the report, it might be best to ask your employer what the reasoning is behind the request. Wanting to protect your privacy shouldn't be held against you. If your employer still insists, be honest. Say that you reluctantly give your permission, but want to state from the outset that there is some negative information on the report, which you have since settled, or are in the process of settling. There's little else you can do here, and much of it depends on the fairness of your employer. Honesty seems to be the best policy here.

Q: What if I am denied employment because of information contained in the credit report?

A: Again, you must be supplied with the name and address of the credit bureau that made the report, and you have the same rights to learn the nature and substance of the report.

WOMEN AND CREDIT

The Fair Credit Reporting Act and the Equal Credit Opportunity Act both attempt to combat credit discrimination against women. The questions and answers in this section cover the laws and regulations of both of these acts, which overlap somewhat.

Women who are divorced or widowed might not have separate credit histories because all past credit accounts were listed in their husbands' names. But they can benefit from this record. Under the ECOA, creditors must consider the credit history of any account women have held jointly with their husbands. Creditors must also look at the record of any account held only in the husband's name if a woman can show it also reflects her own creditworthiness. If the record is unfavorable — if an ex-husband was a bad credit risk — she can try to show that the record does not reflect her own reputation.

Also under the ECOA, reports to credit bureaus must now be made in the names of both husband and wife if both use an account or are responsible for repaying the debt. Also remember that a wife may open her own account, and thus be sure of beginning her own credit history.

If you are denied credit and feel that you have been discriminated against, the first step to take is to contact the creditor and talk the matter over.

Keep accurate records of all contacts you make. If you still aren't satisfied, you can always go to another creditor. There are many creditors who are fair in the equal granting of credit. If the loan you want isn't, in your mind, worth the trouble of an ongoing battle with an unfair creditor, you shouldn't feel guilty about moving along. Taking your business away, and asking your friends to do the same, can be protest enough. If you are convinced that illegal discrimination is involved, talk to the Federal Trade Commission or the consumer affairs office in your area.

To state your rights simply and clearly, these are the most important rules regarding women and credit, according to the Federal Reserve:

WOMEN AND CREDIT: YOUR RIGHTS AT A GLANCE

1. You can't be refused credit just because you are a woman.
2. You can't be refused credit just because of your marital status: single, married, separated, widowed, or divorced.
3. You can't be refused credit because a creditor decides you're of child-bearing age and, as a consequence, won't count your income.
4. You can't be refused credit because a creditor won't count income you receive regularly from alimony or child support.
5. You can have credit in your own name if you're creditworthy.
6. When you apply for your own credit and rely on your own income, information about your spouse or his co-signature can be required only under certain circumstances.
7. You can keep your own accounts and your own credit history if your marital status changes.
8. You can build your own credit record because new accounts must be carried in the names of both husband and wife if both use the account or are liable on it.
9. If you are denied credit, you can find out why.

Q: Can my credit accounts be closed just because I've changed my marital status?

A: No. A creditor cannot close your account or change its terms unless you demonstrate an inability or unwillingness to pay. However, the creditor can require you to submit a new application, if the original charge account was based on your former husband's income.

Q: When can a creditor ask for information about my spouse or former spouse?

A: When you apply for credit, the creditor can only ask for information about your spouse or former spouse when:

— that spouse will be permitted to use the account;
— that spouse will be contractually liable on the account;

— you are relying on your spouse's income as a basis for repayment of the credit for which you are asking; or

— you live in a community property state — such as California, where everything a husband and wife have is divided 50/50 among them — or you are relying on property located in a community property state as a basis for repayment of the credit for which you are asking.

— you are relying on alimony, child support, or separate-maintenance payments from a spouse or former spouse as a basis for repayment of the credit for which you are asking.

Q: Does a creditor have to accept child support or alimony payments as regular income?
A: Yes, as long as these payments are made regularly.

Q: Can I be asked about my marital status when I apply for credit in my own name, on an unsecured basis?
A: No. When you apply for an individual, unsecured credit account the creditor may not ask about your marital status unless you live in a community property state or rely on property located in a community property state for repayment of the credit you request.

Q: When *can* a creditor ask about my spouse or former spouse, or about my marital status?
A: Whenever you apply for a credit account that is not an individual, unsecured account. For example, if you apply for a joint account, or a secured account. Also, you may be asked about your marital status when you apply for a home mortgage — but you are not required to supply information about your marital status in this case.

Q: If I qualify on an individual basis under the creditor's standards for creditworthiness for the amount and the terms of credit I ask for, may a creditor require my spouse to sign any agreements?
A: No, unless your spouse has, or will have, an interest in the property you are offering as security, or if you live in a community property state. In those cases, the creditor has a right to ask your spouse to sign agreements making his interest in the property available for payment of the loan.

Q: Can the creditor require my spouse to co-sign a credit agreement or act as a guarantor?

A: No. The creditor may ask you to find someone to be personally liable on your account, such as when he asks for a co-signer, but he can't require that this person be your spouse.

THE EQUAL CREDIT OPPORTUNITY ACT

The ECOA ensures that you will be considered for credit only on the basis of your ability to repay. It prohibits certain forms of discrimination, and provides the consumer with ways of getting a fair consideration of his or her credit application.

The ECOA explicitly prohibits creditors from denying you credit because of your race, religion, national origin, sex, marital status, age (as long as you have the legal capacity to enter into a contract), because you receive all or part of your income from a public assistance program, or because you have exercised in good faith any right under the consumer protection acts.

A creditor can ask you about your race, color, and national origin *only* when you apply for a home mortgage and the credit is secured by a lien on the property. In such a case, the creditor must request information about your race and national origin (it's for census statistics), but you do not have to supply the information. Failure to supply it will not affect your credit application, since the request is made only to provide evidence that the creditor is complying with equal credit laws.

A creditor may ask you about your permanent residence, your immigration status, any income you have from part-time employment or alimony, and if you receive money from a public assistance program — although participation in such a program cannot be a reason for denying you credit.

The ECOA also contains strict provisions concerning how a creditor must go about turning you down for credit. When a creditor turns you down, they must provide you with a written notice that contains:

1. a statement of the action he has taken in connection with your application;

2. a statement of the provisions of the ECOA (similar to the requirements stated above);
3. the name and address of the federal agency that administers compliance concerning the creditor giving you notification; and
4. a statement of the specific reasons for turning you down; or a notice that he must respond to you within 30 days after he receives such a request. This notice must contain the name, address, and phone number from which you can obtain the statement of reasons.

Q: Does a creditor have to give me a written notification of having been turned down, or can he tell me orally?
A: If the creditor has received 150 or less credit applications in the last year, he is allowed to notify all applicants orally.

Q: When is a creditor permitted to require me to reapply for a credit account?
A: The creditor may require you to reapply if you were originally granted credit based on the income earned by your spouse, and your income — by itself — at the time you originally applied for credit would not be enough to obtain the amount of credit currently extended to you.

A creditor cannot require you to reapply for an account, change the terms of the account, or close your account on the basis of:
— your reaching a certain age;
— retiring; or
— changing your name or marital status.

Q: When is someone too old to get credit?
A: Never. As long as there is evidence that you are willing and able to pay your bills, age cannot be used as a reason for denying you credit.

If a creditor relies on a credit scoring system to filter his applications, the number of age points given to a person 62 or older must be at least as many points as any person under 62 would receive. The law permits a creditor to consider information related to age that has a direct bearing on a person's ability and willingness to repay a debt, such as loss of income, rising expenses, etc., but age itself is not a legitimate criteria.

CREDITOR'S REMEDIES

The average debtor is largely unaware of his rights but is often all too familiar with what his creditors might do next: take him to court, press for a judgment, or begin the process of repossession.

Collectors and creditors often threaten legal action when they do not usually take such action, or when they're not authorized to do so. (In some states, this is illegal, but not under the FDCPA.) It's important, then, to know what they can do, and when, so that you can maintain a realistic picture of how you are able to handle your debts.

This section can be used in conjunction with the chapter that describes emergency situations and how to deal with them.

The basic creditor's remedies are garnishment, also known as income execution; wage assignment; repossession; and writ of execution.

Garnishment is the seizure of part of your paycheck or other income to be used to pay a money judgment for which you have been found liable. Garnishment is available to a creditor only *after* a court judgment. An employer cannot withhold anything from your wages until a court action is completed against you.

Federal employees (except for postal workers) are exempt from garnishment, as are working people receiving supplemental welfare. You can't have your paycheck reduced to less than the minimum wage for garnishment payments, and there can be only one garnishment against you at any one time — other creditors must wait in line to settle their debts, and often do so since a judgment can be carried out against you any time within 10 years, and is easily renewable for another 10 years.

Once a judgment is filed against you, you can enter into voluntary garnishment, therefore stopping the sheriff from notifying your employer, by paying a certain amount of your income per pay period, as determined by state law.

The difference between a wage assignment and a garnishment is that a wage assignment is voluntary. It is offered to you by the creditor, before the creditor seeks a judgment. In a wage assignment, you assign a portion of every paycheck to your creditor toward repayment of a debt. Finance companies use the method as a standard procedure.

There are two major disadvantages to wage assignment. First, your employer learns of your debt problems and, while your employer may not have moral objections to your debt, he may not be pleased by the extra paperwork it causes. Second, a wage assignment takes away your right to due process in court. (In some states, debtors have the right to go to court and *vacate*, or wipe out, a wage assignment if the creditor has not followed the procedures for obtaining it to the letter of the law.)

A writ of execution takes place after a money judgment has been awarded against you in court. If you are unable or will not pay what has been specified in the judgment, the court may grant an order directing the seizure of your personal property to satisfy the judgment. Exactly what will be seized is specified by the creditor in the request to the court for an execution.

State and federal laws protect your rights to retain some items of an essential or purely personal nature. Unless, of course, it is the purchase price of these items that is subject to the judgment. The state attorney general's office can tell you which items are covered by personal exemptions.

When you borrow money, often the loan or credit agreement will state that the creditor, if you default, can take back the goods purchased or any goods pledged as collateral. This is called repossession.

The main difference between a repossession and a writ of execution is that, when a secured loan is made, the collateral is agreed upon and this is what will be repossessed if you default. In an execution after levy, any of a number of items of worth can be taken from you, provided they are not protected by law.

Repossessions are governed under the Universal Commercial Code, which is applicable in most states. (It is not in Louisiana, for example.) The code states the following:

- A creditor may take possession of collateral on the default of the debtor, "if this can be done without a breach of the peace."
- In cases in which a debtor has paid 60 percent of the cash price of a

purchase or of a loan for goods, the creditor must dispose of the collateral and return to the consumer any amount in excess of the debt and any reasonable expenses incurred by the creditor in the collection.

If you owned a boat, for example, which you had paid for with a loan that was secured by the boat, and had paid 60 percent or more of the loan when the boat was repossessed, the creditor would have to sell the boat, and give you any "profit" he made from the sale — minus the "reasonable expenses" and what was owing at the time of the repossession.

• The debtor has the right, up to the time the creditor has disposed of the property seized, to redeem the collateral by payment of the remaining debt plus expenses.
• The creditor must notify the debtor before disposing of the collateral.

Unfortunately, the debtor has very few rights that would guarantee that the repossessed property was sold at a reasonable price. Most autos that have been repossessed, for example, are sold at public auction, where the bids can be fairly low. If the money received in the resale does not equal the amount owed by the debtor, the creditor can go back to court for an execution after levy — basically a garnishment to recover the deficit of the debt.

A debtor can fight what he or she feels is an unreasonable sale of repossessed property, but only by going to court and proving that the price received for the goods was "commercially unreasonable," and that the method of resale was unconscionable on the part of the creditor or repossessor. Short of proving that your creditor sold your four-month-old car to his brother for $25, and is garnishing you for the difference, it is hard to prove either charge.

If the creditor fails to comply with these rules, the consumer can seek an injunction against him or receive punitive damages if the collateral has already been disposed of. (For more information about this, see the section in this chapter on "Debtor's Remedies.")

The creditor's timetables for these actions are explained in "Your Creditors" and "Collection Agencies."

YOU'VE BEEN SUMMONSED

Most debtors, on receiving a summons to appear in court for a judgment hearing, feel that the worst has happened to them. Getting to this point with their creditor is usually the result of a series of misunderstandings and failures of communication, complicated by ignorance and fear. By this time, the creditor thinks the debtor is a deadbeat, and the debtor sees the creditor as one of those silent-movie villains who wants to grab the deed to Little Nell's ranch. In fact, the majority of those who receive consumer credit summonses don't go to court for the hearing—a big mistake.

It's not as bad as you might think. Like the many other crises we've discussed, receiving a summons can also provide an opportunity.

The one thing you should *not* do if you receive a summons is ignore it. If you fail to appear in court after receiving a summons, you will be found in default. You will have given up your right to have your case heard, and the judgment will enter into your credit report.

When you receive a summons, you have two alternatives — to answer the summons by filing with the court clerk on your own, or to seek a lawyer's help. (First of all, you'll want to check to make sure that what you have received is an actual summons. See pages 164–165.) Later in this chapter, I'll discuss how to find a lawyer.

The first advantage to filing an answer is that a court date will be assigned to your case which, most likely, will be a month or two away from the time you received your summons. This gives you a little more time to settle any fair debts with your creditors.

Depending on where you live, when you appear at court to file an answer, you will either be given a form to take with you and return by mail, or a court clerk will help you fill out the form right there. The form seeks to find why you have not paid the creditor, and what the circumstances of your relationship with the creditor are.

The points you list in your answer will, of necessity, pertain directly to your case. Although I can't list all of the possibilities, here are a few examples, to show the nature of the responses you might give:

- The collectors have been abusive, and you may feel that they violated state or federal laws. This constitutes a counterclaim against the collectors. If you are planning to do this, get all of your evidence of the violations together, including the names of all witnesses, the times and dates of all abusive calls and visits, the name of the collector, the exact (or near-exact) words used, and any other details you can use to support your case.
- The goods you purchased were defective. This and the next point are defenses, as opposed to counterclaims. Again, you'll need evidence: receipts, letters, notes on phone calls, etc.
- You did not receive the services for which you contracted.

In all of these instances, prepare a detailed, written, chronological statement of all the facts relevant to your answer.

It's important to know that you have a right to have your response to a summons filed correctly, no matter what the clerk thinks of your reasons. Court clerks vary — some are encouraging, some are helpful, others just shuffle papers.

Consumer credit cases rarely, if ever, go to trial — although you might very much like to see your collection agent grilled by Perry Mason. In some states, your answer to the summons will be challenged — in other papers filed at the court — by the attorney for the creditor, who will provide evidence that the collector was not abusive, the goods were not defective, etc. The judge will decide, in a procedure known as a summary judgment, whether or not the judgment is warranted based on your answers and the creditor's arguments. You and the creditor *may* be brought in for an open hearing of the case, or the judge may simply have the court notify you of his decision.

The other thing that can keep your case out of court is that your creditor will contact you, seeing that you have filed an answer to the summons, and attempt to settle with you. At this point you'll have to decide for yourself how cooperative you want to be with the creditor. If he has made efforts in the past to negotiate with you, in good faith, then you should take this advantage to settle. If he has been difficult to negotiate with, and you feel the judge will look favorably on your past attempts to seek a settlement, it might be worth your while to go to court. One reason the creditor might not want to go to court is because of the expense involved for him.

If your creditor does not show up on your court day, the judgment will be denied without prejudice, which means that the court has not been able to "judge" the case based on what was before it. This does *not* mean that you have "won" the case, merely that your creditor must now start the whole process over again.

Going to court is a business proposition for most creditors, and they have to decide if the time and money invested in it will be worthwhile. In many cases, a creditor is willing to take the time to file a judgment, since it's a fairly straightforward thing and the paperwork can be done in a wholesale manner. But going to court is another matter entirely, and some creditors will not show up rather than pay a lawyer to appear in court and, in essence, wipe out any profit that might be made from collecting on your balance.

If your creditor does show, the judge may tell the two of you to go out in the hall and make a settlement. The pressure will be placed on you to settle, and the creditor will also be a little more amenable at this point to accepting your debt-management program. In a few rare cases, the judge will hear about the way you worked to propose a reasonable debt-management program with the creditor over a period of a month or so, and he will rule in your favor — probably to force the creditor to accept your program.

Q: I really want to challenge my creditor — how do I go about it?
A: After all of this, my advice is, if you are planning seriously to challenge a default judgment and the amount of money is substantial, get a lawyer.

Q: What's the worst that can happen to me?
A: First thing — there are no debtor's prisons.

The question at hand is actually two questions — what they can do to you and what might happen to you. The worst thing they can do is repossess your property or get an execution after levy. Or, if you've offered your home as collateral, foreclose on your home. Whatever enters the public record as a result of legal action will go on your credit report. (By the way, if you feel your home is in danger of being foreclosed — GET A LAWYER. The stakes are too high to go through this process without one.)

As for what happens to you, a great deal depends on how the people you live with and work for view your being in debt. It is illegal for an employer to fire someone who has a garnishment on his salary just because he has a garnishment. On the other hand, it's hard to prove that someone who was fired on grounds of poor performance or personality conflicts was actually fired because of a garnishment.

Before you get to this point, I hope that this book has given you enough solid advice to deal with your debts completely. If not, then there is always bankruptcy, which I'll discuss in the next chapter.

DEBTOR'S REMEDIES

Ah-hah! So you thought *they* held all the cards!

Creditors assume two things of most debtors: they don't know their rights, and they won't exercise their rights. Up to now, this chapter has concerned itself with telling you what your rights are. Let's look at how you can exercise them — from filing a complaint with your creditor to finding a lawyer.

To begin with, complaining does make a difference. If you are complaining about immediate behavior, such as harassment, you can stop the abuse by complaining to the proper agencies. If you are complaining about a debt you feel you do not owe, or about a legal process that is being used against you unfairly, you can at least temporarily put a halt to the process until the proper agency determines if it is just.

In a larger sense, complaining against creditors and collectors who are abusing their privileges to do business helps to tilt the balance a little bit toward debtors in general. As David Samuels of the New York Office of Consumer Affairs told me, "It's difficult to enforce a federal or local regulation against a business if only one or two people complain. But if we get thirty or forty people complaining, then we can build a case." I think that it's pretty safe to assume that if you are being harassed or your rights are being violated, thirty or forty other people are having the same problem. The greater percentage of people we have complaining about legitimate abuses, the less abuse we will see in the future.

The New York City Department of Consumer Affairs has had a good degree of success in enforcing their regulations concerning debt collections. Fines have been levied against collectors using obscene language with debtors, making repeated phone calls, sending out dunning notices that implied legal action would be taken, and against collectors who did not advise consumers of their rights to dispute the validity of a debt.

The penalties for violating the federal laws are fairly stiff, and can provide a direct benefit to you. Here's a brief rundown:

- Fair Debt Collection Practices Act. You may sue a third-party debt collector for violating your rights under the FDCPA. You are entitled to actual damages and punitive damages up to $1,000, costs and attorney's fees. Also, the creditor who hired the third party is liable. Class action suits are allowed, and the FTC can also sue the agency, depending on the type of agency involved and the number of complaints.
- Fair Credit Billing Act. A creditor who fails to follow — to the letter of the law — those rules applying to the correction of billing errors *automatically forfeits the amount owed* on the item in question and any finance charges on it, up to a combined total of $50 — even if the bill was correct. As an individual, you may also sue for actual damages plus twice the amount of any finance charges, but in any case not less than $100 nor more than $1,000. You are also entitled to court costs and attorney's fees in a successful lawsuit. Class action suits are also permitted.
- Fair Credit Reporting Act. You may sue any credit-reporting agency or creditor for violating the rules about who may have access to your credit records and correcting errors in your file. Again, you are entitled to actual damages, plus punitive damages as the court may allow if the violation is proven to be intentional. In any successful lawsuit, you will be awarded court costs and attorney's fees. An unauthorized person who secures a credit report — or any employee of a credit-reporting agency who supplies a credit report to unauthorized persons — may be fined up to $5,000 or imprisoned for one year, or both.
- Equal Credit Opportunity Act. If a creditor has discriminated

against you for any reason prohibited by the act, you as an individual can sue for actual damages (any money loss you suffer) plus punitive damages (damages for the fact that the law has been violated) of up to $10,000. In a successful lawsuit, the court will award you court costs and a reasonable amount of attorney's fees. Class action suits are also permitted.

I can't stress enough the importance of complaining when you feel that you have a legitimate beef. In some cases, a lawyer or a small claims court is needed to get full resolution. But more often than not, you can solve a problem by following a few guidelines.

- Get your facts straight. Collect your warranties, bills of sales, credit agreements, and other documents. Sit down and write out a straight account of your experience stating the problem, what you have done, and what the creditor or collector has done and said. This will be an important reference throughout the process.
- Go to the top and get names. Talk to the person with the most authority. Don't waste time on clerks. Make sure that the person you are talking with has the power to help you. Always find out whom you are talking to, and write down the name.
- Send letters. Describe all the facts and the contacts. State what you want and give a deadline for a response. Send a copy of the letter to your local consumer affairs office and to the state attorney general's office, if you don't receive a reply after three weeks. This will act as a formal filing of a complaint and get a third party involved. (A sample letter is shown here.)

SAMPLE OF A GOOD COMPLAINT LETTER

> Your Address
> Town, State, Zip
> Date

Appropriate Person
Company Name
Street Address
City, State, Zip

Dear [appropriate person]:
    Last week I purchased [or had repaired] a [name of product, with serial or model number, or service performed]. I made this purchase at [location, date, and other important details of the transaction.].

Unfortunately, this product [or service] has not performed satisfactorily [or the service was inadequate] because [concisely describe the problem].

Therefore, to solve the problem, I would appreciate it if you would [state the specific action you want]. Enclosed are copies (not originals) of my records [include copies of receipts, guarantees, warranties, canceled checks, contracts, models and serial numbers, and any other pertinent documents].

I am looking forward to your reply and resolution of my problem, and will wait three weeks before seeking third-party assistance. Contact me at the above address or by phone at [home and office numbers here].

Sincerely,

Your Name

Before you send off your complaint letter, check this list of items to make sure you don't leave any "loopholes" for your creditors:

1. Have you stated what the purchase was, the service contracted for, or the agreement that was made?
2. Did you give all pertinent product names, serial numbers, model numbers, or service numbers?
3. Have you included the date and location of the purchase and other details, including the names of anyone you spoke with about your matter, if the names are available?
4. Have you clearly stated the problem?
5. Did you give a concise history of the problem?
6. Have you made clear to the creditor that you want your complaint satisfied by them?
7. Have you enclosed copies of all documents, with the items you are complaining about circled?
8. Have you offered a reasonable amount of time for action to be taken?
9. Have you included your address, work and home phone numbers?
10. Have you made a copy of your letter and all related documents and information for your own files?

Don't forget — send all complaint letters by certified mail, return receipt requested.

Either the attorney general's office of your state or the local consumer affairs office will help you to settle your claim. Neither, however, will go to court for you.

The basic thing to remember is to be assertive. You have your rights and most stores and creditors don't want to lose your business. You have to decide yourself how far you want to go, what your claim is worth to you, and how angry you are.

GETTING A LAWYER

After hearing all of the arguments for and against having a lawyer for consumer credit problems, I've arrived at a simple, exact test of the issue: how much is it worth to you? Lawyers cost money. Very often a lawyer's fees and your court costs are recoverable if a creditor or collector is found in violation of the law. Add to this that very often it is only a knowledgeable consumer credit lawyer who will be able to spot if the creditor has broken the law. But — you can never count on the outcome of a court case to pay your lawyer's bills. The best advice is to weigh the cost of a lawyer's services against the cost of not using one and, perhaps, losing in court.

Very simply, you should get a lawyer when your property is threatened by repossession, foreclosure, or some other legal action, or when it is obvious that the cost of a lawyer is no more than or less than the cost of what your creditor's lawyers have planned for you.

A lawyer can be helpful to you in consumer credit matters for a variety of purposes. If you are going to court, either because your creditor is taking you or you are taking him, it is good to consider getting a consumer credit lawyer. If you have been unable to negotiate a debt-management program with your creditors, or through a credit-counseling service, a lawyer can do this for you, as well.

You should take the job of finding a lawyer as seriously as you do that of finding a doctor.

There are five sources of legal aid open to the average consumer. The first of these is a private lawyer.

The best way to contact lawyers is through referrals, although you should be careful to consider the source of any referral. The bar association is not always the best source, although they will give you some names to call. It is better to go through people and agencies who have experience with consumer credit, who know what lawyers currently have expertise in the area and are doing a good job for their clients. Good referrals can be made by the trustees of the bankruptcy court in your area, even if you are not considering bankruptcy and only need help with one or two problems. Other referrals can be made by the office of consumer affairs in your area. If neither of these sources pans out, check the court records in your area (a court clerk can help you find your way through them) for names of lawyers who have successfully handled cases like yours. You can check with consumer credit counseling agencies, who generally know the names of good lawyers in their area.

Don't assume that your family attorney can handle the case, until you've asked him if he has had past experience with your particular kind of problem. Finally, if you have any friends who have had situations similar to your own, you can ask for the name of their lawyer if they are happy with the service he provided.

The second source of legal aid is a public-interest law center. These are nonprofit, tax-exempt groups offering legal representation to consumers and others who would not otherwise be represented before federal agencies or the courts. There are nationally more than a hundred public-interest law centers involved in consumer issues. Although the law centers generally do not handle individual cases, they can help you understand your rights, and direct you to positive, helpful ways of defending them. A national clearing house for public-interest law firms is operated by the Council of Public Interest Law, 1250 Connecticut Ave., N.W., Washington, D.C. 20036. You can also find them through your local consumer offices.

The third source is prepaid legal services, which are now available to people through prepaid legal plans—a form of insurance where consumers, for a small monthly fee, receive basic legal services. There are more than two thousand of these plans on file with the Department of Labor. Check with your insurance company or your union or employer to see if you currently participate in, or can join, such a plan.

The fourth source of legal aid is legal aid services, which help people who cannot afford to hire private lawyers, and who meet financial eligibility requirements. There are more than a thousand of these offices around the country, staffed by lawyers, paralegals, and law students. These offices can give you help with your credit problems, and in some cases they have one or two staff members exclusively assigned to them.

Even if you have doubts about your eligibility for free legal assistance, it's worth contacting an office to see if you are eligible. If you are not, or if the office cannot help you with your problem for some other reason, they will try to refer you to other sources of help. You can find legal aid services under "Legal Aid," or "Legal Services" in your local phone book.

Recently a fifth kind of legal service has been making an appearance around the country. The legal clinic provides routine services at relatively low cost. They depend on high volume and rapid turnover to operate successfully. Unfortunately, consumer cases don't fit neatly into this pattern. Legal clinics are of limited help to people with consumer credit problems.

Once you get the names of a few lawyers, call and make an appointment. If you are in an emergency, explain this to the attorney or the person taking his calls. Most lawyers have some time which they leave open for emergencies, particularly if they handle consumer work, and will be able to see you sometimes within 24 hours.

The first purpose of sitting down with a lawyer is to review the facts of the case with him. Give him as complete a review of the matter as possible. After that, there are some questions you should ask. Has he handled this kind of case before? What are the alternatives he sees, and which of these does he suggest to you? And finally, what will the fee be for his services? You might want to ask him about some of the rights outlined in this book, to see if he is familiar with these laws and what they guarantee for the consumer.

Lawyers charge for their services with one of three plans: an hourly rate, a flat fee, or a contingency fee.

When a lawyer charges on an hourly basis, he keeps records of the time spent on your case, and you are billed for that time multiplied by the hourly rate — which can vary anywhere from $50 to $150 an hour. You will be entitled to an accounting of the hours you have been charged for, and many lawyers will give you a written estimate of the time it will take to handle your case.

A flat fee arrangement is the simplest of the arrangements. You will be charged a certain amount, plus costs, for your case. The costs which will be added to the fee include such items as filing fees and deposition charges.

Finally, a contingency fee arrangement gives the lawyer a percentage of any award the court may give you, with a certain amount guaranteed by you whether you win or lose. This kind of arrangement will usually only be made when you are suing a creditor or collector for a violation of your rights, and even in that case it may be difficult to get a lawyer to accept a contingency fee, since many of these cases are settled by judgments that are unenforceable — meaning that the money awarded to the consumer is never actually paid.

None of these fee systems is absolutely preferable over the others. In any case, you should openly discuss with your attorney the costs of your case, and how it will be paid.

Many lawyers offer their first consultation for free. Others charge. As with *all* legal services, don't be shy about asking. These people are in business, and you are a consumer of their services.

This advice is particularly applicable to the large, national legal clinics which have sprung up in the last few years. While their fees may be reasonable, they rely on volume for their profits, and much of the work on your case will probably be done by paralegals. If you are considering one of these clinics, ask which *lawyer* will be handling your case, how often you will see him, and how accessible he will be to you. These considerations will do a great deal to insure that your case will be handled with some sensitivity to personal subtleties.

We are in an age of specialization, and the law is no exception. Ask any lawyer you are considering how many cases like yours he has handled, and what the outcomes were. Ask him what actions he will take on your case, what the cost will be, and how long it will take. The lawyer should be familiar with a number of alternatives in any situation, and should discuss each alternative with you, frankly and openly. Don't be intimidated by him, and don't be afraid to ask questions.

Finally, trust your feelings. If you feel uncomfortable with the lawyer you are talking to, don't do business with him. There are *plenty* of lawyers around, and it won't be hard to find one who can handle your case competently and successfully. Having a bad lawyer can be worse than having no lawyer at all.

The answer, then, to "Can They Do This to Me?" is "Probably not, but they'll try anyway." Knowing your rights as a debtor when trying to keep a businesslike relationship with your creditor is an absolute necessity. Exercising your rights can transform the most cantankerous creditor or collector into someone who — while they may not be a pleasure to deal with — will work with you on a serious, objective level.

Sometimes, though, everything falls through — your plans, your debt-management program, and your relationship with your creditor — and you find that even a knowledge of your rights cannot save you.

If nothing seems to help in your attempt to get out of debt, it might be time to think about bankruptcy.

BANKRUPTCY:
STRONG MEDICINE

At the end of every seven years thou shalt make a release . . . every creditor that lendeth aught unto his neighbour shall release it, he shall not exact it of his neighbour, or of his brother, for it is the Lord's release.

— Deuteronomy 15:2

THE MAIN BANKRUPTCY COURT in the Southern District of New York is situated in the stately granite U.S. Courthouse. Its weekly calendar includes meetings of debtors with trustees and creditors.

All of the bankruptcy hearings are public, and if you were to attend one — say, a final discharge hearing — you would witness none of the Perry Mason–like histrionics you might expect. There is no donning of sackcloths and smearing of ashes. People do not hand the keys to their homes over to greedy bankers. To tell the truth, there isn't even as much drama in a bankruptcy meeting as there is in the usual collection agent's phone call. The trustee for the court sits at a long table, and calls the debtors, lawyers, and the creditors (if they have bothered to show) case by case, spending ten or fifteen minutes with each. While he is there to insure that the forms have been filed correctly, that no false statements have been made or assets hidden, the trustee generally does not cross-examine or hector the debtors. He will ask a few questions, but for the most part the hearing is an open-and-shut affair.

Even the swearing-in at the beginning of the session is done en masse — the debtors are called before the trustee and the oath is read. It's interesting to see the line-up of debtors: it provides concrete evidence for the assertion by bankruptcy experts that it is practically impossible to categorize just who is filing for bankruptcy today. There are young professionals, old men and women, the obviously poor, and the uneducated. They are from all walks of life, and are in bankruptcy court for a variety of causes. One thing unites them: they can't pay their bills.

What brought these people to this point? Will bankruptcy help them? How will their financial status change because of bankruptcy? As you watch their faces, when they approach the trustee, answer his questions, and walk away from the table, you come to realize completely that bankruptcy is serious business. It is strong medicine that, even if taken lightly at first, enforces its own effect upon the patient. The faces of the debtors tell you that this is strong stuff. No one who is considering bankruptcy should do so without witnessing a bankruptcy hearing.

There are plenty of books on the market today that will tell you how to go through bankruptcy. I won't attempt to cover that ground in this chapter. This book is about financial recovery, and I want to discuss bankruptcy in that light. When is it right for you? What changes will bankruptcy bring about in your life? What are the short-range and long-range effects? How will the controversy currently going on among bankers and other lenders over bankruptcy affect people who have gone through bankruptcy? These are the essential issues surrounding bankruptcy.

Will bankruptcy lead you to financial recovery? In many cases, yes. But like strong medicine, it is best to attempt other treatments before undertaking the most severe. I have written this book so that those other treatments can be carried out successfully. If they've failed, then bankruptcy might be right for you. That's a big *if*, though, and one that too few people put to the test.

WHAT'S BEHIND THE CURRENT RISE IN BANK-RUPTCIES?

The tremendous rise in bankruptcies over the last two years is the result of three major factors: the new Federal Bankruptcy Reform

Act — now called the Bankruptcy Code — which became effective in 1979, the ability of lawyers to advertise their services in ads featuring the option of bankruptcy (which not only indicated its availability but subtly "legitimized" it by placing bankruptcy on a level with suing your landlord or making a will), and the severe effects of the economy on debtors.

The new bankruptcy law is a tremendous boon to consumers in genuine need. Even its simplest change — making the consumer a "debtor" instead of a "bankrupt" — points the way to a more humane, balanced system of giving people a "fresh start." There are some abuses that occur with the law, but I don't think that they have as profound an effect on the credit industry as creditors claim. What I am wary of, though, are the wholesale bankruptcy mills — those law firms "specializing" in bankruptcy cases which, in fact, handle such a high volume of cases and give so much of their work to paralegals that they neither serve nor protect debtors — and the reactionary attitude that creditors are taking to former debtors.

If at all possible, debtors should avoid bankruptcy completely. Many can't.

Almost three hundred thousand people went through bankruptcy in 1980, and 228,549 cases were filed in the first six months of 1981. That fact has angered bankers and creditors all over America, and made them a little scared. Some critics of the credit industry say that the lenders are getting their just rewards, and that the rise in bankruptcies is merely the result of indiscriminate lending and other credit practices.

Another factor that has affected the rise in bankruptcies is the removal of the stigma that once surrounded going bankrupt. "It's become the fashionable way to get rid of your debts," one New York banker told me, "and people just don't understand what they're getting into." Another creditor claimed that bankruptcy "more than ever before has become a viable option in the minds of consumers."

Add to this a general attitude towards credit which distinguishes this generation of consumers from that of twenty years ago. "The baby boom people regard credit differently," commented Nancy Teeters, Governor of the Federal Reserve Board. "They have a cavalier attitude toward being cut-off from credit. It's going to have a major effect in the years to come."

Finally, "going bankrupt" means a variety of different things to people. In many cases, there are false expectations associated with the process. Among these are:

- Going bankrupt will be easy.
- You will be able to get revenge on your creditors.
- You won't have to go through the hassle of credit counselors and budget plans.

All of these are, in their own way, myths. Going through bankruptcy is a difficult, emotionally draining, time-consuming, often expensive proposition. And, once you've had to fill out all of the bankruptcy forms and — in the case of a "regular income" plan (I'll explain that later) — completely overhauled your finances, you'll probably think that credit counselors and budget plans would have been the easy way out.

The rise in bankruptcies has created a "backlash" among creditors. They feel taken advantage of by "abusive debtors" who have left them holding the bag. What people involved with credit are witnessing today is a highly emotional atmosphere: in response to the rise in bankruptcies, creditors are becoming more stringent in their standards for would-be borrowers. And when it comes to those who have gone bankrupt in the past, many banks and loan companies are closing their doors entirely, in retaliation. This can become the most direct reason for not going bankrupt.

WHY BANKRUPTCY DRIVES
THE CREDITORS CRAZY

Creditors have seen the new wave of bankruptcies and they are digging in their heels — hard. "The law is fraught with abuse," one New York banker told me.

Jack Downing, a vice-president of Household Finance Corporation, called the new bankruptcy act "the worst law in the last two hundred years. We are alarmed at the things that are happening since it was passed. We've seen a sharp increase in the number of bankruptcies, and our policy is that we will not make a loan to a person who has a bankruptcy on his record, unless he can prove to us that the bankruptcy was caused by extenuating circumstances."

Commercial banks' losses increased 46 percent during 1980, due to many causes, but largely as a result of the rise in personal bankruptcies, according to Keefe, Bruyette & Woods, a New York research company.

Just how creditors will react to the problems engendered by their bankruptcy losses is unknown. One creditor I questioned told me "our bank hasn't decided how to handle the new bankruptcy code. It's very new, and the impact has yet to be felt. We're a little gun-shy right now, and the only sure thing is that we will be making lending and obtaining credit on the part of the bankruptee much more difficult."

Besides limiting the credit granted to bankrupts, creditors are also planning on covering the losses they've suffered by raising the rates charged to their other credit customers. However, many creditors have found themselves unable to pass through added costs — state usury laws keep their rates at a certain level. As I wrote in "Making a Plan You Can Stick To," amending these laws both at the state and the federal level is a prime goal on bankers' agendas in the coming decade.

But the area that causes creditors the greatest distress, and has led to the most reactionary statements on their part, is the question of proof of financial distress. Under the present code, there is no requirement for establishment of any financial disability before someone files for bankruptcy. Some creditors claim that they have seen huge increases in bankruptcy filings among customers who had always before paid promptly. The manager of the San Antonio, Texas, office of a consumer lender reported to the *Wall Street Journal* that nearly a third of the office's $250,000 in bankrupt accounts came from "out of the blue," by customers who had been "excellent payers." Half of these were accounts of customers who could afford to pay all of their bills without filing bankruptcy.

The definition of financial need, though, raises a good deal of controversy. "What does need mean?" asks credit counselor Luther Gatling. "Who judges what need is? Does someone have to be facing a total mental breakdown before they *need* to go bankrupt?"

Lenders want two changes in the bankruptcy act, although they are asking for many more. They want to require a showing of financial distress as a prerequisite for bankruptcy and another amendment to force judges and trustees to be more strict in what they will accept as a "good faith" payment in Chapter 13 plans. Until they get those amendments, and possibly after, credit is going to be tight for the bankrupt, and creditors will spread that tough stance as far as possible.

WHAT IS BANKRUPTCY?

Essentially there are two types of bankruptcy for consumers. The first involves a straight liquidation of all but certain exempt debts: this is the Chapter 7 proceeding. The second involves a regular income plan under which the consumer's debts are restructured in accordance with court approval and repayment of a percentage of creditors claims are paid over a period of three years: this is the Chapter 13 proceeding, and to qualify you must have some form of regular income from which you can draw funds for repayment.

Filing for bankruptcy is not a question of how much money you have or how much you owe. Rather, it is the relationship between the two that indicates the need for bankruptcy. In making your decision, you should consider a variety of facts about your income, assets, and debts.

First, you have to know how much you earn and what you are likely to earn in the future. It's also important not to overestimate the stability of your current employment.

Then, you must take into account what you own and how much it is worth. Is any of your property pledged to creditors as security or collateral?

Finally, the nature of your debts and liabilities must be looked into. Will any co-signer — including a spouse or relative — be left vulnerable by your bankruptcy? How much do you owe and to whom?

As you can see, these first considerations closely parallel the questions you ask at the beginning of a debt-management program. In many ways, bankruptcy can accomplish the same goals, but at a higher price, as we'll see later.

INVOLUNTARY BANKRUPTCY

Although the great majority of bankruptcies in this country are voluntary, you can be taken to court by your creditors in involuntary bankruptcy. (The ratio of voluntary filings to involuntary is about 150 to 1.)

In an involuntary bankruptcy, a petition must be filed by three or more creditors who can prove claims amounting to a total of at least $5,000. If you owe less than twelve creditors, any one with a claim of more than $5,000 can file a petition.

The decision of whether or not you can be subject to involuntary bankruptcy proceedings is based on the ability of your creditors to prove that you are unable to pay debts as they become due, or if a custodian — someone assigned by the civil court for the benefit of your creditors — has been appointed to take charge of your property.

Obtaining this proof and bringing it before the court takes a long time and can be very expensive for the creditor. That's why there are so few involuntary bankruptcies. Creditors will often accept reasonable payment plans before taking such a step. If this isn't the case, you have four alternatives:

1. You can allow the bankruptcy to "go through" by doing nothing. The court will follow the usual procedures, and in essence you will receive the same discharge as if you had initiated the bankruptcy.

2. You can "consent" to the bankruptcy, making it a matter of record that you fully participated in the case, and receiving the same discharge as in Point 1.

3. You can, with the aid of a lawyer, fight the bankruptcy and ask for a dismissal.

4. You can file a conversion to another, more suitable, chapter of the bankruptcy act — a Chapter 11 (business reorganization, if your debts are largely derived from business obligations) or a Chapter 13.

HOW A CHAPTER 7 BANKRUPTCY WORKS

Here's what happens in a reasonably simple Chapter 7 bankruptcy:

1. Your petition for bankruptcy is filed, and a fee ($60 for one person, or for a husband and wife filing together) is paid to the court. Included in your petition is a detailed list of all your debts, all your assets, and any exemptions you claim.

2. The court will then schedule a meeting of your creditors, which will be held, usually, within 20 to 40 days after you have filed. You and your creditors will be notified of this meeting, and you will be required to attend. Depending on where you live, this may be the only time you will have to appear at a hearing until your discharge hearing.

3. At the meeting of creditors, the trustee appointed to your case will run the meeting. The trustee will ask you some questions about how the papers were filed, about your property, about how you got into your present situation, and attempt to verify the statements in your petition.

4. The trustee will decide which of your nonexempt property will be used to repay your debts. He will then demand that these items be turned over to the court. If you do not comply with the demand, there is a subsequent proceeding to obtain the property. Most often, the trustee will accept the value of the equity due to your creditors in lieu of selling your nonexempt property. For example, if you owe $250 on your car, the trustee will often accept payment of the $250 rather than your car. The nonexempt property that is collected will be sold, and the money from the sale will be distributed among your creditors. The trustee will carefully examine your financial affairs and make a detailed report to the court.

5. After you file, you must not give away, return, or lose any property that is not exempt. That property belongs to the creditors, to be held by the trustee and disbursed as is prescribed by the bankruptcy act.

6. Immediately after you file for bankruptcy, the "automatic stay" takes effect — you (or your attorney) are responsible for notifying your creditors that you have commenced bankruptcy

proceedings. This makes it illegal for them to attempt to collect their debts, and they are subject to strict penalties if they do so. The automatic stay does *not* apply to your co-signers, and your creditor will most likely pursue them immediately.

7. Your creditors have at least 30 but no more than 90 days after you file to object to your discharge or to claim that certain debts are nondischargable, unless the court grants them an extension. If a creditor does challenge your discharge, the court will hold a hearing and the bankruptcy judge will decide whether or not the creditor is right.

8. Unless your creditors have objected, about 90 days after filing, a Notice of Discharge Hearing will be mailed to you by the court. You will have to attend this hearing, and shortly thereafter a discharge will be sent to you.

9. Once you have received your Notice of Discharge, you have a document that prevents your creditors from collecting the debts listed in the bankruptcy papers. Your case is officially closed when the trustee files his report with the court.

During your bankruptcy proceedings, there are a number of strategies your creditors will employ in an attempt to regain as much of the money owed to them as possible. A number of these strategies were outlined by William Mapother, a lawyer, in the December 1980 issue of *Credit* magazine, a publication of the National Consumer Finance Association.

Those of your creditors who hold unsecured loans, according to Mapother, "might as well close [their] files when receiving a Chapter 7 Bankruptcy notice, unless there is a possible fraud suit." As I've already pointed out, if you have co-signers on any of these loans, your creditor can pursue them immediately after you file for bankruptcy — and without the permission of the court.

If you have secured loans, you can expect that, soon after you file for bankruptcy, your creditors will contact you to see, as best as possible, what you intend to do about their particular debts. Creditors can best make this type of contact, according to Mapother, "with the debtor and his attorney after they are together, immediately after the first meeting of the creditors."

During bankruptcy proceedings, a creditor might also contact you, asking you to reaffirm your debt. To reaffirm the debt is to recognize, despite your bankruptcy, that *this* debt is just and that you are willing to repay it. Creditors often pursue you to reaffirm a debt, claiming that the debt will be affordable after others are discharged, and that reaffirmation will place you in good standing with them.

One of the major changes in the new act was the strict limitations placed upon the consumer's ability to reaffirm a debt. This limitation applies to both Chapter 7 and Chapter 13 cases. Under the new restrictions, you can reaffirm a debt only (1) before discharge; (2) after you have had 30 days to cancel the reaffirmation; (3) after the court has explained your rights in a reaffirmation to you and; (4) if, in the case of a non–real estate debt, the judge has ruled that reaffirmation is in your best interest.

WHAT YOU CAN KEEP IN A CHAPTER 7 BANKRUPTCY: EXEMPTIONS

There are items of property which cannot be taken from you when you file for bankruptcy. State and federal laws differ in the exemptions allowed, although the federal law guarantees you the right to choose under which law you wish to declare exemptions — unless, frustratingly enough, your state has "opted out" of the federal law, in which case only state exemptions apply. The choice you make between state and federal exemptions can be as important as the choice of whether or not to go bankrupt at all. You should carefully compare the exemptions available under each law and choose the law which is best for you.

Under federal law, some of the assets which you can keep when you file for bankruptcy are:

1. Your interest in your home, up to a total value of $7,500. If you do not own a home or you do not use part of the amount of this to exempt your home, you may use any unused part of the exemption for any other property you own.
2. Equity in a motor vehicle of up to $1,200.
3. $500 worth of personal jewelry.
4. Any household or personal property up to $200 per item.
5. Your rights to social security, unemployment, compensation, public assistance, veterans' benefits, disability benefits, and cer-

tain pensions or annuities, alimony, maintenance or support payments, or life insurance proceeds.

6. Any additional property worth up to $400.

There are also federal exemptions that cover property you may need to earn a living (professional tools), to keep yourself healthy, or for a number of specified other purposes. If you feel you have other property to protect in a bankruptcy proceeding, your lawyer will be able to help you.

If you file a joint return with your spouse, each of you is entitled to the full exemptions allowed under state or federal law, and each of you may choose which law is best for you — thus, your spouse may choose federal law, and you may choose state law. The determination of which is best depends upon the nature of the property you own.

WHAT WILL YOU HAVE TO PAY IN A CHAPTER 7 BANKRUPTCY?

Along with certain property that is exempt from bankruptcy proceedings, there are also certain debts which cannot be discharged. They include:

1. Any debts which you did not list on your petition.
2. Alimony, maintenance, and child support.
3. Taxes due within the past three years, or for which you filed a false return or no return.
4. Any interest in real estate or personal property which you have offered as security on a loan. In this the creditor has the right to go into court and vacate the automatic stay and then proceed with his lawful remedies. If the trustee doesn't claim equity, the debtor is free to deal with the secured creditor.
5. Debts that resulted from your obtaining money or property under false pretenses. This includes any credit obtained, renewed, or refinanced where you misstated to your creditor, in writing, your financial condition.
6. Debts resulting from your taking someone's property without permission, or from fraud and embezzlement.

The following cannot be discharged in a Chapter 7 liquidation, but can be discharged through a Chapter 13 plan:

7. Fines or penalties payable to the government, including traffic or parking tickets.
8. Debts for student loans, unless they have been due and owing for five years, or unless repayment would cause you undue hardship.

HOW A CHAPTER 13 BANKRUPTCY WORKS

The Chapter 13 plan is also called a "regular income" plan because it is available to anyone with a stable or regular income, such as a wage earner. Anyone who has unsecured debts of less than $100,000 and secured debts of less than $350,000 can commence a case under Chapter 13.

Your offer of a settlement with your creditors in a Chapter 13 plan allows three years to pay your debts (the plan can be extended another two years), or for the reduction of the amount you intend to pay your creditors (you may offer each creditor a percentage of the amount you owe), or a combination of both. If the court finds your settlement to be equal to at least what the creditors would receive in a Chapter 7 liquidation, and is satisfied that you can make the payments you propose, the settlement becomes binding on your creditors.

For example, if you owe $900 on an unsecured home-improvement loan from a commercial bank, and propose to pay back $300 of that loan (and if the bank is getting the same deal as everyone else — an equal percentage of the loan or indebtedness paid back), the court — if it is satisfied that the proposal is in good faith and that you will make the payments — will automatically discharge the other $600 when the $300 is paid.

Another important aspect of a Chapter 13 bankruptcy case is the "cram down" provision of the code. The "cram down" provision operates only in Chapter 13, and works in this way: if, for example, you own a refrigerator that cost you $750, and you owe $550 on it, the court might determine that the refrigerator, if it were resold, would have a value of only $300. In that case, you would only have to pay the creditor $300, and the remaining $250 of the debt would be discharged after that payment.

To gain a more personalized view of the Chapter 13 process, I spoke with one partner of a law firm that specializes in bankruptcies. She offered a description of a typical Chapter 13 case at her firm.

The first thing this particular firm does when a debtor decides to file for Chapter 13 is to make moves to protect the secured property. If the mortgage has been in arrears, they will notify the bank that the debtor is filing for Chapter 13, and make assurances that the mortgage will be brought up to date. The same procedure will be made for other secured loans.

The lawyer handling the case will then separate the debts between priority and nonpriority items. Tax claims, alimony, and child support will have to be paid 100 percent, so they get first priority.

The debtor and the lawyer will then figure out a monthly budget. If no budget can be made that will satisfy the Chapter 13 plan, then the lawyer will suggest that the debtor reconsider going into a Chapter 7 plan.

After the budget has been drawn up, the lawyer will go through all of the exemptions available to the debtor. In addition, the debtor and the lawyer will work to ascertain the value of any secured item that might be subject to the "cram down" provision of the Chapter 13 law.

After this preliminary work, the process of filing, amendments, and objections proceeds in the court. The trustee in a Chapter 13 proceeding accounts for property, investigates the finances of the debtor, examines proofs and claims, collects monthly payments and distributes them to creditors, and makes a final report. In addition, the trustee in a Chapter 13 case has the duty to appear and be heard at any hearing concerning the value of property subject to a lien, or confirmation of the proposed plan, or modification of the plan.

After your creditors have been notified, the court will hold a hearing to confirm the plan. You will then begin to make monthly payments to the trustee.

Once you have made all the payments specified in the plan, a discharge will be granted. If you have not made all of the payments, the court may still grant a discharge if: (1) you cannot make payments due to circumstances beyond your control, such as natural disasters, extreme medical expenses, or total loss of future income that would have allowed you to complete the plan; (2) you have paid an amount of money on all unsecured claims that is not less than what your creditors would have received under a straight bankruptcy proceeding.

Chapter 13 has a variety of values. In many ways, it is a more ethical version of Chapter 7, both because it pays back more to the creditors, and allows the debtor to keep more of his property. For those who can handle the demands of a Chapter 13 plan, and who complete the plan successfully, there is a feeling of satisfaction, and a better sense of living on a budget, within your means. For those who fail, straight Chapter 7 bankruptcy is always available.

BANKRUPTCY: THE PROS AND CONS

What, then, are the advantages and disadvantages of Chapter 7 and Chapter 13 bankruptcies, and how can you decide if either is the best way for you to get out of debt?

First, let's look at the disadvantages and advantages of Chapter 7 bankruptcy:

1. Depending on how much property you own, you can lose some of it. The laws of exemption are complicated, and anyone with property to protect would do best to have a lawyer take them through the bankruptcy proceeding.
2. Some of your losses may hurt your co-signers, including friends and relatives. (Although reaffirmation is available in these cases.)
3. Your credit rating will suffer, and the fact that you went bankrupt will be on your record for 14 years. The long-term effect of this, as we have seen, could result in credit being denied to you for major purchases.
4. Some debts will not be discharged and will remain to be paid.
5. There is a possible bad effect on future employment, particularly if your work includes handling money, an area where many employers regularly check the credit reports of their employees.
6. You can not be discharged in bankruptcy again for another six years. If you find yourself overwhelmed by debt again — facing summonses, foreclosure, etc. — you're on your own, although you can enter Chapter 13 (with no recourse to convert your Chapter 13 plan to a Chapter 7 liquidation).
7. There is a certain psychological hazard to going bankrupt, rang-

ing from loss of self-esteem to severe emotional burdens, especially if friends or relatives are involved.

8. Bankruptcy is not easy. It costs time, money, and effort — at least equal to, if not more than, the debt-management program outlined in this book. In the long run, it pays to seek an alternative means of meeting your debts.

There are, of course, a variety of advantages to Chapter 7 bankruptcy. Among these are:

1. You will discharge most of your debts, and will be able to start again without a deficit budget.
2. All collection and garnishment attempts will stop.
3. You can usually decide before you file what property you will maintain as exempt.
4. You can fulfill any ethical or moral obligations by voluntarily repaying or making partial payment to anyone after you are discharged, by reaffirming — with court approval — that debt.
5. If money problems have been having a serious effect on your psychological well-being, or on your marriage, these problems may be alleviated by proceeding with a bankruptcy.

Judging whether a Chapter 13 plan is right for you or not should be done with the help of a credit counselor or a lawyer. You must first consider whether you will be able to make those payments to your creditors which your plan contemplates. While the first months of Chapter 13 proceedings under the new code saw a number of plans which offered 1 to 19 percent of the total debt as payment being approved by the courts, lawyers and bankruptcy experts agree that in certain parts of the country, courts are getting tougher on the plans, and you could now expect to pay closer to 50 percent of your original debt. To accommodate this new strictness, plans are being extended from the typical three years to five years.

The two major disadvantages of a Chapter 13 plan are:

1. Your credit rating receives the same damage as with a Chapter 7 liquidation.

2. It can take up to five years of strict budgeting and supervision to complete a Chapter 13 plan. You have to ask yourself if you and

your family are able to make such a commitment, compared to the relatively short time a Chapter 7 liquidation takes.

There are two factors which, depending on your individual case, may be advantages or disadvantages:

1. While some people are able to handle the commitment to a Chapter 13 in their marriage, others are not.

2. You will end up paying more to your creditors in a Chapter 13 plan than you would in a "straight" Chapter 7 bankruptcy.

In comparison with a Chapter 7 liquidation, the advantages of Chapter 13 bankruptcy are:

1. You don't have to turn over your property and assets above and beyond those which are exempt to the court for distribution to your creditors. Instead, you will promise to turn over a portion of your future earnings to the court.

2. Once you've made all the payments under the plan you receive a much broader discharge — in that more types of debts are discharged — than you would in a regular bankruptcy. You are discharged in a Chapter 13 from all debts except alimony, child support, and any unpaid taxes or debts to the government such as tickets and fines.

3. As with a regular bankruptcy, collection attempts and garnishments will stop. In addition, the commencement of a Chapter 13 case will stop all collection attempts and garnishments of your co-signers and co-debtors, forever, if you successfully complete the plan.

4. While you are making payments under your plan, your secured creditors are prevented from reclaiming the goods or real estate which secure your debt.

5. The fees for a Chapter 13 are tax-deductible, since you are protecting your assets.

GETTING A BANKRUPTCY LAWYER

Even from the brief details of bankruptcy which have already been given, you can see that this is a complicated legal process. Lawyers will tell you that it is absolutely necessary to have an attorney when you go through bankruptcy. (One of their favorite lines is, "Sure there are books and kits for do-it-yourself bankruptcy. And you can buy a scalpel and a medical book and take out your own appendix, too.")

Others, including credit counselors and family counselors, will say that it is possible, and sometimes preferable, for the debtor to file for bankruptcy himself—thus saving legal fees and even paying the $60 filing fee in installments.

The bottom line in whether or not you use a lawyer is the monetary value of what you have to protect. If you have practically no assets, you can't really be hurt by filing for bankruptcy on your own. (Unless you have recently transferred assets to another party, in which case the court will still claim them for your creditors.) On the other hand, if you own your home, have a relatively new car, or own anything of value which might conceivably not be exempt under state or federal law, you should get a good lawyer.

How can you judge whether or not a particular lawyer will handle your bankruptcy proceedings well? The bottom line, I feel, is if he regards bankruptcy as a last resort, and has encouraged and aided you in exercising all of your alternatives prior to bankruptcy. If he does this, you can trust that he will handle your case with competence and professionalism. This "bottom line" separates the bankruptcy mills from the competent, knowledgeable attorneys.

Experts point to the rise in lawyer advertising as one of the major reasons for the high level of bankruptcies over the last two years. What kind of service did those who filed through the advertised bankruptcy attorneys receive? According to one attorney I spoke with, the advertised lawyers were "the lowest of the low." He criticized them for misrepresenting their clients, for filing bankruptcies when they weren't called for, for not offering personal attorney-client service, and for collecting fees that were at least twice as high as the fees permitted by state law.

Another attorney told me that the bankruptcy courts, in the first few years that lawyers were allowed to advertise, were seeing several dozen cases a year in which debtors who had gone to a lawyer for the advertised "debt relief" were put through bankruptcy without knowing exactly what they were doing.

According to Herbert Minkel, a nationally recognized expert on bankruptcy, "The only way for these firms to economically handle the cases that come to them is through paralegals." And in that wholesale handling of bankruptcies is where the basic problem for debtors has arisen.

Some people do just as well on their own. One clerk for the bankruptcy court in New York told a debtor, "Go to a stationery store and get yourself a bankruptcy kit. Look at the forms and if you can't fill them out, come back here and I'll show you a set of completed papers that will show you how to fill out your own."

"Forty percent of our cases are filed without lawyers," said Irving Picard, U.S. Trustee for the Southern District of New York, in an interview with the *New York Daily News*. "And we don't want to get burned on these applications. So if people make a mistake on their forms, we try to help them."

If you feel you need a lawyer, a good starting place in your search is the local bar association, friends who may have been in a situation similar to yours, and credit counselors. After you've gathered a list of names, set up some interviews. In the few minutes it takes to explain your situation and set up an appointment on the phone, you might even be able to cross a few names off your list — some lawyers will tell you that they don't have time to discuss all of your alternatives with you, or might want to begin bankruptcy proceedings immediately.

When you have set up a few interviews, begin to extensively prepare all of the facts of your situation for your attorney. Bring with you the three worksheets from the third and fifth chapters in this book, and also bring your bills, installment agreements, loan books, etc., and prepare the beginnings of the "priority list," on page 70.

The attorney, after looking over the facts of your case, should discuss with you:

1. Whether or not you should file for bankruptcy. At this point, he should outline the feasibility of debt consolidation or prorating, and the workability of any debt-management program you may come up with. An attorney can be a powerful tool in getting creditors to accept such a program, since his involvement signals that the next step for you could be bankruptcy.
2. What steps you should take before filing bankruptcy. At this time, for example, it might be wise to begin making solid repayment

arrangements with secured creditors so that you won't lose secured property in a bankruptcy proceeding.

3. How to complete the bankruptcy forms. Some attorneys will ask you to fill out a series of bankruptcy forms, which they will then revise and amend. The twofold process can make for a more complete and comprehensive filing.

4. What to do if your proceeding becomes complicated. After reviewing the facts of your case, the attorney should be able to anticipate some particular complications or objections from your specific creditors.

In addition, an attorney might be able to see that you have a defense against some of your debts because of violations of the Truth in Lending Act — which encompasses the Fair Credit Reporting Act, the Equal Credit Opportunity Act, and others which are discussed in "Can They Do This to Me?" He can enter a defense against these claims, enabling you to wipe out some debts and thus begin repaying others.

Here are a few guidelines consumers should have when talking to their lawyers:

- A lawyer should be prepared to stick with his client through the entire bankruptcy proceeding, even if it's a complicated Chapter 13 plan. Also, the client should have a clean means of contacting his lawyer at any time — and not just someone working with the same firm.
- Many lawyers do not consider Chapter 13 as an option for their clients because it is more time-consuming for them and they may not be familiar with its ins and outs. Make sure your lawyer discusses both Chapter 7 and Chapter 13 with you completely.
- The lawyer should discuss the state and federal exemptions with you thoroughly, spelling out which laws apply most directly to your situation. As I said before, the difference between the two can be crucial.
- Your lawyer should express an interest in your overall financial picture. He should outline what financial position you will be in after bankruptcy, and at what points he will be able to intervene on your behalf with your creditors.
- Although practices differ among lawyers, every lawyer should be able to explain to your satisfaction why he practices as he does. In

some cases, he may have an understanding of the particular court or judge handling a case which another lawyer may not have.

- The lawyer should take up any "hidden costs," aside from his fee and filing fees, at the first meeting. Especially in the bankruptcies involving taxes owed, or cases that might prove to be "test cases" in bankruptcy law, these hidden costs can become a significant factor.
- Your lawyer should be aware of the ways in which bankruptcy law is tied into other branches of the law — including tax law, real estate law, and matrimonial law. Although most attorneys handling bankruptcies specialize in this area, they should have some familiarity with any area you have a special problem in.

WILL YOU HATE YOURSELF IN THE MORNING?

"The bankruptcy court is the dentist of the judicial system," wrote a lawyer for Beneficial Management Corporation in *Credit* magazine. "The relief it affords always hurts."

What many debtors are surprised to find, after going through bankruptcy, is that its effects are rarely what they had imagined. Few of us ever have the opportunity or the need to overhaul our financial machinery completely, and yet that is what you do in bankruptcy. For some, it is truly a fresh start. For others, it can be a serious mistake.

Bankruptcy can succeed for many debtors. There are some problems in the new federal act, and in the way bankruptcy is sold to the public by unscrupulous lawyers. But I don't think the real problem, as the creditors claim, is the number of people filing without financial need. Rather, I think that the problem is that more people who aren't able to meet their obligations in any realistic program do not file for bankruptcy. I'm not advocating bankruptcy as the rule — but what seems clear to me is that there are more people *not* going bankrupt because of their drastic circumstances who really should than there are people who abuse the system. The scale is still tipped *against* the debtor.

Bankruptcy will succeed for you, if you have tried every other alternative, if you have a good lawyer, and if you work conscientiously to keep your financial house in order both before and after you file.

The verdict on your creditworthiness after bankruptcy has yet to be delivered. You should be aware of the strong feelings credit grantors have against the formerly bankrupt — it looks as though this attitude is here to stay. If you truly want to gain control of your financial future, it would be best to avoid the creditor's backlash surrounding bankruptcy.

And there are still thousands of merchants, bankers, and other credit grantors who feel that the recently bankrupt individual is their best customer. If your goal is a fresh start, you'd best stay away from them. Don't take on new credit until you are absolutely sure that your financial affairs are under control.

Of course, there are still the major purchases of life — cars, homes, appliances. For these, most of us depend on credit. If you had to file bankruptcy because of basic mismanagement of your financial resources, it might be almost impossible to prove to your creditors that you've turned over a new leaf.

Which brings up the question of who gets hurt in a bankruptcy, and how. My advice to anyone considering bankruptcy who has a co-signed debt is to make every effort with your lawyer to protect the person who signed with you. Money is only money, and family and friends are far more valuable than dollars — especially with the way inflation is running. There are also the psychological and emotional issues which surround bankruptcy. Not many people talk about them, but most bankruptees experience the upheaval that comes from assessing completely their financial lives. Before having a couple file for bankruptcy, for example, Luther Gatling of the Budget Credit Couseling Service in New York will offer them the services of a family counselor. "What can happen in the midst of a bankruptcy can be very hard on people," he claims.

If you are married, bring your spouse into the process right away — you'll need each other's strength. Do the same with your children, to the degree that their age and maturity allows them to understand the family's finances. As with a sound debt-management program, a well-conceived bankruptcy can renew family members' ties to one another.

Finally, everyone considering bankruptcy should ask himself if he could accomplish the same goals any other way. It seems to be a large question, although it can be easily answered with another question: Have you tried the other ways? I wrote this book so that you would have a knowledgeable, complete guide to getting out of debt. Use the techniques outlined in it. If you make your way to this chapter, then use *it*, as well. But I hope you don't have to.

IS THERE LIFE
AFTER DEBT?

"A man in debt is so far a slave."
— RALPH WALDO EMERSON

A GOOD DEBT-MANAGEMENT PROGRAM is an enormous commitment, and one that is not necessarily measured by the amount of debt you owe. The person with an "average" amount of debt, who might feel that he is beginning to slip into trouble, has to do his own work of examining and isolating all of his financial activities. The person with a serious debt problem receives frequent calls and letters telling him where the trouble lies. Both have their work cut out for them.

Anyone with serious debt problems, reading this book, must have thought to himself at one time or another, "But what if something happens while I'm doing this? What if I lose my job? What if the creditor changes his mind? What if inflation ruins my budget?" For many people, these little nagging questions can be enough to keep them prisoners of debt and prevent them from starting a debt-management program in the first place.

In my interviews for the book, I asked many debtors and credit counselors what kind of situations arose that could throw people off course, and how they could prepare for the unexpected. In general, their responses confirmed that, despite minor setbacks and even the occasional major disaster, anyone who is already on the road to financial solvency is in better shape to handle emergencies than someone who continues to sink slowly in a pool of debt.

Debt is a state of mind, and a style of life, as much as it is a financial condition. Getting out of debt *now* means no longer being a victim of creditors and collectors. It means knowing that the money you earn every week is yours and doesn't belong to two or three, or more, different collectors and creditors. When you get out of debt, you say no to the vicious cycle of credit cards and personal loans — to the house of cards so many Americans live in today. Certainly, you can't pay off all that you owe in one fell swoop — if you could, you wouldn't be in debt. But you can stop being a helpless debtor, and that can change your life.

Getting out of debt now lets you draw on your own self-reliance. No longer will you be the "slave" Emerson refers to in the quotation at the beginning of the chapter. Although you can receive help from counselors, lawyers, and even creditors, unless you know your situation completely, know how you plan to handle it, and what all of the alternatives mean to you, you can still fall victim to those who prey on the debtor. You *must* take full personal responsibility for your personal finances.

But if you have taken a realistic assessment of the situation, and made knowledgeable plans for the future, even those who might have taken advantage of your indebtedness will have to deal with you on a direct, businesslike level.

With that kind of energy behind you, you can't fail.

You're leaving one way of life behind you, and starting another. The perspective you'll have on practically every one of your financial decisions will change completely — from the clothing you buy to where you might be thinking of living. Debt has a way of pervading every aspect of your finances, and by releasing yourself from its grip, you can truly gain control of your financial affairs — once and for all.

STAYING ON COURSE

Particularly if you've had bad financial habits in the past, staying on course in a debt-management program can be tough sailing indeed. Promises you've made to creditors for monthly payments, deadlines you have to meet for getting money in, and the everyday pressures of making a living can all mount up to an uncontrollable mess. But a good system can save you headaches, and leave you free to concentrate on your job, your family, and enjoying your new independence.

At least three times a year, you should redo the worksheets in the third and fifth chapters. Needs change, children grow, your career may take a jump, or your means of income may alter. One of the easiest ways to get thrown off your debt-management program is not to take new factors into account. The minute you think, "Oh, that detail will take care of itself," you're leaving yourself open for financial mismanagement.

It's important, too, to keep accurate records of everything coming in and going out. Except for pocket money and small day-to-day expenses, write checks or use money orders. (Unless, of course, you are on the cash-only system described in "Making a Plan You Can Stick To.") You'll have to fight the temptation to disguise any little splurges by paying cash for them, but if you write a check for some "luxury" item you purchase (I'm speaking here of a $5 or $10 "luxury" — you really can't afford any more), it gives you an opportunity to think twice about the purchase, and also provides a record later, when you're wondering "Now, where did that money go to?" Sometimes, it can even help to have a record of impulse items so that you can be reminded that you *did* do something for yourself once in a while, and things really aren't as totally bleak as they may seem.

Being open about impulse spending is the best defense against the ruinous effect it can have on your budget. If you find yourself keeping secrets from your family — and even from yourself — about your spending habits, think about the larger consequences of these little dishonesties. A solid debt-management program is a way of building a lifelong atmosphere of trust and cooperation within a family. It's an invaluable opportunity, and you owe it to yourself and your family to give it your best shot.

The day-to-day, month-to-month rigors of a debt-management program can become monotonous, and that routine alone can place difficult pressures on the person responsible for holding the program together. If it's possible, change roles once in a while within your family. For example, you might let your oldest child take the helm for a month, once things have assumed a steady course. This will provide you with a break in the process, your son or daughter will receive an important lesson in family finance, and it might even be fun.

You probably pay your bills once or twice a month. If your debt management is fairly strict, though, you might want to pay some bills on a certain week of every month, so that you won't spend the money on other things. This will enable you to be even more on top of your finances. Keep a list of bills you pay on the first week of the month, the second, etc. If you have minor emergencies, you can "juggle" your payments, substituting a small bill from the third week when it's impossible to meet a large bill in the second week. Be careful, though, not to let all of the large bills in one month fall together.

Paying your bills on a weekly basis, counting on four weeks in every month, has another advantage: there are, on the average, three months in every year in which five paydays occur — for those who are paid weekly. That money can be saved for an emergency fund, or used for some other purpose. (See the section in this chapter "Building a New Financial Foundation.")

Just as a sidelight, I'd like to tell you about an interview I had with a computer specialist in the credit field. He told me that the technology is now available to place a device in your car that would make it impossible for you to use the vehicle if you hadn't made your monthly loan payment. The idea is pretty farfetched, but the mere threat of that little gizmo is enough to keep anyone to their payment schedule.

You might also want to get in the habit of stretching your dollars by buying things on sale or off-season. The January white sales, the holiday bargains just before and after the summer crush, and other annual events can really help the person who plans to take advantage of them. Most of the general "money books" include information on seasonal bargains, and you can always watch for sales in your local newspaper.

Keeping organized files of all your papers, including correspondence with creditors and any agreements you sign with them, is a must for a successful debt-management program. The first thing to remember is to keep your system simple. If it's too complex, important details will start to fall through the cracks, and you'll be wasting time and energy on filing that could be better spent on actually managing your money.

In an article in the *New York Times*, Leon Nad, national director for taxes for Price Waterhouse Company (the large accounting firm that tallies the votes for the Oscars, among other things), offered some hints for developing a home filing system. Use simple folding files or manila folders, he advised. Find the important areas of your financial life — income, possessions, personal papers, and credit agreements. The most important strategy, and also the most overlooked, he said, is for all records to be stored in one place. "It sounds so simple, but many people just don't seem to be able to discipline themselves to do that," Mr. Nad claimed. "They throw some bills in a kitchen drawer, others in a bedroom closet, and leave their checkbooks in the office."

This advice applies to everyone in the family. Anything that has to do with the overall finances must be kept in a central place.

Finally, one of the most important steps you can take to keep you on course in your debt-management program is to maintain a good relationship with your creditors. Not only will good relationships lead to open doors, in many instances, for credit when you have completed your repayments, but a good relationship will see you through any emergencies that might develop.

At the beginning of your debt-management program, keep in close touch with your creditor. You should have already established that there will be one person whom you can contact throughout the program. When you first begin making payments on your new arrangements, call that person to tell him that the payment is on the way. For the first 3 or 4 months, a monthly call to say all is well, and perhaps to voice your satisfaction with the arrangement, can impress the creditor with your character and ability to repay. After that period of time, call every 3 or 4 months, and ask for a confirmation of the amount you calculate as still owing.

If an emergency crops up later on, the creditor will remember your name, and your past record, and will be more willing to work out whatever arrangement needs to be made to help you over your rough spot. If you don't exercise this personal relationship, you'll be just another debtor to them, and you won't be able to expect personal consideration.

According to one New York banker, keeping to your repayment plan won't wipe the slate of your credit record clean, but it will reestablish with the creditor that you have the ability to pay back on your debts, and that you have made an honest effort to stay on good terms with them.

If you fall seriously behind in payments, for two or three months, don't despair. Your creditors and collectors will no doubt start hounding you again, and when that happens it's easy to forget the progress you've made. But getting behind in your debt-management program isn't like falling off your diet — you don't pile up new calories on your debts. What you've paid off is *gone*. Remind your creditors of your past efforts and your record of repayment. Explain to them your difficult circumstances. Most creditors and collectors will allow you one or two mistakes, as long as you keep the lines of communication open.

Remember that emergencies do happen. Some debt-management programs can take a year to three years, and in that amount of time anything can occur. Your car might blow three tires. You may be hit by sickness, or some other unexpected disaster. In cases like these, it's good to have a small emergency fund, to have good relationships with your creditors, and if at all possible, to have a line of credit open to you for just such occasions.

"A line of credit? Emergency savings?" you may ask. Yes, both are possibilities in a debt-management program, as the next section will show.

RECYCLING YOUR DEBTS

After all you've been through, it would be unnecessary for me to lecture you on the intelligent uses of credit. The fact that you're using this book to get out of debt is proof enough that you've learned from your mistakes. But credit is still a fact of life for most of us, and once you've begun to relieve your debt burdens, the opportunities will arise to begin developing new credit relationships. It may also be a possibility that, although you were in debt, not all of your credit relationships were severed, and you may have preserved a bankcard or retail store card. It's important to ask yourself why you may need to use credit again, and how you can avoid past mistakes.

Applying for renewed credit can be a difficult process. According to Meredith Fernstrom, consumer affairs director at American Express, rebuilding your creditworthiness after you've been in debt takes a great deal of extra initiative and energy. "You have to let the creditor know you've straightened yourself out," she claims. "You have to be assertive, be willing to question why you've been turned down, if you have been turned down. You should know what's on your credit report, since it weighs pretty heavily on most creditors' decisions." But most creditors, according to Ms. Fernstrom, also recognize that other circumstances might override the credit report. "Sometimes the report is outdated. You may have had a job change, or a change in income, or you might have cleared up your situation with your creditors. In most cases, it is your responsibility to let the creditor know what your situation is."

The best prospect for new credit is still the relationship you have with an old creditor. According to Jack Downing of Household Finance Corporation, "We recognize that our customers may have had problems. When they come to us after clearing up some of these problems, we look at three things: whether their obligations have been reduced, whether they demonstrate stability, and whether they've maintained their position of employment. If there hasn't been a significant change in their profile from when we first granted them credit, we will consider their application."

As I pointed out in a previous chapter, if your creditor is willing to grant you credit after you have completed a successful debt-management program with them, you can expect that they will offer you a level of credit that matches what you *have* been repaying them. Their best means of assessing what you are good for is what you have demonstrated you can handle. I call that process "recycling your debts". . . basically, you'll be allowed to borrow what you've been repaying, and it can become an important part of your financial base in the future. If you have a major purchase such as an appliance, furniture, or a necessary home repair, which you have been putting off because no credit was available to you, you might want to recycle your debt this way. However, this also raises some difficult questions. Do you want to channel what you have been paying to a creditor for past debts into new credit? Are you sure that you won't get into trouble again?

The problem with recycling is that many people can't help but fall into the trap of using credit for nonessential purposes, and spending beyond affordable levels. Essentially, that's how they got into trouble in the first place. This only serves to point up one of the most difficult, but important, aspects of anyone's debt-management program — examining *how* money is spent.

Given that you have probably learned your lesson about credit, and have demonstrated to your creditors that you are again creditworthy, there is no reason why you shouldn't, with a certain amount of self-discipline and caution, renew relationships with some of your creditors. Especially in regard to large-ticket purchases, having access to credit can make life easier for you and your family.

Here are some dos and don'ts of borrowing from the vantage point of the credit-wary:

1. Don't borrow money unless you've already established an "emergency account" equal to three months' salary, or $3,000 — whichever is less. Of course, one can not be totally unrealistic about this — if an emergency comes up and you have to raise money quickly, there's nothing else you can do. But be aware of the risk you are taking.

2. Know what the loan is going to cost you — read the contract carefully, calculate the annual percentage rate, and figure in any finance charges. Ask yourself: Can I really handle this? Would it be better to save and buy this free and clear in several months' time?

3. Don't try and live by the "20 percent of your take-home pay" rule when judging the amount of installment debt you can handle. Until bad debts, collectors, and angry creditors are a fading memory, keep your installment commitments below 10 percent of your take-home pay.

4. *Do* talk with your spouse and your family about borrowing

money or using credit to make a purchase. They've gone the distance with you on the road to financial recovery, and they deserve your honesty and trust in the future.

5. Don't borrow money or use credit to celebrate getting out of debt. The consumer credit counseling offices regularly see people who were almost out of debt and then decided to celebrate with a little spending spree that set them back another six months to a year.

JUST WHEN YOU THOUGHT IT WAS SAFE TO GET BACK IN THE WATER . . .

Unfortunately, the consumer-credit picture isn't as easy as all that. Coming off some of their worst years ever, the consumer lenders have geared up for the coming decade with a tough, lean, profit-oriented strategy that could leave the average consumer wondering what hit him.

The first effect that consumers will feel will be the higher costs of credit. According to one New York banker with whom I spoke, "The public will have to become accustomed to being treated by bankers as they have been by every other merchant." What this means is that pricing of bank services will become more competitive in the future, and will most likely rise in a fairly consistent pattern. Most banks today are trying very hard to get rid of usury ceilings in their various states, allowing them to charge more for credit and assume a higher risk among their customers. Consumers can expect, in the years to come, that credit will be readily available, but that it will cost a great deal more. Again, the responsibility for separating the value of the credit being offered from the cost of the credit will fall squarely on the consumer's shoulders.

Banks will also be allowed, in many states, to take security interest in homes for consumer credit and credit cards. Because of this, many consumers will be faced with extremely large lines of credit on their cards, and extremely high penalties for defaulting on that credit. Although the legislation to make it possible is only in the proposal stage, it's entirely possible that debtors in the future could face the loss of their home or other valuable property when they have trouble paying their credit-card bills.

Another development that consumers can expect to see everywhere in the 1980s is the variable-rate loan, not just in mortgages, but in many other types of consumer lending as well. Although it should be stressed from the outset that these loans were developed by creditors to enable them to offer more mortgages — and the great advantage of them is that they place the "American Dream" of buying a home closer to reality for many people — the loans are more complicated than previous standard mortgages, and deserve some careful scrutiny.

The variable-rate loan ties the interest charge over the life of the loan to some index — the prime rate, for example. If the prime is at 12 percent, then you might be paying 14 percent on your loan. If the prime rises to 15 percent, you'll be paying 17 percent. It sounds simple, but variable-rate loans have some sticky complications. The first question you have to ask is what kind of "index" your rate is tied to. While many banks will use the prime rate or the Federal Funds rate, others may not. The index will be stated in your credit agreement, and you'll have to read it carefully to make sure you won't be burned in the future. You'll also have to be aware of when the rate will be calculated within a billing period or payment period of a loan. Will your rate vary according to the prime rate on the first of the month? The fifteenth? For an average of the prime rates over a 3- to 6-month period?

Another aspect of consumer credit that bodes poorly for you is the tremendous competition currently going on among states to attract credit banking operations. For instance, in early 1981, the Delaware legislature passed a bill to eliminate all usury rate ceilings on credit-card accounts, and give income-tax breaks to banks earning more than $20 million a year. New York's Chase Manhattan Bank and J.P. Morgan and Co. promptly filed papers for their proposed moves into Delaware (Chase plans to move their entire credit-card operation there) after the bill was signed.

The Delaware legislation was modeled on similar laws made in South Dakota in 1980, which resulted in Citibank moving its credit-card operations from New York.

The atmosphere of fierce competition between banks will definitely affect the consumer. The real survivors will be those who understand what the banks are doing to increase their profit margin, and who are able to distinguish between using credit in their lives and offering their lives over to their creditors.

BUILDING A NEW FINANCIAL FOUNDATION

Let's say you've made the last payment on a debt. You enclose a letter with your final remittance. The letter should state that, by your understanding, you have completely repaid the debt and no longer owe the creditor. You should also ask that the creditor send you a letter acknowledging full repayment of the debt.

The next month rolls around, and the money which would ordinarily have gone toward the obligation is now available for something else. What can you do about it?

- First, you should make sure you don't need the money somewhere else in your budget. When was the last time you assessed the effects of inflation on your grocery bill? Has your car insurance gone up? What about your heating bill? Your transportation costs? If you see a gaping hole in your budget, now is the time to fill it.
- If you still have money left over, you can save it. Have you built an emergency fund yet? I realize that it's not exactly the most glamorous idea in the world, but it is a necessity. You've got a spare tire in your trunk, haven't you? A basic emergency fund, as I've said, should hold three months' salary or at least $3,000.
- Chances are, you've been postponing some purchase until some extra money came in. Now's the time to take care of it. Someone might need new shoes or clothing, something in your home might need repair. If there are several of these postponed purchases around, you might consider using what would normally have gone to pay back the old debt for the next few months to take care of them. If you have an "emergency fund" you might want to keep a "necessity fund" also, to dip into when these kind of expenses come up.
- How close are you to paying off another debt? If you took the money that is now available and put it toward another debt, could you wipe out a second or third debt within a few months? Doing so

would soon give you an even larger chunk of "free" money every month.

• Finally, you could celebrate. Take that first month's free money and do something fun!

If you don't feel the urge or the necessity to do any of those things, then it's time to start thinking about long-range financial goals.

What if, at the age of thirty, you were to streamline your budget and pay off debts so that you were able to put away $50 a week? If you put the money in a tax-deferred investment, yielding 15 percent, at the age of 65 you would have an accumulated $3,000,000!!

What could happen to $50 a week in the course of a year? If you had opened a money market account at the beginning of 1981 with $1,000, and added just one-half of your $50 a week beginning in February, you would have entered 1982 with close to $2,400 (calculating with the average 1980 money fund rate of 12 percent).

The benefit of these investment tools, while not the subject of this book, is just beginning to be realized by consumers. What many people are seeing happen very quickly is that you can begin to develop, with a small amount of money regularly saved, the kind of principal that leads to a financially secure future. You'll never have to be seriously in debt again.

Inflation, of course, is the enemy of the saver. In the last couple of years in America, regular savings accounts have diminished in proportions that industry officials have termed "disastrous." There are two reasons for this "outflow" of money. (If you really want to know the fancy term for it, the flow of money from one investment to another is called "disintermediation." Now you know something only bankers know). First, people who are finding it hard to make ends meet are tapping into their savings just to get by. Second, those who can afford to put something away for the future do not find the average 5 to 6 percent savings account attractive. They are moving their funds into the very popular money markets. Or they are just plain spending it on what they want, when they want it — true inflationary psychology.

What does this mean for the savings and loans? Nothing but bad news. They have less in their funds to cover current deposits, and very little to lend — especially for mortgages. In addition, the outflow of savings hurts the economy as well. While funds deposited in savings and loans traditionally went toward lending for housing or local business, the cash in money market funds follows the hot tickets on the stock exchange.

If it sounds to you like the end of the savings and loan industry, you're not the only one to hear the distant thunder. Recently, Richard Pratt assumed his new duties as the chief regulator of savings and loan associations in America by paraphrasing Churchill. "I have not been appointed Chairman of the Federal Home Loan Bank Board to preside over the demise of this industry," he told reporters.

It's no secret that the American economy faces stiff competition from the Japanese. Many analysts are fond of pointing out that the Japanese workers save at a far higher rate than their American counterparts — and that their saving very often involves turning their wages back into their nation's economy. One reason this occurs in Japan is that the Japanese have more faith, of late, in their yen than we have in our dollar. Another reason is that Americans, over the last few years, have grown relatively sophisticated when it comes to managing their money. What they do to "invest in the future" can no longer be measured by what they put in savings and loans. Americans, more and more, are putting their money where the high interest rates are. It will only be up to the banking system to see how well, in the future, Americans will be able to churn their dollars back into their nation's economy.

Now that you've seen your way out of debt, you might be confused by this virtual "monetary supermarket" before you. Savings and loans, unless they receive substantial legislative help, might not be the answer for you. But when you turn away from the traditional means of savings, where do you turn?

One thing that you might consider is working with a family financial planner. Consumers have realized the value of tax-deferred investments, money markets, mutual funds, real estate, and even IRA and Keogh funds. Financial planning has become a booming business. Like any other professional service, looking for a financial planner involves a lot of shopping around. Be sure to find one who sees your financial life-style the same way you do, who knows your needs and is able to help you meet them and perhaps even surpass them.

The areas a financial planner will counsel you in are: budget, savings, home purchase, life insurance, establishing an IRA or Keogh account, investing in stocks and other markets, career assessment, taxes, and long-term goals such as education for your children or retirement.

Whether you decide to get professional help or not, planning for your family's financial future will be essential in the coming years. For one thing, inflation will drive many unprepared people into difficult financial straits. For example:

- Owning your own home — one of the staples of the American dream — is already out of reach for many people.
- A college education in 1990 will cost *at least* $11,500 per year. Many Ivy League schools posted $10,000-plus tuitions in the early eighties.
- Some of the projected prices for 1990: a pound of hamburger, $4.60; a loaf of white bread, $1.03; cornflakes, $1.12; and coffee $12.10 a pound!

On the other hand, according to *Fortune* magazine, the 1980s will be a time of relative prosperity. The median family income will rise 23 percent. And at the end of the eighties, two out of five families will qualify as "upper-income," earning more than $25,000 a year (this is calculated in 1977 dollars — about equal to $29,000 in 1980). If inflation is reined in to single-digit levels, we may begin to enjoy some of our prosperity as we haven't been able to since the sixties.

There are many good guides to financial planning and money management. After having battled your way out of debt, it should be a pleasure to consult them on your road to financial control.

LIFE AFTER DEBT

As Aristotle said, "The unexamined life is not worth living." You've now had the opportunity to examine your financial life closely; to make difficult, yet productive changes; and to make your life and that of your family better. You now have a degree of control over your money that the average American has long ago relinquished to bankers and creditors.

Use that control. Maintain your self-reliance. Enjoy your new-found prosperity.

And may you never be in debt again.

BIBLIOGRAPHY

The following books are either referred to in *Get Out of Debt Now*, or would be of help to anyone using this book.

Super Threats: How to Sound like a Lawyer and Get Your Rights on Your Own, by John M. Striker and Andrew O. Shapiro. Dell Books, New York, NY.

Levin's Laws: Tactics for Winning without Intimidation, by Edward Levin. Fawcett Books, New York, NY.

Credit Where Credit Is Due: A Legal Guide to Your Credit Rights and How to Assert Them, by Glen Walker. Holt, Rinehart and Winston, New York, NY.

How to Get Creditors off Your Back without Losing Your Shirt: A Consumer's Guide to the Federal Bankruptcy Code, by Melvin J. Kaplan. Contemporary Books, Chicago., Ill.

Winning with Your Lawyer: What Every Client Should Know about How the Legal System Works, by Burton Marks and Gerald Goldfarb, McGraw-Hill, New York, NY.

The Consumer's Almanac, published by the National Consumer Finance Association, 1000 Sixteenth St., NW, Washington, D.C., available for $2.

Sylvia Porter's Money Book for the 80s, by Sylvia Porter. Avon, New York, NY.

The Overspenders Anonymous Newsletter, c/o Overspenders Anonymous, P.O. Box 243, Middleton, Wis. 53562.

INDEX

Account Review Service Program (CBI's), 98
Acrofile. *See* CBI
adjusted balance method (interest calculation), 40–41
age discrimination, 179, 180
Alert System (TRW's), 98, 115
American Bankers Association, 113
American Bankers Association Bulletin, 14
American Collectors Association, 143
American Creditor's Bureau, 144, 146
American Express, 120, 121–122
Amoco, 123
Anderson, Jack, 28
annual percentage rate (APR), 40, 41, 225
Ashby, Dean, 10
attorney-collectors, 143, 157
attorneys. *See* lawyers
automobile loans, 12, 21, 71, 130–131, 134; comparing costs of, 41–42; refinancing, 82–83
average daily balance method (interest calculation), 41

bad debt. *See* charge-offs
bankcards, 13–14, 26, 108–109; billing practices, 113; collection practices, 47–48, 116–120; credit lines, 113, 226; and debt-management program, 65–68, 224; the economy and, 111, 112, 226–227; interest rates, 26–28 (*see also* usury laws); pricing structures, 114–115
Bank of America, 108
bankruptcy, 7, 15, 54, 80, 82, 107, 196–197, 215–217; Chapter 7 proceeding, 201, 203–207, 209–211, 214; Chapter 11 proceeding, 202; Chapter 13 proceeding, 201, 206, 207–211, 214; in credit reports, 92, 93, 104; creditors' response to, 15–16, 197–201, 203–205, 207, 208, 210, 211, 216, 222–224, 228; debt-management program versus, 202, 213, 215–217; emotional/psychological factors in, 199, 209–210; exemptions in, 205–206, 207; factors involved, 197–199, 201–202; involuntary, 202; lawyers for, 198, 201, 208, 210, 211–215; undischargeable debts in, 207–208
Bankruptcy Code. *See* Federal Bankruptcy Reform Act
banks and banking industry, 17, 23–25, 48, 72, 80, 107; bankruptcy and, 197, 200, 216; and credit reports, 92, 93; dunning cycle of, 47–48, 116–120; the economy and, 108–110, 111, 226–228, 229; interest rates, 26, 27; *see also* bankcards; mortgages; thrift institutions
Bell System, 128, 160
Beneficial Finance Corporation, 108, 134
billing errors. *See* disputed bills/billing errors
billing methods: of bankcards, 113; of lawyers, 193–194; *see also* collection processes
Booth, S. Lees, 28
borrowing, rules for, 225–226
Boyle, James, 31
Broadman, Ellen, 87, 110
Budget and Credit Counseling Service (BUCC$), 78, 80–81
budgeting and budgets: "cash-only" policy in, 65–68, 220; determining, 33–38, 39, 43, 54–63; impact of inflation on, 5, 7, 14, 65–68, 229–231; utilities in, 126–127, 128, 129; *see also* debt-management program
"bugetism," 19
Bureau of Labor Statistics, 63–65

Capital Credit, 144
Carte Blanche, 120, 121
Carter, James Earl, 27
"cash-only" policy, 65–68, 220
CBI (consumer reporting agency, 89, 90, 95–96, 98, 165